COMPARATIVE
ECONOMIC
S·Y·S·T·E·M·S

COMPARATIVE
ECONOMIC
S·Y·S·T·E·M·S

Richard L. Carson

M. E. Sharpe, Inc.
Armonk, New York
London, England

Available in the United Kingdom and Europe from M. E. Sharpe,
Publishers, 3 Henrietta Street, London WC2E 8LU.

Library of Congress Cataloging-in-Publication Data

Carson, Richard L.
    Comparative economic systems / Richard L. Carson.
        p.   cm.
    Includes bibliographical references.
    ISBN 0-87332-583-4
    ISBN 0-87332-580-X P (Vol. I)
    ISBN 0-87332-581-8 P (Vol. II)
    ISBN 0-87332-582-6 P (Vol. III)
    ISBN 0-87332-680-6 (3 volume paper set)
    1. Comparative economics. I. Title.
HB90.C37   1989
330—dc20   89-10888
                                                                      CIP

Printed in the United States of America

                    ∞

ED   10   9   8   7   6   5   4   3   2   1

To those who have struggled for reform
in China, Eastern Europe, and the Soviet Union.

—— CONTENTS ——

Comparative Economic Systems is being published simultaneously in one clothbound edition, which includes the complete text, and three paperback editions, one for each major part. The complete table of contents and the complete index are included in the clothbound edition and in each of the paperback editions.

FIGURES

TABLES

PREFACE

This book is mainly an effort to understand contemporary economic systems, using an approach based on property rights plus elements from standard supply, demand, and cost analysis. The basic framework is developed within the first four chapters. More space is devoted to socialism than to capitalism in the early chapters, since the majority of readers are likely to be less familiar with and/or more curious about the former. Over the course of the book, however, this deficit is largely made up, so that space is more or less evenly divided between the two. There are analyses of several modern economies as well as of historical topics of interest. The political dimension of an economic system is developed, and the compatibility of different economic and political organizations is examined briefly. I also discuss the impact of sociocultural factors on economic organization and development when these are particularly important (as in the case of Japan), although my focus is on economic causes and consequences.

I view the traditional Soviet-type economy as a system based on disequilibrium and more precisely on shortage, a notion which I attribute to the well-known Hungarian economist, Janos Kornai. Portions of the first two chapters develop the properties of this system and pave the way for later discussion and analysis of socialist reforms, especially in chapter 5. In-depth treatment of the current reform movement includes careful consideration of the causes of reform, as well as the reasons for the failure of past reforms and the barriers to successful reform, plus progress reports and examination of the relationship between political and economic reform. The 1980s have been an exciting time to study comparative systems, and the revitalization of socialist reforms has been a major reason for this. Yet the traditional Soviet-type economy has demonstrated staying power again and again in the face of reform efforts, and while there is a growing feeling that its days are numbered in most places, the pace and exact direction of change remain treacherous to forecast. Reform and counterreform will continue to produce tension and surprise in these societies for years to come.

The 1980s have also witnessed efforts to redefine the economic role of government in capitalist market economies. Chapter 1 gives reasons for the expansion of this role since World War II, as well as efficiency arguments for and against widespread social insurance, now the largest category of public-sector outlays. In addition, it introduces the idea of national planning in a market economy and identifies common denominators with Soviet-style planning.

Nowadays, authors sometimes use the term "industrial policy" to describe a type or an aspect of planning. The last section in chapter 2 shows how this can be a tool for coping with market failure, although later discussion makes it clear that industrial policy has sometimes in practice held back structural change, thereby reducing growth and raising unemployment. I also give extensive treatment to two modern economies (Japan and Sweden), which are often cited as models and within which the government's policy role has been substantial, but which contrast in many ways as well. This includes Swedish labor market policy—attractive to socialist reformers as a way to combine full employment with flexibility in production in response to shifts in demand and cost—and the system of (limited) lifetime employment in Japan. Historical topics include National Socialism in Germany plus an analysis of the causes of Hitler's rise to power, including the role of the "debt crisis" growing out of World War I and the reparations levied on Germany in the Treaty of Versailles.

In addition, current "insider-outsider" explanations of unemployment and rigid wages in capitalist countries are outlined and contrasted with the Marxian explanation of unemployment. This is done mainly in chapter 3, which also gives the basic elements of Marx's theory of the evolution of capitalism and analyzes several precapitalist economies in the context of a theory of history based primarily on the writings of Marx and Engels, but also on those of modern economic historians. Although Marx devoted most of his energies to a critique of capitalism, Marx and Engels had more to say about the nature of the socialist system that they foresaw than is sometimes realized, and they did experience a leap of the "future into the present" (the Paris Commune) during their lifetimes. A socialist system meeting their requirements would not be a traditional Soviet-type economy. As is explained in chapter 4, however, efforts to implement the former would probably lead either to the latter or to some form of market socialism, under the pressure of a continuing need to resolve conflicts over resource allocation. ("Socialism" within the Marx-Engels historical evolution occurs when resources are still scarce.)

I intend this work to appeal to a variety of readers in terms of background and interests. It should be accessible to anyone who has completed a standard one-year course in principles of economics, but I have also found this material to be interesting to graduate students (not only in economics) and believe it will be useful and interesting as well to specialists and businessmen dealing with one or more of the countries covered here.

I view the study of comparative systems primarily as a study of systems alternative to one's own and also as a study of phenomena not readily encountered in other branches of economics. In such a context, "model" aspects are important, but exclusion of a specific economy from coverage does not necessarily imply any judgment on my part as to its importance or significance. Space and my own competence are both limited!

Special thanks are due to Gwen McBride, without whose help I never would have been able to get this manuscript in shape for publication, as well as to several others who did portions of the word processing along the way—notably, Norma Rankin, Charlotte Burba, and Ginette Harte. Special thanks also to Susan Klement of Information Resources in Toronto, who compiled the index on very short notice and against an extremely tight deadline. Finally, I would thank students and colleagues who have given me moral support. I have always found my students' enthusiasm for this subject a source of strength.

Richard L. Carson
Ottawa, Canada
December 1989

PART II

SOCIALIST ALTERNATIVES

6

THE HUNGARIAN ECONOMY

6-1. The Nature of Hungary's Economy and Government

A. Introduction

In chapter 6, we focus attention on Hungary. One author writes that, during the 1950s, "industrialization [was] carried out in Hungary more extensively, with greater brutality, than in any other East European country."[1] Under Communist party leader Matyas Rakosi and economics minister Ernö Gerö, Hungary adopted the Soviet-style command economy, with its emphasis on priority development of heavy industry, despite its questionable application in Hungary's circumstances. Eighty-six percent of all investment in industry was earmarked for heavy industry during the first half of the 1950s, to turn Hungary into a "country of iron and steel." This flew in the face of comparative advantage, since it cost Hungary more to import the raw materials needed to produce steel domestically than the steel was worth on the world market. These priorities were dictated by the Soviet Union, although they were also supported by Rakosi and Gerö. Hungary's purchase of low-quality Soviet iron ore—and its partial payment via steel products made from this ore, which were also of modest quality—became a symbol of the economic relationship between the Soviet Union and Eastern Europe.

The climax of forced draft industrialization was an uprising that lasted for two weeks, October 23 to November 4, 1956, and turned Budapest into a battleground. The insurrection was suppressed by Soviet troops, but it led to a willingness by

Hungarian authorities to experiment with the structure of the economy and to pay more attention to comparative advantage. Soviet leaders became more tolerant of such experiments, and there was a break for the Hungarian consumer, by comparison with the early 1950s. Thus, the next few years witnessed modest efforts to reform the economy, which were largely unsuccessful. By the mid-1960s, Hungary's labor reserves were also disappearing, along with the possibilities for further extensive growth.

Because partial decentralization had not worked, the party decided in 1966 to launch a major reform to replace administrative planning with a quasi-market system. Both planners and politicians carefully laid the groundwork, and New Year's Day, 1968, saw the launching of the New Economic Mechanism (NEM). Despite the wave of reforms in the USSR and Eastern Europe around the same time, Hungary became the only country to pass significantly beyond the basic command-economy model. Although there was again recentralization, over 1972–78, the oil price explosion led to a balance-of-payments crisis marked by growing indebtedness to the West. This created new pressures for decentralization and for closer ties between rewards and performance. At the end of 1978, Hungary renewed its commitment to reform, apparently with the blessing of the Soviet Union. In 1982, it joined the International Monetary Fund and World Bank. Hungary's experience with reform, which is more extensive than that of any socialist country, is the main reason for our interest in this small nation.

First, to orient the reader, we note that Hungary is a landlocked country of about 36,000 square miles, centered on the Danubian plain of East Central Europe. It covers approximately the geographical area of Indiana and is a bit larger than New Brunswick. Its population of 10.7 million (1988) is about the same as that of Ohio—which has a slightly larger territory—or just over 40 percent of Canada's. Hungary shares common borders, in order of length, with Czechoslovakia to the north, Yugoslavia to the southwest, Romania to the southeast, Austria to the west, and the Soviet Union to the east. The capital is Budapest (population 2.1 million), the largest city of Central Europe, which lies not far from the Czech border. Historically, the Hungarians, or Magyars, entered the Danubian basin under their chieftain, Arpad, in the winter of 895–96. Farming was their main occupation for centuries, and industry did not surpass agriculture, in terms of contribution to national income, until after 1955. Because Hungary fought on the losing side in both world wars, its present territory is less than the area inhabited by ethnic Magyars, a source of some frustration since the Treaty of Trianon, signed after World War I.[2] Romania, Yugoslavia, and Czechoslovakia have significant Magyar minorities, totalling about 3 million in all.

Like all socialist economies, Hungary has passed through a structural evolution—outlined above in Table 4.2—which continues. In this chapter, we shall take a snapshot of the system as of 1988 and deal more specifically with reform in chapter 9, although it will receive some attention below.

B. Main Features of the Hungarian Economy

Hungary is still primarily a planned economy of the Soviet type, although the role of the market has been growing, and fundamental changes in 1988 and 1989 may lead to a major breakthrough of market forces. The Communist party and the state determine in broad outline the composition of goods and services produced and the direction of economic growth. In industry, and to a lesser degree in agriculture, state management of production and interenterprise exchange takes place through a hierarchy that stretches from central planners—and ultimately from the political leadership—at the top to workplaces at the bottom. Beneath the political leadership, Hungary's top planning organ is the State Planning Commission (SPC), with responsibility for drawing up and implementing national economic plans and for harmonizing these with other government policies. Formally, SPC is a staff agency to the Council of Ministers (the prime minister and his cabinet), which is the top executive authority of government. In practice, SPC takes many major decisions itself, although it shares its authority with the National Bank, as well as the Prices and Materials Board (PMB) and the State Economic Commission (SEC). While SPC focuses on conceptual and longer-range planning problems, PMB and SEC cope with day-to-day distribution, exchange, and pricing, in a context where most producer goods are in short supply.

Below this level, ministries supervise most large and medium-sized firms, while smaller state enterprises and cooperatives usually come under local government control or are subject to the market. Prior to a 1980 reorganization, there were Ministries of Light Industry, Heavy Industry, Metallurgy and Engineering, Agriculture and Food, and Construction, besides the more usual functional ministries, such as the Ministry of Finance. In 1980, the first three of these were merged into a single Ministry of Industry, which is supposed to give looser guidance to firms, more along the lines of a mixed economy. To encourage this, it has fewer employees than the combined staffs of the ministries it replaced. However, some of their powers—including control over interenterprise trade—devolved onto PMB and SEC.

Because of an extensive merger movement, Hungarian firms are large relative to the domestic market, and as recently as 1979, half of all state-owned enterprises were organized into twenty-four trusts or cartels, which exercised extensive management rights over them. Since then, at least fifteen trusts have been dissolved, as part of efforts to decentralize, although some may continue to operate *de facto*. In 1987, there were 1,043 state industrial enterprises, which produced over 80 percent of industrial output. This was nearly a 50 percent increase over the 699 firms existing in 1980 and was achieved mainly by splitting up large enterprises and trusts. Yet, most product groups are still dominated by one or two big domestic suppliers, each of which has several factories that are often geographically dispersed. Import competition is next to nonexistent.[3] The trust or large enterprise is, itself, a link in the planning chain of command. The factories below have little autonomy, unless this has been delegated to them by enterprise or trust management (and the extent of such delegation varies widely).

As is normal in a command economy, industrial firms have concentrated on production, leaving most finance, supply, and marketing to be handled above the enterprise level. Because of the restricted autonomy of firms, a different type of manager tends to emerge than in a market economy. These are "people who, although very capable of effectively carrying out directions from above, [are] incapable of displaying independent initiative. Their basic quality and strength [lie] in their excellent knowledge of a particular factory or enterprise."[4] In Hungary, most executives have been with their firms at least ten years (and often more than twenty) and have come up the ladder within the company, which reinforces this internal knowledge. The centralized nature of the system often causes the central planners and the ministries to be overwhelmed by the volume and complexity of decisions thrust upon them. Yet, if they fail to act, "there is nothing which forces and hardly anything which stimulates enterprises to carry out desirable changes . . . some workplaces use the same methods and have been turning out the same products for 10–20 years; they cannot understand that their products and methods are no longer up-to-date."[5] These observations by the Hungarian Finance Minister in 1975 remain valid today. A 1988 report by the Minister of Industry estimated that just 3–4 percent of industrial equipment and machinery in Hungary was up-to-date. Only 5 percent of Hungarian engineering products were five years or less behind their Western counterparts, while 75 percent were six to sixteen years behind, and 20 percent were over sixteen years behind.

Many goods and services with a low state priority are in especially short supply because the overworked planners fail to provide adequately (or at all) for their production. One result is a network of private artisans, shops, and repairmen, many of them moonlighting, who fill gaps in the supply network. Officially, the private sector produced just 14 percent of net material product in 1987, including less than 2 percent of value added in industry. Unofficially, it is larger, accounting for a third or more of all time spent at work and an even higher share of personal disposable income. (Price receipts of small firms per labor hour are 2.5 times those of large state enterprises, and underreporting is greater in the case of small companies, many of which operate illegally.) It also accounts for 55–60 percent of new homebuilding and for 85–90 percent of the value of all repair and maintenance services. It is especially prominent in the service sector, most of whose output is not counted as part of net material product, and where shortages have been acute, owing to low state priority and to difficulties of supply within the framework of state planning and management.[6]

As part of reform renewal after 1979, the government passed laws to encourage private business and small cooperatives by reducing taxes and red tape, making it easier to start such enterprises, raising access to credit and supplies, and giving people working in the private sector the same rights to social welfare benefits as state and cooperative employees. After a long decline, this sector began to grow again, although much of its apparent growth during the 1980s represents legalization of previously illegal private activity or efforts to get around wage control in the state sector.[7] By 1986, over 80 percent of all retail shops and restaurants were in private hands. However, a key 1949 law forced private firms to remain small by requiring nationalization of enterprises with more than 9 permanent employees, except in commerce where the legal limit was 12. Taxes on private businesses were also high and had tended to rise since 1982, because of budget deficits and popular resentment toward the high incomes that private businessmen were often able to earn. Then, in October 1988, after a change of political leaders, a new Corporation Law raised the employment limit for private firms to 500 (and abolished it altogether for foreign-owned companies). This law may herald a fundamental change in the nature of the Hungarian economy.

As with other systems originally based on the Soviet model, Hungary is ruled by its Communist party, and other political parties were effectively outlawed until recently. The Patriotic Peoples' Front, a mass organization dominated by the party formally recommended all candidates for election to political office. Historically, most elections have been uncontested, although the government has allowed electoral competition between party-approved candidates and, in recent years, has required this. At some cost, voters have also been able to register negative votes (against all party-approved candidates), although less than one percent of the Hungarian electorate has done this. Hungary has a Parliament, called the National Assembly, whose membership includes leading party figures. It meets in Budapest for a total of about two weeks each year. Aside from the party élite, a 1983 reform requires there to be at least two candidates in each election for every seat in the National Assembly, as well as for seats in local assemblies. A complementary 1985 reform allows employees of state firms to elect councils with power to choose enterprise directors, although only from candidates approved by the party and by the firm's planning superior. In each case, the increase in democracy may also be viewed as a reduction in preselection by party and state officials—since the planning superior used to hire and fire all top enterprise officials.

As a rule, the organs of government and Communist party remain distinct in socialist countries, but for every government agency which carries out the tasks of day-to-day administration, there is a party authority to supervise and to guide it. Thus, the Council of Ministers is, in practice, subordinate to the Politburo of the party's central committee—the country's top political authority—and there is a substantial membership overlap between the two. The party sets basic policy. About 11 percent of Hungary's adult population belongs to the party, officially called the Hungarian Socialist Workers' party (HSWP), and they come from all walks of life. More than half are blue-collar workers or farmers, although many of these are retired. They are supposed to be the most politically active and able individuals, and they join the party through invitation. Within the party, there can be discussion of issues and candidates for office, but once a decision has been taken or candidates have been named, party members must close ranks behind the party line. This is democratic centralism, the political legacy of Lenin. However, a law passed in 1988 has allowed new political parties to form in Hungary. They will engage in electoral competition for legislative seats with the Communists in 1990, for the first time since 1947.

HSWP control over economic life has increased the role of political, ideological, and administrative criteria in guiding resource allocation. These have often crowded out economic cost-benefit analysis, a task made easier by the absence of rational prices in which to value costs and benefits. Selection and promotion of enterprise managers has depended as much on party and government ties as on job performance, and until quite recently, there has been little risk of bankruptcy for enterprises of any size or consequence. The budget constraint for state-owned firms has been soft (or elastic), in the sense that over 80 percent of enterprise profits have been taxed away and most losses subsidized. In 1987, new efforts got underway to cut subsidies to loss-making firms and to restructure them for more efficient production. Hungary now has a formal bankruptcy law, and a major tax reform took place in 1988.

C. Excess Demand

Where production of a few consumer goods is concerned, Hungarian markets are almost competitive. But this is still the exception to the general rule of a sellers' market. Historically, there has been an excess demand for both producer and consumer durables, as is normal in a command economy. Prices have been held below market-clearing levels, making goods scarce. For consumers, there are fewer shortages today, but higher prices than in the past, although chronic excess demand persists for some items—notably, public housing. The latter is attractively priced, and tenants may leave their apartments to heirs (even though the state is the legal owner). However, the average waiting time for a government flat is more than 15 years in Budapest, and long waits are common as well in other cities, despite large rental increases in recent years (averaging about 130 percent over 1983–88). Increasingly, the housing stock is in private hands—about 75 percent of all dwellings in 1985 and over 85 percent of new dwellings—as a result of deliberate policy. In the private sector, access to a home is faster and depends more on ability to pay (or to obtain materials and build it yourself), with the result that prices and rents have been rising much more rapidly than average incomes in the state sector. Today, even a small apartment may cost the equivalent of twenty years' average earnings in a typical state enterprise.

Although the number of rooms of housing space per person rose by more than 90 percent over 1949–85, many people are also forced to live with relatives or even to squat in condemned buildings or other substandard dwellings. By no means all of these people are in poverty, as measured by income. In recent years, for example, young professionals have found it harder and harder to obtain housing, and most do not have their own quarters by age 35, since they do not qualify for means-tested government housing, and privately built dwellings are increasingly beyond their financial reach. Despite the growing shortage, as measured by excess demand for subsidized apartments, housing construction peaked in 1975, and output has since fallen by more than 40 percent (over 1975–87). This sector does not enjoy a high priority in access to resources, although housing is a basic need that a socialist state is supposed to satisfy. Instead, the housing market has a dual character, also found in the West. Publicly assisted housing is in excess demand. Access to it is means tested and requires long average waiting times for those who pass the test. Private housing is beyond or barely at the margin of affordability for growing numbers of families. One author writes that "the problem of acquiring a dwelling is today the single most important cause of social tensions . . . social inequality in Hungary is increasingly related to the quality of dwelling occupied by the individual or family and to the inequality of opportunity in the acquisition of a new dwelling."[8]

In the past, subsidized housing was more prominent in the total supply, but distribution was not necessarily more egalitarian. In 1967, implicit rent subsidies for apartments occupied by managers and professionals ran eight times, and for apartments occupied by other white-collar workers, four times subsidies on unskilled workers' flats. The latter were smaller and of much lower quality, then as now. Moreover, the old system did not provide good incentives to maintain the housing stock or to cater to demand. Apartments were highly standardized. Over 1970–80, Hungary completed 890,000 new dwellings, one of the highest rates, per capita, in the world (and one unlikely to be repeated soon). But nearly half as many dwellings were removed from the stock—a demolition rate that was also one of the world's highest.

The last twenty-five years have witnessed an explosion in the number of autos and smaller consumer durables in Hungary. In 1960, there was just one car, on average, for every hundred households. By 1985, there were over thirty-five, although the expansion of roads and repair services has not kept pace. Moreover, waiting times for new autos still average two to three years, and range up to six years, depending on make and model. Since new-car prices are set below market-clearing levels, while prices of used cars respond to supply and demand, the latter are often above the former. Sometimes, people even buy new cars primarily in order to resell them for a profit on the used-car market. There are also chronic shortages of medical care—as sometimes happens in Western countries when such care is largely financed by social insurance—and of telephone service. Average waiting time for a telephone line is now around fifteen years, and phone service is poor. Recently, the government sold "telephone bonds" to help finance an expansion of service. It promised phone lines for buyers within three years.

The other side of an excess demand for consumer goods is an excess supply of savings and of cash balances—in the sense that many individuals save more than they want to because goods or services they want to buy are in short supply. A leading Hungarian economist (Janos Kornai) wrote in 1971 that ". . . on a number of markets, shortages are continuous." Later, Kornai noted that "supply has much improved in Hungary in past years, yet a shortage of some goods and services occurs repeatedly.''[9] Around 5 percent of all savings deposits are placed in an account known as the ''auto lottery.'' Winners of the lottery do not receive a free car. Instead, they are allowed to jump the queue and take immediate delivery, provided they pay the full purchase price.

Thus, possession of money has not always ensured access to goods and services. This is still generally true of producer goods, unless the would-be buyer can find what he wants on the second economy. Through official channels, the Prices and Materials Board, SEC, and other government organs control the allocation of these goods to designated users. Rationing is more flexible than before 1968, but access still usually depends on having a government authorization. For the most part, consumer goods have not been formally rationed in Hungary for many years, however, and especially since the late 1960s, retail prices have played a growing role in their allocation. Constraints facing Hungarian households have become more financial and less physical—or more like budget constraints in the West—and Hungary has gone further in this direction than any other Soviet-type economy. (In the USSR, for example, 80–85 percent of all housing is state subsidized and usually priced far below market-clearing levels.) Increasingly, it is lack of money rather than a shortage of goods to buy that constrains the Hungarian consumer. This reflects government efforts to raise the incentive to earn higher incomes, as well as to reduce subsidies (which causes prices to rise). Yet, product selection remains poor by Western standards, consumer credit has been negligible to low, and dual allocation persists for housing and some other goods. Here, part of the supply is sold at low, controlled prices and the other part at prices which clear the market.

Finally, in Hungary as in other Soviet-type economies, there is a financial plan, which has historically been used to monitor performance in fulfilling the physical plan. The principal monitor, on behalf of the state, has been the National Bank of Hungary. Until recently, it combined the functions of a central bank with those of commercial banks and other financial intermediaries. Prior to 1968, the National Bank's main task, through its local branches, was to serve as watchdog over plan performance by monitoring flows of funds. This was ''control by the forint,'' the forint being Hungary's unit of currency. More recently, the bank has played a role in allocating investment loans (for which there is a strong excess demand) according to state priority. By increasing its reliance on financial levers, Hungarian planning has moved a step closer to planning in Japan, France, and other nonsocialist countries, as practiced during the 1950s and 1960s.

Hungary's financial system has also moved closer to Western models. Since 1982, a thriving bond market has sprung up, and bonds financed about 5 percent of enterprise investment in 1987. Some bonds have yields that vary with enterprise profitability, and the new Corporation Law referred to earlier provides the legal framework for limited liability and a full-fledged stock exchange, beginning in 1989. The National Bank of Hungary has also given up its commercial banking functions to 5 quasi-independent banks founded in 1987, which are supposed to compete for customers, both in attracting deposits and in granting loans. Although the central bank retains basic control over interest rates and owns a majority of shares in each commercial bank, the availability of loanable funds to each is to depend on its profitability. If this happens, borrower credit-worthiness should become more important in determining how much access to loanable funds each enterprise will enjoy. The same reform established nine smaller, specialized investment banks, besides which there continues to be a State Development Bank, financing major investments under the five-year plans, and a Foreign Trade Bank. The government budget will also continue to finance many investments, although the role of credit (which must be repaid) has been growing. Finally, to serve households, Hungary maintains a network of cooperative and savings banks, under a National Savings Bank. As the volume of consumer credit is small, this is largely to collect the savings of the public. Beginning in 1989, all banks were allowed to compete for these savings.

6-2. Approach to Planning and Development

A. The "New Economic Mechanism"

State control over the Hungarian economy has undergone modification and relaxation as a result of reforms begun in 1968 and renewed in 1979 after an intervening recentralization over 1972–78. The system ushered in by the reforms was baptized "New Economic Mechanism" (NEM), and the impression originally created in the West was that Hungary had gone from command to market socialism. While this may come to pass during the 1990s, it does not indicate the present state of affairs. In 1986, Kornai wrote that

> the Hungarian economy [has become] a symbiosis of a state sector under indirect bureaucratic control and a non-state [private and cooperative] sector, market-oriented, but operating under strong bureaucratic restrictions. Coexistence and conflict exist between [these] sectors in many ways and all the time.[10]

After 1968, the main task of reform in Hungary, as in other East European countries, became that of improving planning by freeing the ministries and central planners from involvement in day-to-day management of the economy. This was to allow them to concentrate on the basic strategy of development. "Relieved of the vast, circumstantial work of a mainly technical kind connected with elaboration of the national economic plan in details, our planning organs devote considerably greater attention to the main . . . development trends of the national economy and to forecasting domestic and international economic activity."[11] In 1974, this assessment was optimistic, but it indicates what Hungarian officials felt the reform had achieved prior to the 1980s. Arguably, this was not enough to resolve the problems which led to reform (and which were then made worse by the energy crisis).

Pressures for reform stem from comparative advantages and disadvantages of

Soviet-type economies. As a rule, these systems maintain high levels of job security and low levels of open unemployment. Employment security exists behind the pressure to produce more that command planning usually generates, together with the general state of excess demand and the reduced concern of management for cost control, in an environment where profitability is a secondary consideration. In fact, enterprise managers have an incentive to hoard labor, capital, and scarce materials as a reserve to ensure that they will be able to meet output targets. This leads to excessive inventories of material inputs and to periodic campaigns by the planners to uncover these hidden reserves. It also leads to underemployment of labor, in the form of overstaffing of work places.[12] Efforts by Hungarian planners to control wage increases (described below) have reinforced overmanning in some sectors, together with labor shortages elsewhere.

Command economies have also generated rapid growth. For the most part, however, this has been *extensive* growth—output increases due to increases in productive inputs—rather than *intensive* growth, due to technological improvement. State management has provided an excellent vehicle for mobilizing large forced savings and for plowing these into industries where investments could produce large, quick yields in higher output—as long as they were combined with rapid increases in energy, raw materials, and industrial labor. Hungarian industry has used generous quantities of these inputs, by Western standards.[13] But by the late 1960s, the sustainable size of Hungary's industrial labor force was approaching a limit. Labor force participation was already high, unemployment had long since been eliminated, and agriculture, the main source of new workers for industry, was beginning to be short of labor itself. Economic development was also increasing the range and variety of products and making the matrix of flows of intermediate goods between workplaces more complex. This was raising the management burden on state planners. Later, the energy crisis would lead to a worsening of Hungary's terms of trade with the rest of the world. The resulting balance-of-payments constraint has reduced growth further by restricting Hungary's ability to import energy, raw materials, and industrial machinery made in the West.

Until the early 1980s, Hungary continued to expand its stock of domestically produced industrial capital rapidly, by maintaining high rates of saving and investment. But the ability of this investment to generate growth depended more and more on technological progress, which largely depended, in turn, on Hungary's ability to import new capital and better production methods from the West. This was limited by the balance-of-payments constraint and also by the international climate of East–West relations. Thus, Hungary first experienced a growth slowdown in the mid-1960s, followed by roughly a decade of improvement and then a second, more dramatic slowdown, which has persisted into the latter 1980s. The second has been sharpened by a need to cushion the effect of worsening terms of trade on living standards. Maintenance of consumption forced the share of gross investment in national income (measured according to the Marxist definition) to nosedive, from 30 percent in 1978 to 13 percent in 1983. It has since remained near the 1983 ratio, and nearly half of all industrial investment has gone into nuclear power production in recent years—in no small measure, because of high electricity consumption by Hungarian firms.

Input increases are now harder for Hungary to obtain than at any time since the start of command planning in 1949. The basic policy prescription is therefore to decentralize, in order to increase the opportunities for intensive growth. In fact, the low rate of technological progress was becoming a problem as early as the mid-1960s. Then, as now, Hungarian consumers were growing impatient with the slow rise of living standards, which contrasted with the faster growth of heavy industry, and there had already been one violent uprising which no one wanted to repeat. This is why HSWP decided to launch NEM in 1968. Enterprises were to receive greater autonomy and to be judged more on the basis of profitability. The central planning apparatus has not withered away, but in principle, firms no longer receive obligatory input and output targets from their superiors, except where national defense or international agreements require this. (Even then, direct interference is only to be allowed when indirect measures would not work, and enterprise losses resulting from this interference are supposed to be reimbursed.) Theoretically, firms now have greater authority to enter into contracts, to decide the output assortments they will produce, and even to determine their investment programs. The central planners are only to decide and carry out the largest and most important investments, which determine the basic strategy of economic development. However, the shift to intensive growth has not yet occurred.

B. The Question of Enterprise Autonomy: Long-Run Decisions

Potentially, decentralization of a Soviet-type economy is a harrowing experience, both for state planners, who lose part of their control over resource allocation, and for enterprise managers and workers, who take on new risks and responsibilities when the protective umbrella of excess demand is stripped away. Ideally, reform would take place in an atmosphere free of pressure, so that individuals have breathing space in which to learn and adapt to their new roles. But decentralization also brings "bourgeois" qualities to the fore, including entrepreneurship and income differences based on success or failure in a market environment, which traditional socialist values deplore. Command economies therefore decline to undertake reform, except under pressure, which makes decentralization less likely to succeed. State planners opposed to reform have also been known to try to subvert it. Ultimately, however, recentralization is no answer to the problems facing the economy, and pressures for decentralization are bound to cumulate again, producing a cycle of reform and counterreform.

In Hungary, enterprise independence in 1988 is still less than was foreseen in 1968, and profitability is not yet a major success indicator for most state firms.

According to a recent series of case studies by the Chamber of Commerce, Hungarian managers in industry feel that they are still more dependent on the comprehensive evaluation of their performance by supervisory authorities than on profits, especially since this evaluation tends to level incomes that [would be] differentiated by enterprise profits results.''[14]

Consider first the sphere of investment decisions. To facilitate greater autonomy, Hungary introduced, along with NEM, a new method of allocating profits within state-owned enterprises and collective farms. Before 1968, most profits were taxed away, and what remained went into an enterprise fund from which bonuses were paid when plan fulfillment was successful.

Since 1968, the portion of enterprise revenue not taken by the turnover (sales) tax goes first to pay the costs of material inputs, depreciation, and the amounts of wages and salaries guaranteed by the state. Until 1988, each firm also paid a tax on its wages and salaries bill that replaced the personal income tax for most people, and it still pays social insurance contributions on behalf of its employees. The remainder of its revenue is profit, of which 40 percent has been directly taxed away in recent years. The rest has been divided among four funds—reserves for contingencies (usually about 15 percent of the total); a welfare fund, fixed in relation to wages and salaries; a development fund to finance investments and from which loans had to be repaid, and a bonus or sharing fund, from which wages or salaries in excess of guaranteed minima had to be paid. The bonus fund was subject to a steeply progressive tax. As a rule, the development fund was not taxed, but most firms had to remit 40 percent of their depreciation allowances to the state. In 1985, the bonus and development funds were abolished and replaced by a single incentive fund. Enterprises may now keep their entire depreciation allowances, which are paid into this fund. However, taxation depends on how the incentive fund is divided between pay increases (still subject to a steeply progressive tax) and investment finance, now subject to an accumulation tax, generally 18 percent in recent years.

The right for firms to invest their development funds as they chose was to be a major component of their new independence. But as a rule, enterprises cannot invest in a new line of production just because this happens to be profitable, nor can they stop producing unprofitable products. Administrative approval at the ministerial level or higher is usually necessary for major changes in a firm's output profile. This tends to stifle the main potential competitive force, although the rules have been eased in recent years to allow more enterprise freedom in choice of inputs and outputs. A state firm can also found a small subsidiary to produce a different line of goods and retain a claim on the profits or losses of its offspring. Cooperatives and collective farms have had freedom for several years to begin or to abandon lines of production (not necessarily related to agriculture) on the basis of profitability. But this freedom is circumscribed: party and government authorities have tried to limit competitive pressures on state enterprises—thus far, with success.

Theoretically, firms in the state sector can invest their retained earnings as they wish, subject to the restriction on major changes in output profile. In practice, however, they will need outside financial help for important projects, and taxation has been designed to ensure this. Such assistance must come as some combination of a bank loan, an investment subsidy, a tax exemption, and borrowing from another firm. However, although interenterprise credit is important, it mainly results from delayed payment for goods and is probably not a major source of investment finance. To get outside help for a major investment, a firm must therefore apply to a bank or to a government committee in control of access to investment loans and subsidies. Given excess demand for these funds, success requires the active support of its parent ministry, in preparing the application and smoothing the way. In the past, credit to finance important investments has usually been awarded to an enterprise only with consent of its supervising ministry. Just 20 percent of investment in the state sector has been financed entirely from enterprise funds.[15]

When the National Bank or the State Development Bank has lent money, it has required the borrower to bear part of the cost of the investment from his own resources, and an investment subsidy usually entails the same commitment. This reduces a firm's control over investment choices, except via lobbying pressures which managers are able to bring to bear on higher authorities (and which are normally proportional to enterprise size and to the priority of its output). Most of the money in development funds has gone to pay back loans or for investments that were partly financed with outside resources. Government authorities have determined the nature of these projects, usually to conform to targets in the national plan. Even when firms finance investments entirely from their own funds, the state exercises indirect leverage, except over enterprises which are relatively small and market-oriented.[16] Thus, state priorities have determined what kinds of investments would be made, although the central authorities have sometimes allowed the total volume of investment to get out of control.

As a rule, state officials have not allocated investment resources to maximize yields as measured by enterprise profitability before taxes and subsidies. They have been about as likely to invest in firms with low as with high expected returns, and large investment subsidies and loans have gone to chronic loss-makers.[17] The latter have been able to survive, pay competitive wages, and even to expand in some cases. At the same time, 80–85 percent of gross enterprise profit has been taxed away. A number of losing enterprises are large, heavy industrial firms, whose products have historically enjoyed a high state priority. For political and social reasons, moreover, the government has been unwilling to jeopardize the jobs or incomes of too many workers or managers, and the state, itself, has been heavily involved in crucial management decisions affecting state enterprises, including the decision to found them and all major expansions. Irrational prices also make profitability a poor measure of efficiency or social return, but freeing prices would result in some dramatic increases, causing hardship and dislocation. Nevertheless, during the 1980s, inflation has been higher, and the budget now redistributes less extensively than during the 1970s or earlier.

Since the central authorities often lack good economic yardsticks to tell them whether an investment is worthwhile, rights to investment resources have been ill defined, and enterprises have found it to their advantage to understate the costs of investment projects when applying for funds. Once granted, the actual cost of these credits to the firm—in terms of their burden on wages and salaries—is apt to be low or nil, because of the high effective marginal tax on profit. A conspicuously high profit is even a liability and could be grounds for criminal prosecution. It is better to argue that a firm supplies useful products at reasonable prices and wishes to expand or improve this capability. Authorities find it hard to turn down applications that meet government guidelines and enjoy ministerial support. As a result, the state wound up financing more investment than it wanted to during the 1970s, and the excess demand for capital—as measured by the ratio of unfinished to total investment—reached an all-time high. The time required to complete projects and to bring them into full operation rose by over 20 percent between 1968 and 1978, until it was twice as long as in Western Europe. Enterprises also tended to overstate the desirability of prospective investments before 1968, as a means of getting their projects into the national plan, which raised the likelihood of obtaining the resources needed to carry them out. Then as now, investment was the principal way to expand output and improve security of supply (since firms often invest in producing their own inputs).

Reforms during the 1980s have sought to improve the allocation of investment resources by moving toward genuine loanable funds markets. In the process, they have also expanded the financial choices open to state and cooperative firms. Since 1982, enterprises have been able to issue their own bonds or to buy bonds issued by other firms. The 1987 Banking Reform allows them to borrow from several different commercial and investment banks, although no longer from the National Bank which is restricted to lending to other banks (as is generally true of Western central banks). This reform may well improve the access to credit of profitable small and medium-sized firms. But persistence of the soft budget constraint would also preserve administrative allocation of credit under conditions of shortage. If banks lend and enterprises borrow with expectations that the state will help to repay loans when the alternative would be hardship to managers or employees of either borrower or lender, the demand for loans will be heavy and banks will be willing to supply most of this demand. To keep down open and repressed inflation, as well as investment completion times, the National Bank will then have to restrain lending with direct or indirect ceilings on credit expansion (including minimum reserve requirements). Since it also controls the cost of borrowing, excess demand for loans is likely to persist, requiring other criteria to help determine how loanable funds will be allocated. Here, government recommendations (which are also apt to look like repayment guarantees to lending banks) will probably serve as a *de facto* quota system. However, if present efforts to harden enterprise budget constraints are successful, they will reduce excess demand for loans, as well as the role of political considerations in their allocation.

C. The Question of Enterprise Autonomy: Short-Run Decisions

In the twenty-odd years since the birth of the New Economic Mechanism, the state planning apparatus has remained intact—albeit with some reorganization—but the formal method of planning has changed. Before NEM, the central planners, the ministries, local governments and, to an extent, the enterprises all drew up annual plans, and there was constant dialogue between the various levels. Central authorities used this to keep aware of production possibilities, although differences between plans being prepared at different levels tended to be resolved in favor of the center. NEM abolished neither the five-year nor the annual plans, which remain the basis for state control of the economy. State planning authorities are still legally obligated to ensure that plan targets are reached. However, the ministries no longer compile independent plans for themselves or for firms within their jurisdictions, and the plans compiled in the National Planning Office, based on Politburo directives, are broken down only to the level of the industry. Instead of breaking down the national plan further and sending production targets to individual firms, the authorities require enterprises to draw up their own plans and to follow these.

In drawing up their plans, Hungarian firms are to be guided by price trends on foreign and domestic markets, and, ultimately, by profitability. But what happens when the sum of enterprise plans is not consistent with plans being prepared by central authorities? The foci of tension will be those institutions charged with reconciliation, notably the ministries and local governments. They will quickly become aware of contradictions between plans being prepared at the two levels, since they are in contact with each; in particular, their representatives sit on enterprise boards of directors. Moreover, they can influence firms through their leverage over credit allocation, their power within HSWP, and their control over managerial rewards.

When such contradictions occur, ministries and local government authorities are duty bound to enforce the national plan, whose targets are likely to be broken down informally by enterprise. (Such a breakdown would normally be based on traditional supply patterns and shares of industry-wide output.)[18] By end-1972, five years after the start of NEM and in the initial phase of recentralization, the ministries had already issued over 500 rules regulating enterprise profits and their use. In the mid-1980s, there were 300 different taxes and subsidies which could be applied to state enterprises, allowing authorities to tailor individual tax-subsidy packages for each firm. "In addition, strong [informal] pressure from government departments, political organs, the press, etc. is put on enterprise management to restrict the role of profitability and economic gain in determining production structure and product mix."[19]

Given the monopoly positions of many large firms—which are strengthened by excess demand—plus the reluctance of bureaucrats to lose control, this was probably inevitable. However, it is also true that many managers, especially of larger firms, had grown dependent on bureaucratic superiors and were unable to cope with the limited increases in responsibility and independence that accompanied or were threatened by the first few years of NEM. These managers preferred the restricted range of decisions under the shelter of excess demand associated with traditional command planning, and they lobbied for protection from market forces, relying on party and government connections they had cultivated over many years. Their superiors obliged, in order to restrengthen their control over economic activity. Thus, the former dependence reasserted itself and was reinforced by fear of many blue-collar workers that reform threatened their living standards or even their jobs. (Until September 1986, Hungary had no provision for unemployment compensation, and it still lacks a good infrastructure for recycling unemployed workers back into productive work, although there is now a system of local employment offices.)

In this context, mergers cut the number of state-owned and cooperative firms almost in half between 1960 and 1980. Small- and medium-sized enterprises were absorbed into larger units, and the share in industrial output of small firms operating legally fell to under 5 percent, before the merger movement was finally reversed during the 1980s. The main reasons for mergers were efforts by enterprise managers to raise their bargaining power with superiors and efforts by the latter to reduce the number of subordinates. By making the structure of industry more monopolistic, the merger movement helped to ensure that major increases in enterprise independence would be intolerable and that profitability would have to remain a relatively minor success indicator. In fact, profits before taxes and subsidies have little effect on the incomes of managers or of workers. The most important determinant of executive salaries in Hungary is the industry to which an enterprise belongs. Managers in heavy industry, metallurgy, construction, and engineering earn more than their counterparts in light industry. Seniority and size of firm are also important.

While formal rationing of scarce industrial goods was reduced after 1968, producer-goods markets did not generally arise to replace the materials balances, nor could they have, since prices remained rigid and below market-clearing levels. For some goods, formal rationing was reintroduced in 1976, only to be relaxed or abandoned again in 1980. In most cases, the rationing process continued, but became more informal and flexible. Planners assign firms the responsibility to supply particular kinds of goods in designated minimum quantities to designated users, normally based on traditional supply patterns. Such assignments must be fulfilled, even if some other pattern of production and supply would be more profitable.

Thus, the reform has produced a more flexible planning process. There is now less need to conform to what was often excessive and unrealistic detail before 1968, and less effort is wasted in working out, writing down, and communicating these details.[20] There is also more room for give and take in drawing up and implementing plans. Financial constraints are somewhat more important, although the government still won't usually force a major firm into bankruptcy, and the effective marginal tax on enterprise profits remains high, even after the 1988 tax reform. Repeated calls for enterprise management to exercise better leadership, show more initiative, and develop entrepreneurial skills have not yet been accompanied by a climate to promote these qualities within most large- and medium-sized firms.

Many traditional problems associated with command planning persist. In particular, planners still do not know what levels of profit (or sales, value added, etc.) would correspond to efficient enterprise management. Thus, they continue to evaluate enterprises on the basis of current *increases* in output, value-added, profit, and other indices. As a result, firms are still reluctant to improve their performance too rapidly, and they continue to hoard scarce inputs, in order to ensure their ability to meet plan commitments, as well as to compensate for defects in the supply system. One consequence is that inventories of goods for processing are three to five times or more higher in Hungarian industry, relative to output, than they are in Western Europe.[21]

In general, the reform has amplified the dual structure of the Hungarian economy. The degree of centralization is greatest for large-scale, capital intensive firms in heavy industry and least for smaller firms in light industry and services, as well as for most collective and state farms. The latter are more subject to market forces. In fact, relations between planning organs and some large enterprises are not much different than before 1968. For political reasons, there can be no widespread demotion of their managers. While many were retiring during the 1980s, selection of replacements may still depend on connections and activities within HSWP, as has traditionally been the case. Such managers often resist reform.

By contrast, collective and state farms, along with a number of medium-sized and small firms in engineering, cosmetics, pharmaceuticals, clothing and textiles, some consumer durables, and in services have gained major increases of independence and responsibility. These companies have greater freedom to set prices and looser ties, both with central development projects and with the national economic plan. They also export greater shares of their outputs, have fewer problems with quality and cost control, and exercise greater autonomy in investment decision making. Their managers are more interested in marketing and technological improvement and display greater initiative in these areas. While they get fewer subsidies, they also receive less intervention from state planning organs and party activists.

Current policy is to promote small- and medium-sized firms, including private and small cooperative enterprises. These now have better access to credit and supplies, and it is easier to found one than before 1982. Government red tape has been reduced, and the number of legal forms that such an undertaking may assume is greater. But government and party policies toward private and small cooperative enterprises have oscillated between periods of tolerance and encouragement and periods of harassment, high taxation, interference, and even confiscation, for nearly forty years. Managers of these companies do not easily develop long time horizons or undertake large investments which require several years to pay off. (The near absence of limited liability prior to 1989 has also reduced the availability of investment capital.) Their attitude has been to make money while the sun shines, which has been unfavorable to the long-run development of this sector and has even helped to cause hostile reactions and policy reversals.

In principle, a state-owned firm can now increase its independence from the state planning hierarchy by compiling an excellent export record to convertible currency (mainly Western) markets. But many managers of state enterprises do not especially want such freedom. The balance-of-payments crisis of the late 1970s caused government to rediscover the market sector, because of its flexibility and cost effectiveness, because of its ability to innovate and to produce a quality product, because of its demand orientation, and because it is capable of putting competitive pressure on large state enterprises. Yet, authorities are of two minds about such pressure, especially when jobs are threatened. They still have a way to go in convincing HSWP members, as well as the general public, that managers able to function efficiently in a market environment deserve the opportunity to prosper.

D. Hungarian Incomes Policy

Over 1945–46, Hungary went through the worst hyperinflation in recorded history, which has given its citizens a basic fear of price increases. Consequently, in 1957—the year after the uprising, when popular acceptance of the régime assumed new importance—the government introduced an incomes policy called average wage control. Together with restraint in expanding the money supply, it kept the annual increase in the official consumer price index below one percent in most years prior to 1973. This contrasts with a 69 percent rise over 1950–52 and with the experience of many other nations. In recent years, inflation has been higher because of external pressures. Officially, the CPI rose by an annual average of 6.5 percent over 1975–85, and the rate of increase has been even greater since then. For the entire period, 1950–85, of Communist rule, consumer price increases averaged a bit more than 3.8 percent per year, which compares favorably with most Western countries, although failure to adequately cover price increases on the second economy gives the official index a downward bias. Hungary has combined moderate inflation with overfull employment. In mid-1987, there were ten vacancies for every job seeker, and registered unemployment was just 1.1 percent of the labor force, although it will rise if current efforts to harden enterprise budget constraints are successful.

Originally, wage control meant that each firm received a binding ceiling on the percentage by which its average wage (total wages and salaries divided by number of employees) could rise from one year to the next.[22] This ceiling became an important success indicator, and the enterprise director who exceeded it had to pay a stiff fine, which came out of his own bonus and those of his colleagues. While all command economies try to control both wages and employment, Hungary has attached a higher priority to wage control and enforced it more severely than in other socialist countries. Elsewhere, targets for wages and labor input are frequently violated or else bargained—by enterprises seeking to build up their labor reserves—to levels that are not very constraining. In Hungary, as in the USSR and elsewhere in Eastern Europe, the government also sets wage rates for each basic skill category, which are minima that firms must pay. After 1971, average wage control was enforced through steeply progressive taxation of pay increases. Mainly because of this and its other taxes, a firm has had to generate anywhere from zero to more than 100 forints of increase in net output, for each forint of average wage increase that it has paid. The exact output expansion required has depended on central regulations, as well as the industry in which a firm operates, and other characteristics of its particular situation. As it grants greater increases, the output expansion needed to cover these rises more than proportionately. Few firms could afford average wage hikes above 6 percent during the latter 1970s, and conditions have since become harsher.

While average wage control helped to contain inflationary pressures, it also encouraged labor hoarding. Suppose a manager wants to give above-average raises to key personnel—possibly, to ensure they will not leave for a better offer elsewhere—without penalizing other employees. If there is a ceiling on the average enterprise wage, he can do this by hiring workers who will accept less than the enterprise average. To an extent, it has even paid to hire people at low wages who did little or no work. During the early and mid-1970s, when 300,000 jobs could not be filled, many firms kept redundant labor, in part because of average wage control.

Consequently, Hungary changed its system of wage control, beginning in 1976, so that a firm could more easily grant wage increases when it reduced its number of employees. In addition, wage control became more complex, and since 1985 has been extended to cover bonuses, as well as wages and salaries. In most enterprises, steeply progressive taxation is now applied either to total earnings (total wages, salaries, and bonuses paid to all employees) or else to the annual increase in total earnings. Under either scheme, an enterprise that cuts its work force while maintaining output can also raise the pay of those workers who remain. However, as soon as a firm's average pay increase (increase in earnings per employee) reaches a preset limit, there is a surtax on further average pay increases. In this sense, an average earnings "brake" exists on top of the ceiling on total earnings. In some years, the brake has been binding on most enterprises, and the net effect has been much the same as with the previous average wage control. State-owned industry still maintains a labor reserve—amounting to 15–20 percent of its total employment, according to some estimates.[23]

Across the state sector as a whole, pay increases have not kept pace with inflation since 1978. Within the first (or official) economy, moreover, earnings regulation has been a tool for levelling incomes. A Hungarian source writes that "[income] differentiation between enterprises is . . . unimportant: it never occurs that personal incomes would be twice as high in an enterprise working with an efficiency twice as high as another one. The extent of material incentive is limited. . . ."[24] Wage and salary differences based on skill and professional ability, willingness to bear risk, aptitude for independent judgment, etc., have been rather low, as well.[25]

Still others argue that pay increases in Hungary have not depended on a firm's profitability. Instead, the reverse has been nearly true. Through selective subsidies and tax exemptions, the government has regulated the post-tax profit of each enterprise, so that each could give about the economy-wide average pay increase.[26] The underlying reasons for this include the unsuitability of profits as an enterprise success indicator, and the unwillingness or (for political reasons) inability of the planners to allow income differences to widen. In fact, wage and salary differentials narrowed through the 1970s, to the point where shortages of workers willing to do hard or unpleasant work and/or work requiring certain skills became chronic.

Consequently, in 1980, the government attacked egalitarian wage practices. The Minister of Labor raised the average wage brake by 25 percent and announced that earnings would depend more closely on performance in the future—an original goal of NEM. In 1981, the Ministry of Labor was abolished and replaced by a State Office for Wages and Labor, with a much smaller staff. This represents an effort to reduce detailed regulation of enterprise pay, and new rules seek to tie pay increases more firmly to productivity gains at the enterprise level.[27] If they are successful, they will probably increase real income and output in Hungary over the long run. But over the next few years, the real earnings of many workers are likely to decline further, because there will be little room for average gains across the country as a whole.

Whereas redistribution of incomes on the first economy has been greater than in most Western countries, redistribution on the second (or market-oriented) economy has been less. Here, firms are smaller, and recent legislation has made it easier to start legal private enterprises and cooperatives, as noted earlier. Thousands of these "new-type" economic units have sprung up, often as a result of individual initiative, although many were previously operating illegally, and the illegal economy has not disappeared. The new enterprises have been able to employ up to 200 workers each if they take the cooperative form, and there have been many reports of large incomes earned by people with the right skills or with good access to capital or scarce supplies. The most prominent kind of new-type unit is the "working community" formed within state enterprises. By 1986, there were over 20,000 of these, each consisting of a group of employees of a state firm, who organized themselves as a cooperative. In effect, state enterprises were getting around wage control by buying the products of overtime work from their own employees at prices allowing comparatively high earnings for the latter.

Altogether, around 75 percent of Hungary's labor force has some association with the second economy, often by way of owning a small farm or garden plot. Thus, Hungarians may work the longest hours in Europe, counting labor input on both the first and second economies. (Over half the adult population works more than sixty hours per week.) A major reason is the high cost of private housing. At some point, dispersion of second-economy incomes may overwhelm government efforts to redistribute on the first economy, and this may lead to new efforts to suppress private ventures, especially if the pressure on Hungary's balance of payments subsides. (Because of foreign debt, however, the latter appears unlikely over the next few years.)

E. Social Insurance

Prior to the 1988 tax reform, most central government tax revenues came from profits or turnover (sales) taxes, while only 3–4 percent or less came from payments by individuals, including personal income taxes. In recent years, 20–25 percent of central government budget revenues have been social insurance contributions, a share that has been rising. These also amount to 40 percent of enterprise payrolls. In 1987, the budget deficit came to about 7 percent of revenues. The state has been financing deficits by creating money, but also by obliging profitable enterprises to buy government bonds, which mature in ten years' time and pay no interest for the first five years. To a degree, these bonds are therefore like a tax and are part of the budget's redistribution activity.

On the expenditure side, over 25 percent of outlays have been investment grants and operating subsidies for enterprises, while another 8–9 percent has been paid as consumption subsidies, to keep down retail prices. Beginning in 1988, both of these shares are to be cut, along with the budget deficit. Over 15 percent has gone for science, culture, education, and sports, while about 4 percent has been officially committed to defense (a figure which understates the total defense burden). Over 20 percent has gone as social insurance outlays, now the largest single expenditure item and the one growing most rapidly. (Over 1979–85, it rose from 14.5 percent to 21.6 percent of total spending.) Government expenditure at all levels was probably 55–60 percent of gross domestic product in 1985, calculated according to Western methods, a ratio comparable to that of Sweden, the world's foremost welfare state. A major difference between the two countries was Sweden's smaller commitment of resources to subsidize loss-making firms.

Within social insurance, pensions have been the fastest growing item, reflecting the aging of Hungary's population, as well as its low retirement ages by comparison with Western nations, and the increasing coverage of state pension programs. Overall, social expenditure amounted to 20–21 percent of GDP in 1981, somewhat below the unweighted average of 25.6 percent for all OECD nations, although above the percentages for Japan and Australia and equal to that of the United States.[28] Hungary's expenditure on unemployment compensation was zero, however, vs. an OECD average of 1.1 percent. It would be fair to include a portion of its subsidies to enterprises under social expenditure, since these subsidies helped to sustain a labor reserve that was Hungary's substitute for open unemployment in the West.

Hungary also trailed the unweighted OECD averages for each of health, pensions, and education in 1981, although real social expenditures have been growing more rapidly in Hungary since 1960, largely as a result of improved coverage and benefits, starting from a low level. (However, like housing, health care has a low priority and a lower share of investment than in most Western countries.) Until recently, the average Hungarian pension was less than half of average blue-collar earnings in state industry and is still under two-thirds of these. Retired farmers still get no more than half the average earnings of active peasants. As a result of changes over time in the pension law, pensions are unequal. The highest are about ten times the lowest, with those who retired earliest generally faring worst. Moreover, while pensions are tied to earnings, most second-economy income does not count in computing them, and wages in the first economy are low. As many as a million pensioners and their spouses (half the total number) live near subsistence or below. In recent years, their real incomes have fallen, as have real earnings in the state sector.

Thus, the main reason for the fairly high (and rising) share of pension payments in GDP is the high percentage of pensioners in Hungary's population. This rose from 6 percent to 20 percent over 1960–85, and will probably reach 25 percent by the year 2000, partly because of low retirement ages—55 for women, 60 for men, and even less for those who do dangerous or heavy manual work. With consent of his or her employer, a person may postpone retirement, and about 10 percent of those past retirement age have done this. Because of low pensions, at least 25 percent of all pensioners also work part-time. The state encourages this by providing improved access to housing, a job placement service for retirees, and the right to earn some income with no cut in one's pension.

Since the mid-1970s, moreover, Hungary has had a relatively good social retirement plan, modeled on those of Western Europe, and applicable to all who have retired in the intervening period. Each retiree who qualifies—usually after ten working years—gets a basic pension equal to 33 percent of his earnings during the best three of his last five working years plus a supplement for each year worked beyond the basic ten. Thus, an individual who retires after twenty-five years receives 63 percent of his earnings and someone retiring after 42 years receives the maximum of 75 percent.[29] There is a further supplement for a live-in spouse over 55 plus annual increments of 2 percent that partially compensate for inflation. Additional income supplements have been paid to offset some specific price increases (notably rent hikes). Nevertheless, inflation has significantly eroded pensioners' purchasing power since the present system went into effect. Beginning in 1991, twenty years of work will be necessary to qualify for a pension, but those who do qualify will receive the same benefits as at present (e.g., 53 percent of earnings after twenty years and 75 percent after forty-two).

6-3. The Organization of Agriculture

As in all command economies except Poland, most farm land in Hungary has been collectivized. The common grounds of collective farms cover 70.5 percent of the agricultural area (as of 1985) vs. 15 percent in the state sector, mainly in state farms, 12 percent farmed privately, and 2.4 percent in various other cooperatives. In principle, state farms are run like state industrial enterprises, and they are supposed to be in the vanguard of agricultural experimentation, research, and development. (In practice, they appear to have little productivity edge, if any, over the collectives.)[30] State farm employees receive wages like workers in state industry.

By contrast, a collective farm is, in principle, a producer cooperative, whose management is ultimately accountable to its membership. In practice, many management decisions have been taken by state officials, who often lack first-hand knowledge of specific crops or of local soil or climatic conditions. In addition, farm management has tended to be government-appointed and party-approved, as in industry, although the membership has had a greater input in recent years. To some degree, collective farm members also share in farm profits and losses. As the farms are large and internal distribution tends to be egalitarian, this has produced a weak bond between reward and performance, especially at the margin of work effort. Since 1968, moreover, the state has had to guarantee minimum income levels for members, and this has helped to blur the distinction between collective and state farms. As in industry, the average size of farm has risen through merger. By 1985, the agricultural area of an average collective covered nearly 9,000 acres, and the average state farm was almost 75 percent larger. There were fewer than 40 percent as many state farms and 30 percent as many collective farms as in 1960. But management personnel decreased by less than 20 percent, while clerical and administrative staff expanded to nearly 4.5 times the previous level.[31] Size increases have probably not raised efficiency, but they have expanded the political and economic leverage of affected farms and, as in industry, simplified the tasks of planning superiors by giving them fewer units to deal with.

Few nations are blessed with a natural endowment as favorable to agriculture as Hungary's. This is why the policy of assigning highest priority to heavy industry and a low priority to agriculture was so costly during the 1950s and 1960s, when farming was collectivized and peasant incomes were squeezed to finance all-out industrial expansion. Although wheat had historically been Hungary's major export, production fell and exports stopped during the first collectivization drive of the early 1950s. Between 1954 and 1966, Hungary had to import wheat to feed its people, and exports did not resume until 1969. Since then, the real value of food exports has more than quintupled, however, and in 1985, they accounted for 20 percent of all exports and almost 30 percent of sales in convertible (mainly Western) currencies. About 30 percent of agricultural output is exported, and net exports (exports minus imports) are far higher than for any other category of goods or services. Today, over 70 percent of Hungary's territory is under cultivation—the highest ratio in Europe—and almost 90 percent of this is cropland.

Since 1970, per capita farm output has grown more rapidly in Hungary than in any other East European nation. Today, it is Europe's fifth largest producer of wheat (after the USSR, France, West Germany, and the United Kingdom), as well as the world's fifth largest per capita producer of meat (after New Zealand, the United Kingdom, Australia, and Argentina). According to official statistics, real investment in agriculture was about 2.5 times as great in 1985 as in 1960. Yet, farming's share of total productive investment (11 percent in 1985) has been declining for some time and is now well below levels of the early 1960s. Although its share of fixed assets was over twice as great (13 percent vs. 6 percent) as during the earlier period, 40 percent of the machinery and tools used in agriculture are worn out or obsolete. The main constraint on expansion of farm output is now shortage of capital, despite higher investment yields here than in most of industry. Moreover, within agriculture as within industry, it is possible to question the wisdom of many specific investment choices.[32]

In the 1950s, agriculture was heavily taxed, and the collectives received obligatory delivery quotas for major crops. Prices paid by the state for these quotas were so low as to amount to virtual confiscation. Between 1950 and 1956, forced savings of the peasantry nearly financed all investment in state industry, in line with the Soviet model of economic development. To ensure delivery, the state controlled most equipment for planting and harvesting, which it kept at equipment stations through the countryside. When harvesting, these stations made sure the state collected its share of the crop, on top of which they charged the collectives for services rendered. The government also paid low prices for farm animals. Thus, "peasants did not report the calving of their cows, since low prices made selling them to the state a poor proposition. If one is to believe the official figures, the 'performance' of bulls, boars, and rams was never so poor as at that time."[33]

Until the late 1960s, members' shares of the income of each collective farm were determined by the residual principle. Whatever was left after the farm had fulfilled its obligations to the state, had satisfied its investment requirements, and had met any other claims, could be divided among the members, based on number of work points earned by each for participating in collective farm chores. Usually, not much was left for distribution, which reinforced the egalitarian bias in assigning work points, and this residual fluctuated sharply from year to year with the size of the harvest. Obligatory deliveries were relatively constant. Farmers therefore absorbed most of the risk of low harvests, but their main burden was poverty. Historically, peasants had been exploited in Hungary, but in 1953 "the national average income paid by collective farms in kind or other forms was about one-third of the compensation [payment in money and kind] of prewar farm hands."[34] In 1938, a farm day laborer earned about 40 percent of the wage of an unskilled worker in industry.

The Soviet development model did not work well in Hungary, and it began to be abandoned after the 1956 uprising. In 1957, the system of compulsory deliveries was ended, and central planning of agricultural production was reduced. Collective farms began to draw up their own plans on the basis of agreements with state purchasing agencies. Equipment stations ceased to exist, and their tools and machinery, along with many of their workers, went to the collectives. Yet, since farms still had little alternative to selling their output to the state, purchase prices for farm produce remained low. Incomes rose, but were still below those in industry, and the collectives had little opportunity to invest from their own resources. They continued to finance investment in industry (and, to a lesser degree, this is still their role today). During the early and mid-1960s, performance did not improve by much, and the countryside was being depopulated, as peasants sought higher and more stable earnings in industry. It was mainly the young and strong who left and the old who stayed behind. Over 1961–65, the farm labor force fell by 200,000, and the collectives were increasingly forced to use hired labor—nonmembers whose wages were guaranteed and who generally received more than members for the same work.

Finally, minimum wages had to be guaranteed for collective farm members as well, starting in 1968. This eventually halted the outflow of labor, and the average age of active members began to decline. In 1986, average peasant incomes were slightly lower than those in state industry, if we leave out receipts from the second economy (including private farming) in both cases. Peasants may have better opportunities here, but they also work longer hours than do state industrial employees, and access to social overhead capital and consumer durables in the countryside is lower than in urban areas. As a rule, local governments in rural districts are starved for tax revenues, which go mainly to benefit cities and towns. Thus, Hungary's villages are chronically short of infrastructure, including good roads, as well as cultural, recreational, and health facilities. In addition, nearly half of collective and state farms are now in financial difficulty, and farm debt is at record levels. About a third of all collectives account for over 80 percent of all collective farm profits.

Following the introduction of NEM, the authorities began to promote production on private plots and other private farms. One compensation to the peasants for giving up their land to join the collectives was the right to keep a small private plot—usually of one to three acres—on which they can raise a few animals and grow food for personal consumption or for sale on the rural free market. State farmers, school teachers in the countryside, and others received small auxiliary farms (in effect, garden plots). Altogether, there were 1.42 million small private holdings in 1985, averaging about 1.4 acres, and only 640,000 belonged to collective farm members. Nearly half of all Hungarian households own a small farm or large garden, although just 20 percent of the labor force officially remains in agriculture (and only 15 percent of those who do some farming now farm full-time). In many village families, the husband works in industry and the wife in collective agriculture, or vice versa. About half of all industrial workers live in rural areas.

Originally, private plots and other private farms were considered temporary institutions—part of the transition to socialist agriculture, while the social consciousness of the peasantry was developing and its private property mentality was withering away. But it has not been possible to get rid of these tiny farms. Here, reward and performance are closely linked, and peasant owners lavish more care and effort on them than on collective or state fields. On 12 percent of the agricultural area, they produced 34 percent of total farm output in 1985, although their share of value added in agriculture was lower. They accounted for a fourth of crop output and over 40 percent of livestock production, including several hundred million dollars in export earnings.[35]

When officials decide to move against the private plots, the unfavorable effect on production usually forces an eventual policy reversal. Following a tax increase in 1974, the number of cattle brought to market fell by 200,000, and the number of pigs by 1.6 million. Before long, authorities were once again encouraging and assisting small-scale private production. The state has expanded supplies of tools and small tractors suitable for use on these farms, along with credit and the services of agricultural research institutes. It has promoted cooperation between the socialist and private sectors and removed all restrictions on the size of private livestock holdings—in part to expand private rearing of animals on behalf of collective and state farms. (The private owner buys the young animal, rears it, and then sells it back.) The state even subsidizes private rearing and breeding of livestock. Nevertheless, the percentage of agricultural area farmed privately has been falling slowly in recent years.

The 1968 reforms also led to an expansion of collective and state farm autonomy and initiative beyond that achieved in industry. Several of the reforms were applied first in agriculture, and farms gained some freedom from the often costly interference by local governments in planting and livestock breeding. In 1977, the collectives founded a joint marketing, supply, and services enterprise, which allows them to bypass the state wholesale trade network. In addition, over 90 percent of collective and state farms have taken up sideline production of industrial goods plus a variety of services, in order to earn extra income and to occupy their workers during the off season. These "sideline" activities now account for more than 40 percent of collective and state farm revenues and are especially important for the many financially weak collectives, who have been starved for investment funds.

According to one author,

> By 1968, 94 percent of all collectives operated one or more subsidiary enterprises embracing 150 different lines of activity. Many . . . flourished because they undercut state or cooperative enterprises. It appears [moreover] that the Hungarian government underestimated the entrepreneurial drive of its farmers. . . . A large proportion [of subsidiary income] came from activities that had nothing to do with agriculture; one enterprising subsidiary built a small airport, while others set up TV servicing and other repair shops. Another . . . tooled up to produce poultry processing equipment for the USSR, and faced with loss of this market when the Russians changed their mind, shifted to subcontracting for [firms] with labor shortages. It then proceeded to hire away skilled industrial workers from state enterprises (presumably by offering higher wages) and ended the year with a handsome profit.[36]

Still another collective opened a restaurant in Budapest, and so forth.

So entrepreneurial were the farms that complaints of "unfair competition" soon arose from state industry and from influential party and trade union officials. Many of the above operations were curtailed, and for a time, farms were largely confined to activities (such as food processing) directly related to agriculture. Nevertheless, sideline output continued to rise, and with the renewed commitment to reform of the late 1970s, farm autonomy again began to increase. By 1980, sideline industrial output was more than 4.5 times as great on collective farms and 6 times as great on state farms as in 1970. Finally, in 1981, most remaining restrictions on sideline production were removed. Today, each farm has 9 industrial workshops, on average, which produce altogether nearly 8 percent of industrial output, and nearly every farm also has a construction organization. As well, the farms run about 2,500 shops and more than 1,000 catering establishments throughout the country.

Hungarian collectives have also been innovative within agriculture. In 1971, they began introducing "closed production systems," which mechanize some farming activities and allow increased use of pesticides, fertilizers, and high-yielding seed varieties. More generally, closed systems use factory production methods—including better management and coordination of inputs than heretofore—to increase land and labor productivity. At present, 90 percent of all state and collective farms apply this technology to at least one crop. Hungarian officials credit it with raising per-acre yields far above average world levels and improving net farm exports.

Even before NEM, a few collective farms introduced share-cropping—which has since spread—as a means of raising the output of labor intensive crops, such as vegetables, fruit, tobacco, and animal husbandry. Here, the application of closed production systems is impractical. Instead, the collective or state land is divided among individual workers, each of whom receives a share of the crops he grows on his assigned plot as payment for his work. These allotments are temporary— often they apply only to secondary crops, which are planted after the main crops are harvested—and the land remains in public ownership. Since mid-1981, any individual or group may sign a share-cropping or other income-sharing agreement with a collective or state farm. Indeed, a farm may also sign contracts with individuals or small groups, who need not be members, to carry out almost any task related to agriculture. These agreements seek to tie rewards more closely to performance by making the individuals or groups in question residual claimants to the net income from their work. Such income is also more lightly taxed than it would be if the farm simply paid it for additional work.

More generally, Hungary has experimented with a variety of flexible contract forms, designed to improve production in agriculture, food, and related industries. As another example, collective farms can voluntarily combine portions of their land, capital, and labor to form a production system, in order to develop and grow crops, raise livestock, process or market their products, purchase or share inputs, spread technological information, and so on. Usually, member farms share the profits or losses of such a venture, and one farm may belong to several different systems. In this way, developments in agriculture continue to set the pace for growth of the legal second economy in industry. Yet, farming is still overregulated. There is too much emphasis on meat and grain, which historically have been the main crops, and too little on other products, where the best possibilities for further growth may now lie, as well as too little allowance for regional differences. Poor planning and management, as well as shortages of equipment, infrastructure, and irrigation facilities continue to plague this sector. One consequence is that gross farm output increased by only 4 percent between 1980 and 1987, while value added in agriculture was scarcely greater than in 1951 and only 13 percent above 1938, according to official statistics. (However, gross farm output was 90 percent greater than in 1938.)

6-4. The Organization of Foreign Trade

Historically, state control over foreign trade has been more centralized than control over the domestic economy. Even today, state trading companies under the Foreign Trade Ministry handle most external trade. As a rule, these firms do not produce, but act as intermediaries between domestic producers or users and foreign governments or firms. In contrast to the market economies of North America, Western Europe, and Japan, command economies are import rather than export oriented. They have traditionally traded mainly to obtain goods deemed essential to plan fulfillment that they could not produce in sufficient quantities at home, and they have tried to export low-priority products in exchange for these. By and large, this is still true, although to a declining extent. In addition, slightly over half of Hungary's trade is with other command economies, most of whom belong to COMECON, the Council for Mutual Economic Assistance. This is a grouping of East European countries dominated by the Soviet Union—and including Cuba, Vietnam, and Mongolia, with Yugoslavia as an associate member—mainly for trade, but also for mutual economic assistance and cooperation. It is an East European answer to the West European Common Market, although COMECON has achieved far less integration than the EEC.

Just under a third of Hungary's foreign trade is with the Soviet Union, its main trading partner, from whom it obtains the bulk of fuel, energy, and raw materials. Another 10 percent is with West Germany, Hungary's second most important partner, behind which come East Germany, Austria, and Czechoslovakia, in that order. For roughly ten years after the first energy crisis (1974), Hungary obtained oil and natural gas from the Soviet Union at less than world market prices. Such trade has had a political dimension which, for the USSR, represents a departure from the lowest-priority-export rule. As the main supplier of energy and raw materials to Eastern Europe, the Soviet Union could severely damage these economies by reducing the flow of supplies. ''Eighty percent of our energy imports, 60 percent of [our] raw materials imports, and three-quarters of [our] imported investment goods derive from [COMECON] countries, the Soviet Union in first place,'' wrote the Hungarian Finance Minister in the mid-1970s. The Soviets take in return many of the manufactures of these countries, which have often been too low in quality to be sold on Western markets. ''Ninety percent of machine exports, two-thirds of industrial consumer-goods exports, and more than half of food exports go to [COMECON] countries.''[37] About 25 percent of Hungarian industrial output is exported, and most of this goes to other socialist countries, primarily the Soviet Union.

Some percentages cited by the former finance minister have fallen since 1975, but Hungary's basic dependence on the USSR remains. Because it is a small, landlocked country without a diversity of natural resources, foreign trade is essential to Hungary. To obtain raw materials and fuel, it exports food and manufactures, with the degree of processing generally higher for exports to the East than for exports to the West. All in all, Hungary exports 35–40 percent of its gross national product—the highest share in Eastern Europe and one of the highest in the world—and 50 percent of its national income (or net material product), calculated according to the Marxian definition. At least 60 percent of the latter derives from foreign trade related activities. Hungary's export volume expanded by more than 7 percent per year, on average, over 1970–85, but because of unfavorable price trends, its share of world export value fell to an all-time low. In 1985, it was less than 0.4 percent vs. 0.65 percent in 1955, 0.66 percent in 1938, and 2 percent before World War I.[38] The decline in Hungary's terms of trade with other nations following the energy crisis—which amounted to about 25 percent over 1973–85—has been costing 9–10 percent of its GNP in recent years, and the cumulative cost since 1975 exceeds its material losses from World War II. In part, this was a consequence of the more competitive export environment to which the energy crisis gave rise, and which caused Hungary to lose export market shares. In addition, Hungarian firms actually increased their use of energy rapidly over 1974–78.

Most of Hungary's trade with other socialist countries is planned in advance and negotiated above the enterprise level. With the exception of Yugoslavia, these nations are all more centralized than Hungary. In effect, specific bundles of goods are exchanged against each other—a form of barter, although traded goods are valued at agreed-on prices. As a rule, each member of COMECON will try to approximately balance its two-way trade with every other over the course of each year. (This is called bilateral balancing.) None of these countries is anxious to build up a trade surplus with another, because a positive balance with one cannot usually be spent in any other country.

The Hungarian forint, like the currencies of all command economies, is not convertible. One cannot freely buy and sell it in exchange for other national currencies at official exchange rates. Instead, a Hungarian firm or individual wanting foreign currency must also have a government authorization. This rationing of foreign exchange is part of the overall control of foreign trade and payments. By excluding part of the demand, it allows the government to keep prices of Western currencies below their market equilibrium levels in terms of the forint. In this sense, the forint is *over*valued, as is the currency of every command economy. Historically, Hungarian firms have been shielded from the profit-and-loss consequences of their exports and imports, even more than from those of domestic transactions. Given excess demand at home, they have also lacked an incentive to produce goods that are readily saleable on Western markets or to conserve on expensive imports.

The 1968 reform was supposed to raise this incentive, first by increasing the importance of enterprise profits as a success indicator, second by raising the autonomy of firms in the area of foreign trade, and third by tying changes in the forint prices of Hungarian imports and exports to changes in world-market prices. Thus, an enterprise which expanded its net exports to the West on a cost-effective basis was supposed to receive higher profits in consequence, which would allow it to pay higher wages and salaries. A firm making excessive use of expensive imports was to be forced to pay lower incomes and to reduce or reorient its investments.

However, this did not happen. The price explosion in raw materials and fuel, beginning with the 1974 energy crisis, forced the authorities to shield enterprises and collective farms from the potential impact of this explosion on their costs and profits. (Without subsidies, firms would have had to cut wages, salaries, and investment.) Instead of raising prices of fuel, fertilizer, raw materials, and energy to domestic users, the state subsidized the difference between low domestic and high foreign prices. Since then, most of the energy-related cost increases have been passed on—mainly through major price revisions in 1979–80—but there have also been large subsidies to firms in financial distress.

These revisions laid down a new principle—namely, that domestic prices for most traded goods (including about 65 percent of industrial output) should vary with world market prices. Previously, movements of the two sets of prices had been largely divorced. When a firm exports at least 5 percent of its output to the West, its product prices are supposed to follow this rule, which is enforced by the National Prices and Materials Board.[39] Domestic prices for fuels, raw materials, and other major imports are supposed to follow the prices Hungary pays for these items. In 1981, Hungary introduced uniform exchange rates between the forint and each convertible currency. These rates now vary over time inversely with the domestic cost of earning foreign exchange via export sales. (As a result, the forint generally declined in value over 1981–87, although it remains overvalued.) Finally, since 1985, enterprises able to show strong export sales, plus the ability to satisfy domestic demand, and which are not considered to be exercising monopoly power in Hungary, may apply to join a "Price Club." To be admitted, they must pledge to follow a pricing policy acceptable to the Prices and Materials Board. Provided they remain faithful to the policies they lay down, they may then set prices without further administrative interference. In 1986, about a third of state enterprises were in the Price Club. On balance, the new pricing policy should give industrial firms stronger incentives to contribute positively to Hungary's trade balance, provided the effective marginal tax on enterprise profits remains well below 100 percent, after the 1988 tax reform.

The energy crisis hit Hungary hard, since it can produce only a fifth of its crude oil requirements and also needs large imports of natural gas, coal, and coke—comprising, in all, over 50 percent of its total energy consumption. In this context, most trade within COMECON takes place at prices which are averages of those pre-vailing on the world market over the past five years.[40] Goods whose prices are rising more rapidly than average therefore tend to be underpriced in COMECON trade, which allowed Hungary to buy 75–80 percent of its imported oil at below-OPEC prices in the years following the first energy crisis. The rising cost of this fuel nevertheless strained Hungary's ability to export, as the quality and volume demands of the USSR escalated. Since Hungary had to increase imports from the West in order to expand exports to the Soviet Union, this escalation also raised its debt to Western nations and increased the pressure on Hungary to join the IMF and World Bank.

In addition, there are quotas to limit purchases at COMECON prices when the goods in question are readily saleable at higher prices on Western markets. Thus, Hungary had to buy part of its oil at world market prices during the latter 1970s, although it could also sell food and some other items within COMECON at such prices, which cover around 15 percent of its trade with other socialist nations. Here, bilateral deficits must be settled with convertible currencies. World oil prices peaked in 1981 and then began to fall. Because of the COMECON pricing formula, the USSR began charging Hungary more than the OPEC price for oil in 1985.

Hungary's balance-of-payments crisis is the root cause of its renewed commitment to reform in the late 1970s, as well as a new approach to pricing. As a small country without a diversity of natural resources, it must rely on international trade, and there are two basic strategies of economic development—export specialization and import substitution—that are open to Hungary. Export specialization requires Hungary to produce goods in which it achieves a cost or quality advantage vis-à-vis the rest of the world. It would export these products in exchange for imports of commodities that can be produced more cheaply abroad. The more successfully a nation carries out such a strategy, the higher its real national income will be and the better will be the terms of trade with other nations. By turning out a restricted range of industrial goods for the world market, it can often realize major scale and experience economies, which improve efficiency further. However, export specialization also dictates rather closely the pattern of production for a small country. Efficient small-market economies—such as Belgium, Sweden, Switzerland, Norway, Holland, and Denmark—have prospered with such a strategy, but they are closely integrated into the international division of labor in consequence.

For Hungary, such specialization would have collided with basic ideological and political priorities, which favored heavy industry. Along with the rest of Eastern Europe, it followed an import substitution strategy by rapidly expanding domestic production of goods previously imported or which would have had to be imported under export specialization. Steel was only the most notorious example of a growth industry in which Hungary lacked (and failed to develop) a cost or quality advantage. A key goal was to reduce Hungary's dependence on imports.

Over a number of years, a policy of import substitution may become one of export specialization, if industries that are initially inefficient by world standards are subsequently able to secure a cost or quality advantage. Here, Japan is Exhibit A. Unfortunately, it more often happens that import substitution both promotes inefficient industries and makes the country in question more dependent on imports, since the industries being subsidized need inputs themselves which cannot be obtained from domestic sources. This is what happened in Hungary, where production came to depend on imports of fuel and raw materials from the USSR plus sophisticated machinery and machine tools from the West. By the latter 1970s, every 1 percent rise in national income (Marxist definition) required an increase of 1.3–2.0 percent or more in imports from the West.[41] As the focus for many years had been on expansion instead of cost effectiveness, each unit of national income also required too much labor, capital, and energy.

Moreover, the industries being promoted generally lacked the export potential on Western markets to pay for their imported inputs. Import substitution did not lead to development of an efficient export sector, which was part of the more general problem that growth was not demand oriented. As a result, Hungary and other Eastern European nations also came to depend on the Soviet Union as a market for their low-quality manufactures. Hungarian planners were aware of these problems, and with the recovery of agriculture from the devastations of the 1940s and 1950s, Hungary was moving cautiously toward export specialization in 1968. NEM was supposed to accelerate this process. But subsequently, Hungary failed to respond to the energy crisis as well as the industrial nations of Western Europe or as well as many developing nations. The most successful among the former expanded exports of high-quality goods (including energy-efficient products), while changing their output profiles toward items whose demand was growing, thereby reducing the fall in their terms of trade. The more highly centralized Hungarian economy could not adapt so quickly or flexibly to deterioration of the external environment.

Hungary did make a special effort to increase sales of machinery and machine tools to the West. But despite the traditionally high priority for these industries, their products did not sell well, even at unfavorable prices. Since heavy industrial enterprises had been shielded from competitive pressures and were not profit oriented, they had problems satisfying user demand, meeting delivery schedules, providing service after the sale, and supplying spare parts. Hungary's competitive position in industry deteriorated vis-à-vis developed nations at the high-technology end and vis-à-vis developing nations at the low-technology end. The share of high-technology products in its exports to advanced market economies fell from 2.4 percent in 1981 to 0.9 percent in 1984, and Hungary became the world's leading per capita producer of electronic vacuum tubes.[42] (Moreover, while machinery exports of developing nations to the West were below those of COMECON in 1970, they were four times as great by 1977.) While Hungary's farm-based exports have done well since 1970, these are vulnerable to government protection of domestic agriculture in the West, and they suffer from investment neglect, as well as organizational problems at home. Until recently, most of the food industry was dominated by eight trusts which generally did not compete, and collective farming, even Hungarian style, is comparatively inefficient.

The initial impact of the energy crisis was to push Hungary further from the decentralizing measures of NEM. Firms were sheltered from the effects of price changes, as noted earlier. The authorities also sought to increase energy supplies through a number of large investment projects, some of which were carried out in cooperation with other COMECON nations. (The latter were mainly designed to improve the flow of Soviet energy to Eastern Europe.) This helped to centralize investment decision making. Over a third of total investment between 1975 and 1980 went to expand energy supplies, partly because of rising consumption by Hungarian industry, and this investment emphasis has continued. Since 1980, however, the organizational thrust has been toward decentralization, with closer specialization according to comparative advantage, in order to expand exports on a cost-effective basis.

Thus, in 1981, over 300 firms received limited rights to import and/or export on their own, without going through the Foreign Trade Ministry or its trading companies (although in 1987, most trade still went through the latter). In principle, an independent trading firm, *Generalimpex*, established in 1980, can export or import any good in competition with these companies, and similar rights were extended to another 100 enterprises over 1986–87. From January 1, 1988, nearly every Hungarian firm is eligible to apply for them. In practice, this means more freedom to export directly; imports have been tightly controlled because of Hungary's large foreign debt and balance-of-payments deficits in convertible-currency markets. (As with domestic producer goods, Hungarian users of imports receive informal quotas, based on use in a base period.) However, despite balance-of-payments deficits, Hungary has also reduced its imports of Soviet iron ore and substituted higher quality and higher priced ore bought on the world market—a potentially far-reaching move in terms of its relationship with the USSR. As well, the forint was devalued against the U.S. dollar by more than 60 percent over 1980–87.

Since 1978, growth has been slow, living standards have been stagnant or falling, and Hungary has lost shares of convertible currency markets. It has tried to solve her balance-of-payments crisis largely by reducing the imports on which growth depends; even so, current account deficits have persisted. A permanent solution will probably require further decentralization, including expansion of private and quasi-private property rights, to produce greater export specialization and intensive growth, which responds more flexibly and efficiently to demand. Ultimately, this must come "from below." A favorable climate must be created for it; it cannot be directly managed by state authorities, although the government can assist enterprises with guidance and technical information, along the lines of Japanese-style planning. This should be complementary with, rather than a substitute for, enterprise initiative and competition for market shares.

Pressures working to create such an environment will run headlong into those trying to preserve comparative equality—or at least to keep income differences from depending too closely on financial or entrepreneurial success—and to insulate enterprise management from exposure to a range of risks and decisions that would be normal in a market economy. Traditionally, Marxists have denounced markets as exploitive and inefficient—part of the irony of the condition in which East European nations now find themselves.

6-5. Growth and Distribution

A. *Growth*

By any reckoning, the Hungarian economy grew at a respectable pace over most of the first thirty-five years, 1950–85, of Communist rule. Living standards rose appreciably, especially between 1960 and 1980. According to official statistics, real national income—deflated for price increases—was about five times as great in 1985 as in 1950, giving an annual average growth of just under 4.7 percent, or 4.3 percent in per capita terms. Hungary's per capita growth exceeded that of nearly every Western country, although it was slightly below the median among socialist nations, and Japan did much better.

However, some economists argue that the above comparison is biased in favor of Hungary vis-à-vis the West. As in other socialist countries, Hungarian statisticians compute national income and output according to the Marxian definition, also called net material product (NMP). NMP excludes many services—which Marx and other economists of his day considered unproductive—and thus counts mainly the output, in value terms, of material goods. Only those service sectors are included whose outputs directly contribute to material production, such as transportation, wholesale and retail trade, crafts, and financial services. The net result is to exclude 10 percent to 20 percent of national income, according to the Western definition, and the excluded sectors have tended to grow more slowly than the economy as a whole.

In addition, official statistics in Eastern Europe and the Soviet Union reflect methods of measurement that tend to assign higher output growth rates and lower rates of inflation to a given performance than do methods used in most Western countries.[43] At times, the Hungarian definition of net material product has been enlarged to include more services than before, and the effect of this has been recorded as growth. Further problems in assuring comparability arise because each command-economy firm is judged according to the value of its output. Under conditions of excess demand, output value increases as product prices go up. Thus, a firm has an incentive to seek effective price increases—for example, by introducing slightly differentiated products, which, it argues, cost more to produce than goods they replace. The use value of the new products may be no higher, yet an increase in output is recorded, which may benefit planning superiors and the political leadership as well, since measured growth and absence of inflation are indicators of their success. On occasion, it is believed, managers or ministers even exaggerate volume increases in production.

Because of these problems, a team of United States economists has launched the Research Project on National Income in East-Central Europe, which recomputes the national accounts of Hungary and other East European countries according to Western definitions and methods.[44] They claim results which are more comparable to Western performance. By their calculations, Hungarian gross national product (GNP) per capita net of price changes, grew by an annual average of just 2.8 percent over 1950–85, to reach slightly more than 2.6 times its 1950 level, rather than 4.33 times, as with net material product. This is below the median among OECD nations (mainly Western Europe, Oceania, North America, and Japan), and Table 1.4, at the end of chapter 1, gives growth comparisons with several Western countries. Hungarian GNP per head was $7,700 or nearly 40 percent of the U.S. level in 1985 vs. less than a third in 1950. GNP comparisons with other capitalist and socialist nations appear in Table 1.3.

In the shorter run, command planning is sometimes associated with relative freedom from cyclical fluctuations in output and employment. Nearly full employment has tended to prevail in Hungary, but according to official statistics, short-term fluctuations in national income were larger during the 1950s and 1960s than in most developed capitalist economies, for two reasons. First, as command planners are usually growth oriented, they have ambitious investment goals. The centralized nature of investment decision making implies that the projects they envisage will be highly interdependent. For example, plans for steel mills, metallurgical complexes, machine-tool factories, electrical and engineering combines, truck-assembly plants, and electric power-generating facilities all emerge from the National Planning Office at about the same time. Because these facilities use one another's outputs as productive inputs, they would ideally be planned together.

However, we have noted that the volume of incomplete investment projects tends to be a high percentage of total investment in a Soviet-type economy, and this has been true of Hungary. Large-scale projects tend to drag out, and the elapsed time between starting one and bringing it into full capacity operation has been long by Western standards. The main cause of this is central planners' overambitiousness, relative to available resources, which is reinforced at lower levels by rent and interest charges that are much too low. Another cause is poor coordination of projects, during either planning or implementation, which leads to construction bottlenecks.

When the value of capital tied up in incomplete projects rises above a critical level, the central planners usually restrict new undertakings and focus on completing projects already begun. This causes the ratio of incomplete to total investment to fall, until the green light for launching major new projects can again be turned on. Then the ratio of unfinished to total investment starts to rise once more, restarting the cycle.[45] Thus, Hungary has tended to oscillate between an emphasis on launching new projects—mainly in the early 1950s, the early 1960s, the late 1960s, and the mid-to-late 1970s—and an emphasis on completing them and bringing them into operation—as in the late 1950s, the mid-1960s, the early 1970s, and the 1980s.

When the ratio of unfinished to total investment is rising, the productivity of

Table 6.1

A. Size Distribution of Income in Hungary vs. Sweden, West Germany, Canada, U.S., U.K., and Japan

Cumulative percentage of income receivers		Cumulative Percentage of Income Received*						
	Hungary 1967	Hungary 1982	Sweden 1972	West Germany	Canada 1972	U.S. 1972	U.K. 1973	Japan 1969
Lowest 20	10.1	11.3	7.3	6.5	5.2	4.9	6.1	7.1
Lowest 40	25.2	26.7	21.4	16.8	17.2	15.8	18.3	19.5
Lowest 60	44	45.1	40.4	31.7	35.2	33.3	36.7	36.3
Lowest 80	67.1	67.7	65.1	53.6	59.4	57.9	60.7	58.1
Top 20	32.9	32.3	34.9	46.4	40.6	42.1	39.3	41.9
Top 20 ÷ bottom 20	3.3	2.9	4.8	7.1	7.8	8.6	6.4	5.9

B. Measures of Inequality in Hungary by Social Stratum

Social Stratum	Average income (national average = 100)**	Percentage with bathroom***	Number of autos per 100 households
Manager and professional	150	92%	55
Other white collar	111	78%	30
Skilled and semi-skilled workers	95	54%	18
Unskilled workers	86	31%	4
Peasants	105	33%	12
Retired	83	31%	1

Sources: Hungary: Rudolf Andorka, "Hungary's Long-Term Social Evolution," *New Hungarian Quarterly*, Fall 1979; Janos Kornai, "The Hungarian Reform Process," *Journal of Economic Literature*, December 1986, p. 1725.

Others: Malcolm Sawyer, "Income Distribution in the OECD Countries," OECD Economic Outlook, Occasional Studies (Paris: OECD, July 1976), Table 10, p. 1725

* Net of personal income taxes and subsidies in Western countries. (In Hungary, these are small.)

** 1972 Data.

*** 1976 Data.

investment forints in generating additional output during the current year or the year to follow will be less than when this ratio is falling. In the latter case, relatively small capital spending outlays will be bringing factories into production, while in the former, much larger outlays will often result in no additional output for some time. Thus, a rising ratio of unfinished to total investment—itself the consequence of overambitious planning and coordination problems—leads to a slowing of growth. A falling ratio leads to a quickening of growth. In this way, the investment cycle leads to short-term fluctuations in output.

A second and related cause of these fluctuations has been Hungary's need to import most of her raw materials, energy, and sophisticated machinery. Rapid growth of output causes a rapid rise in the demand for these imports, which leads to balance-of-payments difficulties. To solve the latter, Hungary must reduce imports (or slow their growth below that of exports), which requires curtailing the growth of output, especially that destined for domestic consumption and use. If this works, the balance of payments will turn around, and reserves of foreign currency and credit will begin to rise. These can be used to raise imports of materials, fuel, and machinery, making it possible to raise the growth rate of national income once again.

B. Distribution

Finally, the distribution of incomes earned on the official economy is more equal in Hungary than in any Western country, as Table 6.1 indicates. In 1967, the poorest 20 percent of Hungarians received just over 10 percent of total household income, while the next poorest 20 percent received 15.1 percent, and so on. According to the table, the distribution of income in Hungary became more equal between 1967 and 1982 and was decidedly more equal than in any of the six Western countries shown. There are two problems, however, with accepting these comparisons at face value.

First, vis-à-vis most market economies, socioeconomic stratification in Hungary is based more on access to goods and services and less on inherited wealth or access to jobs, training, and education. Thus, when we classify Hungarian households by socioeconomic category, the managerial-professional group is wealthiest, but with an average income less than double that of any other group. However, the relative position of white-collar workers appears to improve and that of unskilled workers, peasants, and retired people to worsen when we look at access to housing with indoor bathroom and, to an even greater extent, when we consider access to automobiles for personal use. Differences would probably increase further, if we could take quality into account. During the 1980s, access to housing has become a major determinant of socioeconomic status in Hungary (as noted above in section 6-1).

Second, the official statistics on income distribution also ignore much of the effect of the second economy, which is to increase inequality, since opportunities for personal gain there are unequally distributed, and much of this income is concealed from tax collectors. In the decade after 1972, per capita real income grew by just over a fourth on the official economy, with the lower income categories receiving the largest gains. But income growth on the second economy was probably more rapid, and changes there may have offset officially recorded gains in equity. As much as 15 percent of the population (including many pensioners, unskilled workers, gypsies, those in substandard housing or poorly supplied rural areas) is in poverty, because of low incomes and/or low access to goods or to social overhead capital. In this respect, however, Hungary does not compare unfavorably with most Western nations.

Notes

1. B. Kovrig, *The Hungarian Peoples' Republic* (Baltimore: Johns Hopkins, 1970), p. 97.

2. The Treaty of Trianon, signed June 4, 1920, reduced Hungary to 28.6 percent of its pre–World War I territory. (It had been part of the old Austro-Hungarian Empire.) The desire to regain territory settled by ethnic Magyar groups was a principal reason for Hungary's joining World War II on the side of Germany. As a consequence, it lost a further small enclave, the "Bratislava Bridgehead," to Czechoslovakia, as well as an additional slice of territory to Romania.

3. See Z. Roman, "The Conditions of Market Competition in Hungarian Industry," *Acta Oeconomica* 34, 1–2, 1985 and Tamas Bauer, "The Second Economic Reform and Ownership Relations," *Eastern European Economics*, Spring–Summer 1984.

4. Tamas Bauer, "The Contradictory Position of the Firm in the New Economic Mechanism in Hungary," *Eastern European Economics*, Fall 1976, p. 3.

5. Lajos Faluvegi, "Economic Development; Economic Structure, New Phenomena in the World Economy," *Acta Oeconomica* 14, 2–3, 1975, p. 159.

6. See Janos Kornai, "The Hungarian Reform Process," *Journal of Economic Literature*, December 1986, especially Table 6; K. Falus-Szikra, "Small Enterprises in Private Ownership in Hungary," *Acta Oeconomica* 34, 1–2, 1985, and K. Falus-Szikra, "Wage Disparities Between the First and Second Economies in Hungary," *Acta Oeconomica* 36, 1–2, 1986.

7. One Hungarian author writes:

In accordance with the Civil Code, what are called economic working communities can be formed; this can be done, not only by independent entrepreneurs, but also by the workers of state-owned enterprises and cooperatives. In the latter case, there is an opportunity for the workers of a large enterprise—by forming a working community—to obtain preferentially the waste materials and tools of the enterprise (to be candid: it will hardly be worthwhile any longer to steal these); they may undertake repair and maintenance services locally and they may also contract with their own enterprise for the production of smaller parts and accessories outside working hours.

See Andras Tabori, "Small Businesses in a Socialist Economy," *New Hungarian Quarterly*, Summer 1982. In practice, these working communities have become largely a way of organizing overtime work within large enterprises so as to avoid wage control (discussed below). See T. Laky, "Enterprise Work Partnership and Enterprise Interest," *Acta Oeconomica* 34, 1–2, 1985.

8. See Gyula Partos, "Housing and Housing Policy," *New Hungarian Quarterly*, Spring 1987, p. 172.

9. See Janos Kornai, "Pressure and Suction on the Market," Indiana University Development Research Center, Bloomington, Ind., working paper no. 7, 1971, p. 2 and "The Measurement of Shortage," *Acta Oeconomica* 16, 3–4, 1976, p. 321, as well as "The Hungarian Reform Process." See, as well, Tamas Bauer, "A Note on Money and the Consumer in Eastern Europe," *Soviet Studies*, July 1983. A 1970 survey cited by Kornai in the second article above (p. 326) indicates that most shoes sold in Hungary were "not to the liking" of buyers, who often could not find the style, design, or size they wanted, even though there was no overall shortage of shoes.

10. Kornai, "The Hungarian Reform Process," p. 1715.

11. L. Faluvegi, "Regulation of Enterprise Incomes and the System of Financial Incentives," *Acta Oeconomica* 12, 2, 1974, p. 168.

12. A recent Budapest cabaret joke:
"Where would you rather live, in Hungary or in America?"
"In America, because they have unemployment compensation."
"Oh, but we have that in Hungary too. It's called a wage."

13. If we compare Hungary with Spain, a country with about the same GNP per capita (according to purchasing-power-parity comparisons), Hungary consumed 66 percent more energy per capita and nearly 80 percent more steel per capita, but had only 55 percent as many motor vehicles per 1,000 residents in 1984.

14. Laszlo Csaba, "New Features of the Hungarian Economic Mechanism in the Mid-Eighties," *The New Hungarian Quarterly*, Summer 1983.

15. See Kornai, "The Hungarian Reform Process," pp. 1696–97, and R. Nyers, M. Tardos, "Enterprises in Hungary Before and after the Economic Reform," *Acta Oeconomica* 20, 1–2, 1978.

16. See A. Deak, "Enterprise Investment Decisions and Economic Efficiency in Hungary," *Acta Oeconomica* 20, 1–2, 1978. Deak notes (p. 66) that "If external resources are provided, even to a single investment project of an enterprise, its whole development fund balance is surveyed. . . . When [applying] for outside resources, the enterprise has to prove that it uses its own funds for economical investments that also match the objectives of the national economy." See, as well, K. A. Soos, "Some General Problems of the Hungarian Investment System," *Eastern European Economics*, Fall 1980; also Csaba, "New Features of the Hungarian Economic Mechanism . . . ," and I. Belyacz, "Contradictions between the Investment System and the Requirements of Intensive Development in Hungary," *Acta Oeconomica* 28, 3–4, 1982.

17. Kornai, "The Hungarian Reform Process," p. 1697.

18. See J. Laszlo, "National Plan for the Economy and the Enterprises," *Acta Oeconomica* 14, 2–3, 1975, p. 223. See, as well, Marton Tardos, "The Role of Money: Economic Relations Between the State and the Enterprises in Hungary," *Acta Oeconomica* 25, 1–2, 1980, and Kornai, "The Hungarian Reform Process."

19. Bauer, "The Contradictory Position of the Enterprise."

20. For example, Granick argues that informal rationing of industrial goods, by asserting "responsibility of supply," is more efficient than formal rationing because it saves on paperwork and permits more flexible adjustment of supply patterns. See David Granick, *Enterprise Guidance in Eastern Europe* (Princeton, N.J.: Princeton University Press, 1975), pp. 282–89.

21. See A. Gyulavari, "Stocks and Stockpiling in Hungary—An International Comparison," *Acta Oeconomica* 27, 1–2, 1981, and E. Fabri, "Superficial Changes and Deep Tendencies in Inventory Processes in Hungary," *Acta Oeconomica* 28, 1–2, 1982.

22. The discussion to follow borrows from Jan Adam, "Systems of Wage Regulation in the Soviet Bloc," *Soviet Studies*, January 1976. See, as well, Peter Elek, "The Impact of Revised Economic Stimulators on the Direction of the Hungarian Economy: Phase II of the Reform," *East European Quarterly*, Summer 1979, plus the articles on wage regulation by

S. Balazsy, J. Lökkös, and G. Revesz in *Acta Oeconomica* 20, 3, 1978, and L. Hethy, "Economic Policy and Wage-System in Hungary," *Acta Oeconomica* 28, 1–2, 1982.

23. See, e.g., K. Falus-Szikra, "Wage and Income Disparities between the First and Second Economies in Hungary," *Acta Oeconomica* 36, 1–2, 1986, p. 97.

24. I. Heredi and D. Tarjan, "Results and Further Objectives of the Major National Research Program, 'The Socialist Enterprise'," *Acta Oeconomica* 20, 3, 1978, p. 335. See, as well, K. Szikra Falus, "Wage Differentials in Hungary," *Acta Oeconomica* 25, 1–2, 1980.

25. See K. Szikra Falus, "Some Human Factors of Innovation in Hungary," *Acta Oeconomica* 28, 1–2, 1982, and L. Holtzer, "Educational Level and Incomes in Hungary," *Acta Oeconomica* 29, 3–4, 1982.

26. See article by Revesz, cited in note 22, pp. 296-97.

27. Moreover, until 1983, wage regulation was formally based on *increases* in profits from one year to the next. As noted above, this gave some incentive to conceal reserves, in order to be able to show yearly growth. Since 1983, wages have formally depended on the *level* of a firm's profitability. However, this is profit after taxes and subsidies, and the steeply progressive tax on the bonus fund remains. In addition, the authorities may still be forced to compare present profits with those earned in past years, for want of any other acceptable performance standard.

28. E. Gacs, "Hungary's Social Expenditures in International Comparison," *Acta Oeconomica* 36, 1–2, 1986, especially Tables 1 and 2. From Table 2, the OECD unweighted averages for education, health, and pensions in 1981 were, respectively, 5.7 percent, 5.6 percent, and 8.6 percent, while Hungary's were, respectively, 4.4 percent, 3 percent, and 7.8 percent.

29. The basic formula is 33 percent plus 2 percent for each year of work between 11 and 25 plus one percent for each year between 26 and 32 plus 0.5 percent for each year between 33 and 42.

30. State farms produce more output per acre of land, but less per unit of capital invested in them than do the collectives. State farms also tend to specialize in animal husbandry, from which over half their output derives, while the collectives specialize more in wheat, corn, and other field crops.

31. L. Komlo, "Industrialization of the Hungarian Agriculture," *Acta Oeconomica* 29, 1–2, 1982, pp. 142–43.

32. See K. Lanyi, "Hungarian Agriculture: Export Surplus or Superfluous Growth," *Acta Oeconomica* 34, 3–4, 1985.

33. Istvan Lazar, "The Collective Farm and the Private Plot," *New Hungarian Quarterly*, Autumn 1976, p. 63.

34. Komlo, "Industrialization of the Hungarian Agriculture," p. 133n.

35. Specifically, small private farms produced over 60 percent of all fruit, 52 percent of the wine, over 70 percent of the vegetables, more than 40 percent of the milk and poultry, and more than 55 percent of the pigs brought to slaughter in 1985.

36. Jerzy Karcz, "Agricultural Reform in Eastern Europe," in Morris Bornstein, ed., *Plan and Market* (New Haven: Yale University Press, 1973), pp. 230–31.

37. Faluvegi, "Regulation of Enterprise Incomes . . . ," p. 153.

38. See Bela Kadar, "Preparing to Meet the Challenge," *New Hungarian Quarterly*, Winter 1982, p. 90, and "Structural Policy Dilemmas," *New Hungarian Quarterly*, Winter 1986, pp. 44–45.

39. See Csaba, "New Features of the Hungarian Economic Mechanism . . . ," and Jan Adam, "The Hungarian Economic Reform of the 1980s," *Soviet Studies*, October 1987, especially pp. 618–20 and 622.

40. Before 1975, trade between COMECON nations took place at world-market prices of a previous year, with price revisions every five years. The changeover mainly benefited the Soviet Union, by allowing it to mark up oil and natural gas prices more quickly.

41. Bela Csikos-Nagy, "New Features of Hungarian Economic Policy," *New Hungarian Quarterly*, Spring 1980, pp. 66-67. More precisely (p. 66): "Each percentage point of an annual 3–4 percent increase in national income raises imports from the world market by 1.3–1.5 percent. [This] rises to over 2 percent when the annual increase in national income is on the order of 5 or 6 percent."

42. I. Illes, "Structural changes in the Hungarian Economy (1979–85)," *Acta Oeconomica* 36, 1–2, 1986, pp. 29-30. See, as well, L. Csaba, "Adjustment to the World Economy in Eastern Europe," *Acta Oeconomica* 30, 1–2, 1983.

43. For a thorough discussion of this point, see S. H. Cohn, "National Income Growth Statistics," in V. G. Treml and J. P. Hardt, eds., *Soviet Economic Statistics* (Durham, North Carolina: Duke University Press, 1972). We also note that socialist countries calculate two versions of net material product—respectively, net material product produced (or the sum of value added across material sectors of the economy) and net material product domestically utilized (as public and private consumption plus investment). The text reports on net material product produced. Net material product utilized excludes the foreign trade balance (exports minus imports), as well as some losses in production. Thus, declining terms of trade will depress NMP utilized. For Hungary, per capita NMP utilized grew by an annual average 3.85 percent over 1950–85 to reach 3.75 times its original level. The series has shown less than 1 percent annual average growth since 1975.

44. Regarding this and other recalculated growth figures below, see the following papers by Thad Alton and associates:

(a) "Economic Structure and Growth in Eastern Europe," in U.S. Congress, Joint Economic Committee, *Economic Developments in Countries of Eastern Europe* (U.S. Government Printing Office: Washington, D.C., 1969).

(b) "Economic Growth in Eastern Europe, 1970, and 1975–85," Research Project on National Income in East-Central Europe, occasional paper OP-90, New York, June 1986.

(c) "Official and Alternative-Consumer Price Indexes in Eastern Europe, Selected Years, 1960–80," Research Project on National Income in East-Central Europe, occasional paper OP-68, New York, June 1981.

(d) "Money Income of the Population and Standard of Living in Eastern Europe, 1970–85," Research Project on National Income in East-Central Europe, occasional paper OP-93, New York, June 1986.

(e) "Agricultural Output, Expenses, Gross Product, Depreciation, and Net Product in Eastern Europe, Prewar and 1950–75," Research Project on National Income in East-Central Europe, occasional paper OP-49, New York, March 1976.

(f) "Agricultural Output, Expenses and Depreciation, Gross Product, and Net Product in Eastern Europe, 1965, 1970, and 1975–85," Research Project on National Income in East-Central Europe, occasional paper OP-91, New York, June 1986.

45. This thesis is explained in more detail in Alan Brown, Joseph Licari, and Egon Neuberger, "CES Production Function Analysis of Supply-Determined Growth Cycles," paper presented to Econometric Society meetings, Toronto, December 1972.

Questions for Review, Discussion, Examination

1. Why would the disappearance of Hungary's labor reserve during the 1960s limit the possibilities for further extensive growth?

2. What aspect of the Hungarian and of other Soviet-type economies makes goods easier to sell there than in Western market economies? Explain. Why do firms often invest in producing their own inputs and why is there a tendency to vertical integration at all levels of the planning chain of command?

3. Why do official Hungarian statistics tend to understate the role of the private

sector in the economy? (The same is true of other Soviet-type economies.)

4. Does Hungary grant the basic political rights outlined in section 2-3? Which does it grant and which does it not grant? Discuss, taking recent changes into account.

*5. One author writes that "social inequality in Hungary is increasingly related to the quality of dwelling occupied by the individual or family and to the inequality of opportunity in the acquisition of a new dwelling." Why do you think this is the case? Also, why does Hungary have such a high rate of apartment demolition?

6. The story is told of the Hungarian who proudly took delivery of his new car. During the first weeks of ownership he drove everywhere, entertaining his family and visiting all his friends. Then he took a sledgehammer and put a dent in the right front fender. Assuming the man was rational, why do you suppose he did this? Explain briefly.

7. According to the cabaret expression in footnote 12, a "wage" in Hungary may be analogous to unemployment compensation in the United States, at least in part. Can you explain this analogy?

*8. "Input increases are now harder for Hungary to obtain than at any time since the start of command planning in 1949. The basic policy prescription is therefore to decentralize. . . ." Can you explain why decentralization is advisable?

9. The 1968 reforms were supposed to give state firms in Hungary more freedom to decide on and to control their own investments. But in practice, this freedom has been rather closely circumscribed. Can you explain how?

10. Although the state has been able to control sectoral investment priorities, it has not always been able to control investment volume, which has a tendency to exceed planned levels. Can you explain why? Why is this tendency detrimental to reform?

*11. How has the formal method of planning changed since 1968 in Hungary? In answering, explain how it has changed in theory and how it has changed in practice. Does Hungary have producer goods markets? How are producer goods allocated?

12. Why do decision-making horizons tend to be short in Hungary's second economy?

13. "A firm can now free itself of future obligations under the national plan by compiling an excellent export record to Western markets." Why don't Hungarian managers always want this freedom?

14. Why has average wage control given Hungarian managers an additional incentive to overstaff their enterprises?

15. "[Some] argue that pay increases in Hungary have not depended on a firm's profitability. Instead the reverse has been nearly true." Explain this.

16. As a share of gross domestic product, Hungary's expenditure on social insurance is about the same as in the United States. However, we might argue that official statistics understate Hungary's share relative to that in the U.S. or other Western countries. Explain why this is the case.

*17. Critics of agricultural organization in Soviet-type economies argue that collective and state farms are too large, as management units, to be efficient. Moreover, state officials take many management decisions without sufficient information or knowledge of farm problems, and earnings of collective farm members are divorced from their performance, especially at the margin of work effort. Consequently, they lack incentive to do collective work and misallocate their time, spending too much effort on their private plots, where the private return from additional labor is relatively high.

(a) Recalling the discussion in section 2-1, why might we suspect that collective and state farms are too large, as management units, to be efficient? (Bear in mind that success in farming depends critically on the farmer's judgment.)

(b) Why might guarantees of minimum income levels help to divorce reward from performance in collective agriculture, given the priorities of a Soviet-type economy? Why have these priorities been so costly to Hungary?

18. Generally, the economic reforms in Hungary have gone further in agriculture than in industry. How have Hungarian farms and farmers taken advantage of reform freedoms to increase their incomes and output?

*19. Judging by Hungarian experience, the approach to and organization of foreign trade in a Soviet-type economy differ from standard practice in market economies. Give and briefly discuss at least four differences. How would the structure and organization of a Soviet-type economy help to determine the nature of its trade specialization vis-à-vis Western market economies? (Or, how would the organization of a Soviet-type economy help to determine the nature of its exports to and imports from Western market economies?)

*20. At official exchange rates, are the currencies of Soviet-type economies undervalued or overvalued in terms of convertible Western currencies? Is this practice consistent with domestic exchange in a Soviet-type economy? Explain. Finally, what constraint does currency valuation place on decentralization of control over foreign trade?

21. Some economists argue that Hungary and other East European economies have been in a "dependency trap" vis-à-vis the Soviet Union. Why might they argue this way? Why is it sometimes labeled a "two-way" dependency trap?

*22. What is an "import substitution" strategy, and why did Hungary adopt such a strategy, in place of a strategy of export specialization? Why may such a strategy increase a nation's dependence on imports?

23. Why has Hungary's balance of payments (and her terms of trade with the rest of the world) deteriorated since the 1973–74 energy crisis? How has the balance-of-payments crisis slowed economic growth in Hungary? Has it pushed Hungary toward or away from economic reform? How have the reforms affected the handling of foreign trade?

24. What is COMECON? How is trade handled within COMECON? A Soviet official once said that, after the worldwide revolution, a single capitalist country would have to remain. What purpose do you suppose this would serve? (Alterna-

tively, how are foreign trade prices for exchange within COMECON arrived at?)

25. Soviet-type economies, including Hungary, have experienced short-term fluctuations in output and income that are reminiscent of business-cycle fluctuations in Western market economies. What factors cause these fluctuations in Soviet-type economies? In what way are they *un*like cyclical fluctuations in Western market economies?

26. Official statistics show a greater equality of income distribution in Hungary than in any developed market economy. Moreover, the Hungarian distribution has become more equal since 1967, the year before introduction of NEM. However, there may be problems in accepting these comparisons at face value. Briefly discuss two such problems.

* = more difficult.

Suggested Further Readings

Note: Information on the Hungarian economy in English may be found in *Acta Oeconomica,* a journal of the Hungarian Academy of Sciences and in *Eastern European Economics*, a journal of translations. Another Hungarian journal, *The New Hungarian Quarterly*, contains articles on the economic system, as well as on Hungarian society and culture, more generally.

Adam, Jan. "The System of Wage Regulation in Hungary." *Canadian Journal of Economics* 7 (November 1974): 578–593.
———. "Systems of Wage Regulation in the Soviet Bloc." *Soviet Studies* 28 (January 1976): 91–109.
———. "The Hungarian Economic Reform of the 1980s." *Soviet Studies* 39 (October 1987): 610–627.
Andorka, Rudolf. "Deviant Behaviour in Hungary." *New Hungarian Quarterly* 26 (Autumn 1985): 134–140.
Andorka, Rudolf, and Istvan Harcsa. "Changes in Village Society During the Last Ten Years." *New Hungarian Quarterly* 24 (Winter 1983): 30–44.
Balassa, Bela. "The Firm in the New Economic Mechanism in Hungary." In Bornstein, Morris, ed. *The Hungarian Experience in Economic Planning.* New Haven: Yale University Press, 1959.
———. *Plan and Market.* New Haven: Yale University Press, 1973), pp. 347–372.
Balazsy, S. "The 'Unsolvable' Dilemma of Regulating Earnings in Hungary." *Acta Oeconomica* 20, 3 (1978): 247–267.
Bauer, Tamas. "The Contradictory Position of the Firm in the New Economic Mechanism in Hungary." *Eastern European Economics* 15 (Fall 1976): 3–23.
———. "The Second Economic Reform and Ownership Relations." *Eastern European Economics* 22 (Spring–Summer 1984): 33–87.
———. "Reform Policy in the Complexity of Economic Policy." *Acta Oeconomica* 34, 3–4 (1985): 263–273.
Bélyacz, I. "Contradictions Between the Investment System and the Requirements of Intensive Development in Hungary." *Acta Oeconomica* 28, 3–4 (1982): 317–336.
Bihari, P. "On (Structural) Unemployment." *Acta Oeconomica* 28, 1–2 (1982).
Csaba, Laszlo "Adjustment to the World Economy in Eastern Europe." *Acta Oeconomica* 30, 1 (1983a): 53–75.
———. "New Features of the Hungarian Economic Mechanism in the Mid-Eighties." *New*

Hungarian Quarterly 24 (Summer 1983b): 44–63.

Csikos-Nagy, Béla "The Competitiveness of the Hungarian Economy." *New Hungarian Quarterly* 22 (Autumn 1981): 24–35.

——. "Development Problems of the Hungarian Economy." *New Hungarian Quarterly* 23 (Winter 1982): 74–87.

——. "Hungary's Adjustment to the New World Market Relations." *Acta Oeconomica* 30, 1 (1983): 77–88.

Deak, A. "Enterprise Investment Decisions and Economic Efficiency in Hungary." *Acta Oeconomica* 20, 1–2 (1978): 63–82.

Fabri, E. "Superficial Changes and Deep Tendencies in Inventory Processes in Hungary." *Acta Oeconomica* 28, 1–2 (1982): 133–146.

Falus-Szikra, K. "Small Enterprises in Private Ownership in Hungary." *Acta Oeconomica* 34, 1–2 (1985): 13–26.

——. "Wage and Income Disparities Between the First and Second Eonomies in Hungary." *Acta Oeconomica* 36, 2 (1986): 91–103.

Fink, G. "Determinants of Sectoral Investment Allocation in Hungary." *Acta Oeconomica* 28, 3–4 (1982): 375–388.

Gacs, E. "Hungary's Social Expenditures in International Comparison." *Acta Oeconomica* 36, 1–2 (1986): 141–154.

Granick, David. *Enterprise Guidance in Eastern Europe.* Princeton: Princeton University Press, 1975), chapters 8–10.

Gyulavari, A. "Stocks and Stockpiling in Hungary—An International Comparison." *Acta Oeconomica* 27, 1–2 (1981): 57–76.

Halpern, L., and Gy. Molnar "Income Formation, Accumulation, and Price Trends in Hungary in the 1970s." *Acta Oeconomica* 35, 1–2 (1985): 105–132.

Hare, Paul, et al. eds. *Hungary: A Decade of Reform.* London: Allen & Unwin, 1981.

Havas, G. "Public Savings and Production Finance." *Acta Oeconomica* 28, 1–2 (1982): 109–132.

Herceg, Andras. "Energy and the Hungarian Economy." *New Hungarian Quarterly* 23 (Spring 1982): 52–64.

Herédi, I., and O. Tarjan. "Results and Further Objectives of the Major National Research Program 'The Socialist Enterprise,' " *Acta Oeconomica* 20, 3 (1978): 332–338.

Hewett, E. A. "The Hungarian Economy: Lessons of the 1970s and Prospects for the 1980s." In U.S. Congress, Joint Economic Committee. *East European Economic Assessment, Part I.* Washington, D.C.: U.S. Government Printing Office, 1981): 483–548.

Holtzer, I. "Educational Level and Incomes in Hungary." *Acta Oeconomica* 29, 3–4 (1982): 309–328.

Illés, I. "Structural Changes in the Hungarian Economy (1979–85)." *Acta Oeconomica* 36, 1–2 (1986): 21–33.

Inzelt, A. "Economic Sensitivity in Technological Development in Hungary." *Acta Oeconomica* 28, 1–2 (1982): 37–52.

Kadar, Béla. "Major Specialization Tendencies of Hungarian Exports to the West." *Acta Oeconomica* 20, 1–2 (1978): 147–169.

——. "Changes in the World Economic Environment and Hungarian Industry." *Acta Oeconomica* 30, 1 (1983a): 111–127.

——. "Hungarian Industrial Policy in the Eighties." *New Hungarian Quarterly* 24 (Winter 1983b): 45–61.

——. Structural Policy Dilemmas." *New Hungarian Quarterly* 27 (Winter 1986): 43–60.

Kertesi, G. "Two Types of Development of Small-Scale Industry in Hungary." *Acta Oeconomica* 28, 1–2 (1982): 71–86. Komlo, L. "Industrialization of the Hungarian Agriculture." *Acta Oeconomica* 29, 1–2 (1982): 131–148.

Konya, Lajos "Conditions of Setting Up Simple Forms of Co-operatives in the Hungarian Industry." *Acta Oeconomica* 27, 1–2 (1981): 77–92.

——. "Income Regulation of Small Industrial Co-operatives in Hungary." *Acta Oeconomica* 28, 3–4 (1982): 363–374.

Kornai, Janos. *Overcentralization in Economic Administration.* London: Oxford University Press, 1959.

——. *Economics of Shortage* (2 vols). Amsterdam: North Holland, 1980a.

——. " 'Hard' and 'Soft' Budget Constraint." *Acta Oeconomica* 25 (1980b): 231–245.

——. "The Hungarian Reform Process." *Journal of Economic Literature* 24 (December 1986): 1687–1737.

Kovrig, Bennett. *The Hungarian People's Republic.* Baltimore: Johns Hopkins University Press, 1970.

Kozma, G. "Planning in Physical Units and Enterprise Relations in Hungary." *Acta Oeconomica* 29, 3–4 (1982): 259–270.

Kramer, J. C., and J. T. Danyluk. "Economic Reform in Eastern Europe: Hungary at the Forefront." In U.S. Congress, Joint Economic Committee. *Eastern European Economic Assessment, Part I.* Washington, D.C.: U.S. Government Printing Office, 1981, pp. 549–570.

Laki, M. "End-year Rush Work in Hungarian Industry and Foreign Trade." *Acta Oeconomica* 25, 1–2 (1980): 37–65.

——. "Liquidation and Merger in the Hungarian Industry." *Acta Oeconomica* 28, 1–2 (1982): 87–108.

——. "Central Economic Management and the Enterprise Crisis in Hungary." *Acta Oeconomica* 35, 1–2 (1985): 195–211.

Lakos, I. "Hungarian Export Performance in Western Countries." *Acta Oeconomica* 28, 1–2 (1982): 163–178.

Laky, T. "Attachment to the Enterprise in Hungary." *Acta Oeconomica* 17, 3–4 (1976): 269–284.

——. "The Hidden Mechanisms of Recentralization in Hungary." *Acta Oeconomica* 24, 1–2 (1980): 95–110.

——. "Enterprise Work Partnership and Enterprise Interest." *Acta Oeconomica* Business 34, 1–2 (1985): 27–49.

Lang, Istvan. "Resource Endowment and Hungarian Agriculture." *New Hungarian Quarterly* 21 (Winter 1980): 31–45.

Lanyi, K. "Hungarian Agriculture: Export Surplus or Superfluous Growth?" *Acta Oeconomica* 34, 3–4 (1985): 299–315.

Lazar, Istvan. "The Collective Farm and the Private Plot." *New Hungarian Quarterly* 17 (Autumn 1976): 61–77.

——. "Hungarian Agriculture: Whither and How?" *New Hungarian Quarterly* 23 (Spring 1982): 26–45.

Marer, Paul. "Economic Reform in Hungary: From Central Planning to Regulated Market." In Vol. 3 of U.S. Congress, Joint Economic Committee. *East European Economies: Slow Growth in the 1980s.* Washington, D.C.: U.S. Government Printing Office, 1986: 223–297.

Morva, Tamas. "Planning in Hungary." In Morris Bornstein, ed. *Economic Planning: East and West.* Cambridge, Mass.: Ballinger, 1975, pp. 271–309.

Nyers, J. "Hungarian Ferrous Metallurgy in International Comparison." *Acta Oeconomica* 29, 1–2 (1982): 167–178.

Nyers, Reszo, and Marton Tardos. "Enterprises in Hungary Before and After the Economic Reform." *Acta Oeconomica* 20, 1–2 (1978): 21–44.

Papp, Gabor. "The Aged in Hungary." *New Hungarian Quarterly* 24 (Spring 1983): 130–139.

Partos, Gyula. "Housing and Housing Policy." *New Hungarian Quarterly* 28 (Spring 1987): 172–179.

Révész, G. "Regulation of Earnings in Hungary." *Acta Oeconomica* 20, 3 (1978): 283–303.

———. "On the Expansion and Functioning of the Direct Market Sector of the Hungarian Economy." *Acta Oeconomica* 36, 1–2 (1986): 105–121.

Roman, Z. "The Conditions of Market Competition in the Hungarian Industry." *Acta Oeconomica* 34, 1–2 (1985a): 79–97.

———. "Productivity Growth and Its Slowdown in the Hungarian Economy." *Acta Oeconomica* 35, 1–2 (1985b): 81–104.

Szalai, E. "The New Stage of the Reform Process in Hungary and the Large Enterprises." *Acta Oeconomica* 29, 1–2 (1982): 25–46.

Schweitzer, I. "Central Decisions Enterprise Efforts: Engineering Industry Development Programmes in Hungary in the Early 1960s." *Acta Oeconomica* 24, 3–4 (1980a): 321–340.

———. "On the Economic Nature of a Shortage Phenomenon: The Spare Parts Problem in Hungary." *Acta Oeconomica* 25, 3–4 (1980b): 247–258.

Soos, K. A. "Some General Problems of the Hungarian Investment System." *Eastern European Economics* 19 (Fall 1980): 48–76.

Spulber, Nicholas. *The Economics of Communist East Europe.* New York: Wiley 1957.

Suranyi, E., and Zs. Jarai. "Bonds in Hungary." *Acta Oeconomica* 34, 1–2 (1985): 165–173.

Szabo-Medgyesi, Eva. "Non-Agricultural Activities of Agricultural Enterprises in Hungary." *Acta Oeconomica* 34, 3–4 (1985): 361–381.

Szikra Falus, K. "Wage Differentials in Hungary." *Acta Oeconomica* 25, 1–2 (1980): 163–172.

———. "Some Human Factors of Innovation in Hungary." *Acta Oeconomica* 28, 1–2 (1982a): 19–36.

———. "On Enrichment in Hungary." *Acta Oeconomica* 29, 1–2 (1982b): 47–68.

Tabori, Andras. "Small Businesses in a Socialist Economy." *New Hungarian Quarterly* 23 (Summer 1982): 56–65.

———. "Bankruptcy and the Law." *New Hungarian Quarterly* 28 (Spring 1987): 59–67.

Tardos, Marton. "The Role of Money: Economic Relations Between the State and the Enterprises in Hungary." *Acta Oeconomia* 25, 1–2 (1980): 19–35.

Tatai, Z. "Industrialization in the Villages." *Acta Oeconomica* 24, 1–2 (1980): 169–185.

Tibor, Agnes. "Enterprise and Entrepreneurship." *New Hungarian Quarterly* 28 (Spring 1987): 165–171.

Varga, Gyula. "Enterprise Size Pattern in the Hungarian Industry." *Acta Oeconomica* 20, 3 (1978): 229–246.

———. "Small-Scale Farming in Hungary." *New Hungarian Quarterly* 21 (Summer 1980): 77–84.

———. "Alternatives of the Development of Agriculture and Food Industry in Hungary." *Acta Oeconomica* 29, 3–4 (1982): 285–308.

Winiecki, Jan. "Are Soviet-Type Economies Entering an Era of Long-Term Decline?" *Soviet Studies* 38 (July 1986): 325–348.

7

THE CHINESE ECONOMY: STRUCTURE AND TRENDS

> There are not a few people who are irresponsible in their work, preferring the light
> to the heavy, shoving the heavy loads onto others, and leaving the easy ones for
> themselves. . . . In fact, such people are not true Communists . . . we must all learn
> the spirit of absolute selflessness. . . . A man's ability may be great or small, but if
> he has this spirit, he is already noble-minded and pure, a man of moral integrity
> and above vulgar interests, a man who is of value to the people.
>
> —Mao Zedong
> ("In Memory of Norman Bethune")

7-1. Introduction

Over a fifth of the world's population lives in the People's Republic of China. The
1982 census counted 1.008 billion people, nearly double the number in 1949, when
the Communist party first came to power, and this figure will rise to over 1.1 billion
by mid-1989. Since 1958, the régime has imposed strict controls on urbanization,
with the result that more than 60 percent of China's people still live in rural areas,
although less than half of total output originates there. Over half the population is
under twenty-five, owing to a baby boom in the 1960s, and even the most optimistic
forecasts show more than 10 million new babies every year until the turn of the
century. Since improved health care has halved the death rate during the past twenty
years, restricting population growth has become a major concern of the present
government, which has instituted a draconian family planning program. This goes
hand-in-hand with one of the most ambitious economic reforms of any socialist
country, which seeks to loosen bureaucratic controls and to expand the role of

competition and the market, while retaining China's basic socialist identity.

Geographically, if we were to move China halfway around the world and superimpose her on North America, it would extend from Hudson's Bay to Puerto Rico and from the east to the west coast of the United States. Her longest borders are with Mongolia and the USSR, the latter being in dispute. The administrative capital of China is Beijing in the northeast, with a population of over 9 million. Her largest city—and one of the largest in the world—is Shanghai (pop. 12 million) on the Pacific coast in the lower Yangtze plain of central China. This is also the region with the highest per capita income, and labor productivity. A third major city is Tianjin (pop. 8 million), about sixty miles southeast of Beijing.

In 1985 China's per capita GNP was under 20 percent of the Soviet level or 10 percent of the U.S. level. Whereas the typical Japanese family aspired to own a color TV set, an air conditioner, and a car in the mid-1970s, the representative Chinese family wanted a bicycle, a radio, and a sewing machine. Even by 1980, there was around one bicycle for every two households, a less favorable ratio than exists for cars in most developed countries. Since 1980, the output of bicycles has more than doubled, and living standards have risen sharply under the reform program. Yet, China remains a developing nation, and her economic planners must work with one of the world's most labor-intensive societies. In farming, the labor-to-land ratio is more than 80 times that of the U.S., while electric power input per industrial worker is probably no more than 10–20 percent as great (and power shortages keep about 20 percent of industrial capacity idle). The consequent margin of surplus over subsistence is thin, and the density of population in China's coastal regions is close to being highest in the world. After much wavering, it has adopted a birth control policy which seeks to limit most families to one child each. Enforcement of family planning has been uneven, however, and there is no chance of zero population growth until after the year 2000, when at least 1.25 billion people will live within her borders.

For longer than history records, farming has provided a livelihood for the bulk of China's people. During most of the period of Communist rule since 1949, China has followed the usual priorities for a Soviet-type economy, emphasizing industrial development at the expense of agriculture and services. Yet, agriculture still employed over 60 percent of the labor force in 1986 and contributed just under a third of GNP (vs. 47 percent for industry and 21 percent for services). Peasant sideline occupations, along with rural industry, water conservation, and construction, contributed another 10–15 percent. Agriculture also provides about half the raw materials used by light industry.[1]

While China is a big country—about the size of Canada or the U.S., including Alaska, and over 40 percent as large as the USSR—much of its terrain is hostile, both to humans and to agriculture. Nearly half of China is over one mile above sea level. About a fourth is desert or semiarid, and 10 percent of its terrain is covered by forests (a proportion that the present government is trying to raise). Because of rugged mountains and deserts, most of the western two-thirds of China cannot be farmed. In all, just 10–11 percent of the land area is cultivated, including the sides of steep hills, and about half the cultivated area is now irrigated. Total available farmland is roughly the same as in the United States, with under 25 percent of China's population, and approximately double that of Canada, with under 3 percent. China feeds nearly 23 percent of the world's population on 7 percent of the world's cultivated land. There is about a third of an acre of farmland for each of China's citizens.

Moreover, "floods and drought have occurred more often and have caused greater loss of crops, property, and lives in China than in any other part of the world."[2] By virtue of an extremely labor-intensive effort, the People's Republic is now second in the world (after the United States) in total farm output. However, on average, each of China's grain farmers produces less than 1.5 tons of grain per year. Because of population growth, the average per capita grain ration in 1982 was not much greater than in 1952, when China completed recovery from civil war and war with Japan. And while the poverty of its resource base, relative to its population, is the main reason for China's low living standards, it has also paid a high price for ideological and political strife within the Communist party and for major errors in planning and execution which grew out of this.

7-2. Nature of Economy and Government

A. Political and Property Rights

China is a socialist country, in which most of the material means of production and distribution have been nationalized and are either state-owned (in principle, the property of all the people) or collectively owned by rural economic cooperatives (legally, by the membership of each cooperative), generally at the township or village level. The state owns most of the land outside agriculture, along with 5–10 percent of the farm land, while the aforementioned cooperatives own the rest, along with most large farm machinery and many small industrial and service enterprises. In recent years, most collectively owned land has been divided among individual peasant households, who have received long-term use and income rights to it—although not legal ownership—under the rural "responsibility system," a key part of China's reform program. Individuals own means of consumption, such as bicycles, radio and TV sets, clothing, furniture, and other personal effects. In rural areas, they usually own their own homes. Most urban homes are state or cooperatively owned, however, and there are still few automobiles in private hands.

In addition, more than 10 percent of collective farm land is set aside to serve as private plots of peasant farmers. While they are legally collective property, they can be inherited by a family's offspring, although they may not be sold for private gain. The 1982 Constitution explicitly forbids buying or selling of land. Together with a ban on secondary markets in stocks and bonds (although not on primary markets) plus continuing majority state ownership of nearly all industrial assets, this is a socialism-preserving feature of the current reforms. However, many peasants have left farming for industry or services in recent years and have often sold their rights to collectively owned land to their neighbors. China's parliament, the National People's Congress, has legalized these sales. The Constitution also guarantees the basic right of citizens to inherit private property and to find work, although job rights of many individuals have grown weaker under the reforms. China has no independent labor movement.

As with other socialist countries, China is ruled by its Communist party. Other political parties are outlawed or drastically restricted in their activities. However, those in authority are supposed to be acceptable to the people—a requirement that has received varying interpretations in time and space. The 1982 Constitution guarantees individuals the right

> to make criticisms of and proposals to any organ of the state or any functionary therein; citizens have the right to appeal, complain, or report to the relevant organs of the state or any [state] functionary; but no one is allowed to make deliberately false charges. . . . No one shall suppress such appeals, complaints, or reports or retaliate against citizens making them. People suffering loss through infringement of their rights . . . have the right to compensation.

These words admit of interpretation, and we must bear in mind that the police and judiciary are not independent of China's dominant political party. The post-Mao leadership has demonstrated that there are sharp limits to democratization. However, it has also introduced direct election by workers of lower level supervisors in state industry and by peasants of production-team leaders in agriculture. As well, it has encouraged electoral competition for some legislative and lower level administrative posts in party and government, although the most important positions will continue to be filled according to preferences of party leaders. The 1982 Constitution omits the classic phrase "He who does not work, neither shall he eat" found in earlier constitutions. However, it does state that "Work is a glorious duty of every able-bodied citizen" and "The socialist economic system . . . applies the principle 'from each according to his ability, to each according to his work.' " The latter reflects the emphasis of the post-Mao leadership on material incentives to stimulate production—that is, on tying rewards to performance.

In countries ruled by communist parties, the various organs of the party normally remain distinct from those of government, although they share a strong personnel overlap. For every government agency, which carries out the tasks of day-to-day administration, there is a parallel party authority to supervise and to guide it. It is the party that determines basic policy and the direction of economic development. In each workplace, the director or work supervisor has a general responsibility to a committee of party members headed by a party secretary and playing a role analogous to that of the board of directors of a Western company. In China, the subordination of state to party has been more explicit than in other socialist countries, and enterprise party secretaries are still stronger vis-à-vis professional managers and administrators. For many years, party and government were closely fused, and party officials made important management and administrative decisions. The post-Mao leadership has moved to raise the status of professional managers and to restore the usual separation. In contrast to its predecessors, the 1982 Constitution does not explicitly maintain the subordination of state to party—although this is undoubtedly the case—and the Communist party is not mentioned beyond the preamble.

Yet it has proved difficult to suppress the party's role in enterprise management and day-to-day administration, and this has become a central issue within the party itself, in the current struggle over what kind of economic system China will have in the 1990s and beyond. About 4.5 percent of the Chinese population belongs to the party, with membership coming from all walks of life. These are supposed to be the most politically active and able individuals, and they join the party through invitation. Within the party, there can be discussion of issues and candidates for office, but once a decision is taken or an office filled, members must close ranks behind the party line. The latter is supposed to be tempered by the rights of citizens to speak out against officials who fail to serve the people. To what extent this will restrain the arbitrary exercise of authority is uncertain.

B. Organization of Planning

For most of the period since 1949, China has been a planned economy of the Soviet-type, and Chinese planners still exercise strong leverage over the allocation of investment resources. Administratively, China is more decentralized than the Soviet Union, however, in that more decisions are taken further down the chain of command—largely by provincial, municipal, and county authorities. In addition, a major goal of current reforms is to expand enterprise autonomy, and thus the role of the market, and a major theme of reform is that public ownership need not imply direct state management of industry.

Originally, China copied the Soviet planning model, the only operational blueprint of socialism then in existence. In the mid-1950s, the state planning and management hierarchy went from the central planners to about twenty-five industrial ministries, which owned and controlled the most important enterprises directly, and many other firms indirectly, through a regional chain of command. From 1949, the organization of planning grew more centralized, reaching a peak over 1955–56. Eventually, however, as the number of firms nominally under direct control by the ministries expanded, an erosion of actual ministerial control took place, increasing the effective autonomy of regional planners and firms. China had nearly 200,000 separate enterprises, and firms operated with widely varying technologies, product assortments, and levels of efficiency, even within the same industry. Yet, it had only the most rudimentary facilities for gathering, transmitting, and processing data, the latter being largely done on abacuses when these were available.

It also lacked trained specialists. Many planners and managers got their experience as officers in guerrilla warfare or in running the most backward areas of China, which had been longest under Communist control. "In 1955 . . . less than 6 percent of all leadership personnel had a university or equivalent level of technical education."[3] In consequence, the data on which planning was based were often unreliable. The center got out of touch with realities at the enterprise level and dealt with firms in a rigid, routinized way. Frequently, plans were inconsistent, unrealistic, or late in arriving, requiring enterprises and lower level planners to proceed for up to six months and more on the basis of their own target projections. Thus, the degree of centralization prevailing in the USSR during the 1950s was never reached in China. Probably less than half of China's industrial enterprises ever came under firm ministerial control, although those that did were generally the most important. There was also a good deal of unplanned and unauthorized investment.[4]

Then, over 1957–58, China launched an administrative decentralization, effectively acknowledging a *de facto* decentralization that was already underway. Most planning tasks were transferred to officials closer to the scene of production, in an effort to reduce vertical information flows and to loosen the constraints on enterprises. This was also a regionalization of planning, in some ways resembling a Soviet reform of the same period (which was later reversed).[5] A number of industrial ministries were abolished in both countries. For political administration, China is divided into 29 provincial-level governments—21 provinces, 5 autonomous regions (Sinjiang, Guangxi, Ningxia, Tibet, and Inner Mongolia), and 3 large autonomous cities (Beijing, Shanghai, Tianjin).[6] It was on the shoulders of these and of more local authorities that most planning tasks fell. The ministries handed down most of the firms they controlled to these jurisdictions, who also gained more rights to allocate scarce resources. Subsequently, the 60,000-odd communes received an administrative and planning role in rural areas. They replaced the *xiang* or township governments in 1958. However, in 1984, the *xiang* were resurrected, and most communes have effectively been dismantled. In principle, only the most important firms (the "commanding heights" of heavy industry and defense) remained under direct ministerial control. Even many of these were supposed to come under dual subordination to ministries and regional authorities, although in practice, ministerial control soon came to predominate. As far as other sectors were concerned, surviving industrial ministries were to confine themselves to broad guidelines and directives. The number of different kinds of production targets received by major firms fell from twelve to four.

A major goal of the 1957–58 decentralization was to shorten lines of communication. Factories whose products were to be used largely within a given county and whose sources of supply were also within the same county came under county control, for example, and the same was true of provinces, prefectures, and municipalities. Firms under county or provincial control were supposed to have access to goods allocated by the central government only through their regional superiors.

The role of the ministries was also supposed to change qualitatively. They became responsible for coordinating flows of goods between regions and for countervailing excessive regional autarky. In addition, their roles in applied research and development, in technical guidance, and in personnel training were all to increase, and they retained some control over the allocation of investment funds and subsidies among regions and firms.

The 1957–58 decentralization has never been formally reversed, although there was, on balance, recentralization over the next twenty years. A major problem was that the reform left property rights ill defined between the center and the regions, resulting in wasteful competition between different levels of government to expand their control over production. One reason for excess capacity in several industries has been the tendency for various levels to build duplicate production facilities which then compete for supplies of scarce raw materials and intermediate goods. China has also gone through her own version of the cycles of decentralization and recentralization familiar from East European experience. Thus, complaints about mismanagement, rigidity, slowness of decisions, suppression of initiative—and, in China, about income and status differentials based on administrative or professional expertise—have produced pressures for decentralization. However, past decentralizations have not expanded the role of markets and flexible prices in allocating goods or in stimulating production. Until recently, this was not even a goal of reform. As a result, coordination of production has usually become worse following decentralization, and this has sooner or later helped to create pressure for recentralization. In China, local or regional self-sufficiency ("empire-building") has also been a major problem. Moreover, during periods of radical control—notably, the Great Leap Forward, 1958–61, and the height of the Cultural Revolution, 1966–69—decentralization sometimes led to anarchy. State agencies temporarily lost so much staff through purges that they were unable to exercise control, and there was extreme mismanagement by the radicals.

In 1988, the planning hierarchy was topped by the State Council, headed by Prime Minister Li Peng. This is a government body, comparable to the cabinet of a Western country or to the Council of Ministers of the USSR. Thus, it is subordinate in practice to the top Communist party organ—the twenty-member Politburo of the party's Central Committee—which comprises China's political leadership. Formally, the Politbureau was headed by a six-member standing committee, under Party Secretary Zhao Ziyang, but Deng Xiaoping was believed to be the country's most powerful political leader. As a rule, government leaders derive their authority from their party positions. (Prior to their deaths in 1976, for example, Mao Zedong was party chairman, while Zhou Enlai was prime minister.)

After the political leadership, the planning hierarchy is topped by the State Planning and Economic Commission (SPEC), which is China's chief planning authority. From SPEC, the chain of command runs through the ministries to the provinces in some instances and directly to the provinces in others. Beneath the provinces (or autonomous cities or regions) come prefectures, large municipalities, or autonomous prefectures, and beneath these a variety of counties (in the vast majority of instances), districts, and municipalities, which have received greater authority in the current reforms. In particular, an effort has been made to increase the power of municipalities to coordinate economic activity across provincial boundaries in places where the natural trading area associated with a metropolitan district lies in more than one provincial jurisdiction. Below the county level come 90,000 township governments.

Officially, mandatory planning covered just half of total output by early 1988. Unofficially, coverage is probably greater, but efforts have been underway since 1979 to reduce its scope, while expanding that of the market. In 1985, China had about 460,000 industrial firms—excluding small urban and village-level rural enterprises—of which about 94,000 were state owned. These operate with widely varying technologies and product assortments, which makes direct central control virtually impossible. Those firms still subject to mandatory planning receive targets relating to outputs of major products, product assortment and quality, labor productivity, consumption of basic inputs, cost control, and others. Nationally the plans cover "a wide range of activities, including production for industry and agriculture, domestic and foreign trade, transport and communications, public revenue and expenditure, allocation of materials and labor, health, culture, and education."[7]

Since Mao's death, both the degree of centralization in economic decision making and the economy's basic investment priorities have been the focus of political struggle. At first, it seemed the centralizers had won and would entrench the Soviet-type economy. Thus, in early 1978, then Premier and Party Chairman Hua Guofeng, announced an ambitious modernization program that would have obliged China to build 120 large-scale, technologically sophisticated production facilities. These were to be in place by end-1985, giving China fourteen major industrial bases in different parts of the country. In the same year, steel output was to reach 60 million tons—doubling the actual achievement of 1978—and agriculture was to be "85 percent mechanized," despite the near absence of mechanization in 1978.[8]

To reach these goals, China would have had to invest as much over 1978–85 as during the previous thirty years, and it started over 100,000 different investment projects in the first year of the program. Almost from the outset, stresses and strains plagued the economy, along with bottlenecks, delays, and large-scale waste of manpower and materials. Construction projects fell behind schedule—due, in part, to shortages of building materials—and factories that were completed often could not operate at capacity because of shortages of raw materials or power (the latter shortage persisting to this day). The plan's fixation on higher steel production was especially questionable, since this industry was running at less than 60 percent of capacity in 1978, and steel inventories were too high. Indeed, by mid-1978, inventories of industrial goods in the state sector came to over half the annual value of industrial output. Many of these goods were of such low quality as to be unmarketable, despite the prevailing excess demand. Supply-demand mismatches were chronic, industrial productivity was low, and more than a fourth of all state enterprises were regularly operating at a loss. By end-1980, inventories of steel were more than a third above normal levels, while for machinery and electrical products, the excess was over 40 percent.

Part of the problem was a lopsided emphasis on heavy industry, which mainly produced for its own needs, but the planners also failed to grasp the implications for the rest of the economy of a rapid growth of steel output. The ultramodern and expensive Baoshan steel works near Shanghai appears, in particular, to have played a major role in a 1979 purge of centralizers from the Politburo. Originally, Baoshan was to have been China's largest steel complex, producing 6.7 million tons per year, and it was to have been built mainly by Nippon Steel, using the latter's Japanese mills as model. But for a price of $4 billion, China was buying facilities that it would not be able to operate at capacity for some time—because of their high technological level—and which it would have been hard put to supply adequately with raw materials and electric power. Baoshan and other heavy industrial projects played a major role in the budget and trade deficits which developed over 1978–80. Since that time, several of these projects (including Baoshan, itself) have been scaled down or had their completion dates postponed.

Once in power, the decentralizers sought four basic changes: a streamlining and simplification of government administration, a program of population control, a reform of the economic system, and a readjustment of priorities. If we add the "open-door" policy—featuring expansion of China's trade and economic relations with other countries plus a welcoming of foreign investment and other forms of participation in Chinese economic development—we have the five basic components of China's reform program.

In particular, the readjustment of priorities was designed to "redress past imbalances," by reducing the share of investment in national income, and the share of heavy industry in total output. Heavy industry was also reoriented toward serving the needs of light industry and agriculture, whose own growth rates increased. Since the transport network and the energy base had become bottlenecks, their priorities were raised as well. At the same time, the capital-intensive, heavy industrial content of Hua's program was cut back, resulting in the largest cancellation of foreign orders in the history of world trade. Japan alone lost contracts worth close to $2 billion. Whereas heavy industry grew more than 4.5 times as rapidly as light industry between 1949 and 1978, according to official statistics, light industry expanded by 47 percent over 1978–81, vs. 18 percent for agriculture, and just 4 percent for heavy industry. This readjustment ended in 1985, but growth continues to be more balanced than before 1979, although growth targets remain ambitious. The gross value of industrial plus agricultural output is to expand to at least 4 times its 1980 level by 2000.

The decentralizers launched their economic reforms amid a flurry of complaints about the inefficiency of Soviet-style command planning and, in particular, about China's "unwieldy, overlapping, and inefficient" administrative bureaucracy plus the excessive dependence of firms on their planning superiors. To end the latter, the reformers have been seeking to implant a responsibility system (*zeren zhi*), under which producers become more responsible for marketing their output, for procuring supplies, for operating in a cost-effective manner, and for financing their investments from their own earnings or repayable bank loans, in place of the traditional, nonreturnable budget grants. Some authors even compare command-economy distribution to a system of arranged marriages, because producers and users have little opportunity to choose their exchange partners. By contrast, a market system is likened to freedom to choose a marriage partner.[9]

As in other socialist countries, Chinese reformers have followed a dual approach. First, they have allowed the more marketized sector—consisting mainly of small private and cooperative firms—to expand explosively, in both rural and urban areas. In some cases, enterprise capital is still state owned, but the facilities are leased to individuals or groups who operate them on a profit-and-loss basis. Stock and bond markets have also sprung up, although prices of nearly all securities remain fixed (there are legal secondary markets for no more than a handful of different issues), in order to prevent unearned incomes. For the same reason, owners of private firms must work in their enterprises, so that they are considered ''laborers'' rather than ''capitalists.'' In fact, average earnings of owner-managers in private business (where most firms are small) exceed average incomes in the state sector, although the former work longer hours, assume greater risks, and have no claim to the generous welfare benefits available to state employees.

Second, the reformers have sought to expand market links within the state planning network, while reducing control by government agencies. In 1982, the number of ministries and commissions directly under the State Council was cut from 98 to 52 and then to 41, and their total staff was reduced from 49,000 to 32,000. Further cuts are planned before 1990. As their decision-making rights (or use rights over capital) grow, firms are supposed to become more profit oriented (by receiving stronger claims on profits before taxes and subsidies), in order to stimulate them to reduce waste, raise quality and labor productivity, better tailor their products to user needs, and upgrade production. Thus, they are to move away from the one-sided emphasis on output volume, that is a command-economy hallmark.

'' 'Why is it that [foreign] bosses can run a factory efficiently and we can't?' asks a Chinese manager. 'The key is that we never ran a factory as though it was our own.' Whether a manager did well or poorly, the results did not affect his personal interest.'' Within the planning network, many firms still have a primary obligation to meet plan targets, but the latter are supposed to be set low enough to allow a margin of overfulfillment. Production beyond state targets or not covered by targets is to be sold on a more-or-less competitive market, and firms that do this successfully are, in principle, able to keep part of the resulting profit for bonuses and investment under their control. Many loss-making firms have been closed, merged with more viable enterprises, or forced either to change product lines or to revamp production methods. A new bankruptcy law is in effect. Although it has been little used, at least one formal bankruptcy has occurred (of the Shenyang Anti-Explosion Equipment Factory, in August 1986)—the first in China since 1949. Most discharged workers have continued to receive compensation, including early retirement and opportunities to go into business for themselves. In addition, provincial governments and some enterprises now have limited rights to conduct foreign trade on their own.

There has also been a limited decontrol of prices plus a modest gain of worker influence within the firm. However, full price flexibility remains elusive and a major barrier to reform success. The percentage of loss-making firms in state industry remains high, and quality is still a major problem. As one indication, some 60 percent of China's steel output in 1986 went into inventory because domestic producers did not meet users' requirements, while at least 15 million tons (about 30 percent of domestic production) were imported. Full implementation of reforms is scheduled by 1991, although this date appears optimistic, especially after the events of June 1989. Continuing resistance both in state enterprises and in the planning bureaucracy even makes eventual success of the reforms uncertain.

C. State Budget and Banking System

Chinese governments at all levels have exercised financial control over economic activity through the state budget and banking system.[10] As in every command economy, Chinese money circulates in two segregated channels. Within the state sector, all payments take the form of bookkeeping entries, which transfer credit from one enterprise or government institution to another. Between households, units of collective agriculture, and other nonstate entities, as well as between the state and nonstate sectors, payments are usually in cash. The first major goal of the banking system is to keep down the volume of both kinds of money in circulation, so as to limit inflationary pressures. However, since it also grants loans to enterprises on the basis of their inventories (the "Real Bills" doctrine), which have tended to rise out of control, this goal has been difficult to fulfill, although open inflation was officially low in every year between 1952 and 1984.

The second major goal has been to enforce performance according to the plan. Historically, most industrial investment has been financed by budget grants, targeted by the state to specific projects. The government places these grants, which have accounted for about 40 percent of its total expenditure, in the bank accounts of firms assigned to carry out the investments. As a project moves toward completion, funds are transferred to the accounts of construction firms or equipment suppliers. Although the grants are nonreturnable and interest-free, the state has also taxed away nearly all profit, thereby capturing a return on its investments when firms were profitable. It has also covered most losses with subsidies.

This "soft" budget constraint has not given enterprises enough incentive to be profitable, and the state's return on industrial investment has declined dramatically since the 1950s. Beginning in 1985, therefore, most investment is supposed to be financed from bank loans—which are repayable with interest—or from enterprise retained earnings, which have risen under the tax policies associated with reform. Long-term loans come from the Construction Bank, while short and medium-term loans for equipment come from the Industrial and Commercial Bank of China. There is also an Agricultural Bank to serve and to exercise financial control over the rural economy. In particular, it manages the rural credit cooperatives, which handle savings and credit for the *xiang* governments, for small rural industrial enterprises (managed at the township level or below), and for individual peasant households. Despite the increased priority for farming in recent years, loans in rural areas have not risen as rapidly as rural savings deposits, although the peasants have benefited since 1979 from higher prices for their produce. Other specialized banks include the Bank of China and the new China International Trust and Investment Corporation (CITIC), to handle foreign-exchange transactions, plus the China Investment Bank, which raises capital abroad for investment in China. Chinese domestic interest rates have historically been low by Western standards, although they have risen appreciably in recent years—and there is an excess demand for loans.

Until 1984, the only general purpose bank was the People's Bank of China, which combined the functions of central and commercial banking. In practice, this bank was little more than a division of the Finance Ministry over 1956–78 and was formally part of the budgetary system between 1970 and late 1977. It made short-term loans to firms in industry and commerce which were targeted to plan fulfillment and which, on average, covered 60 percent of working-capital needs (the rest coming directly from the state budget). When such loans exceeded amounts allowed by the plan, the borrower was to be charged penalty interest (although since this came out of profit, the state usually paid the penalty, in effect), and the bank had the task of investigating the reasons. While demand for above-plan loans in a command economy may be a sign that firms are surpassing their production targets, it is often the result of difficulties in meeting them, which the central bank is supposed to discover at the earliest possible moment.

More generally, the People's Bank has had the job of supervising plan performance by monitoring financial flows between firms and preventing enterprises from getting hold of funds that could be used for unauthorized investment or acquisition of goods. This was "control by the yuan." In principle, state firms have only been allowed enough funds for three days' normal needs and, thus, have been short of liquidity, which the banking system alone can supply. In practice, financial supervision has been lax in China. Enterprises have enjoyed excessive liquidity, and diversion of funds intended for working capital to investment or acquisition of goods on the second economy has been common. Political pressures on the bank to expand working capital loans have been too great for it to resist—in this respect it has been dominated by local party organs, as well as by the Finance Ministry—and its own internal organization was often under the control of radical elements over 1956–77, who did not believe in financial discipline.

On January 1, 1984, the People's Bank became more like a Western central bank, as its commercial banking operations were turned over to the newly created Industrial and Commercial Bank. Individual bank branches are now to exercise greater control over lending and are to grant loans on the basis of economic (rate-of-return) criteria. The new bank became part of a general expansion of decentralized financial intermediation, which included the fledgling stock and bond markets noted above, and bank-like institutions called investment trust companies (ITCs). The ITCs collect deposits from firms and other organizations, as well as from individuals, and lend to finance a variety of investment projects by cooperative and state enterprises. Depositors have the option of earmarking their funds for specific investments, including joint ventures, and the latter may also be carried out without recourse to the ITCs.

In order to tighten financial supervision of enterprises, the government has created a State Auditing Administration to help enforce financial regulations. Nevertheless, excessive liquidity, uncontrolled investment, and unauthorized use of funds have increased, to the point of threatening to undermine China's industrial reforms. Local bank branches have granted loans indiscriminately and fueled an unsustainable investment boom. Neither borrower nor lender has worried too much about the feasibility of repaying principal and interest. Both have expected that failure to repay would result in little or no financial penalty, with losses being made good by state subsidies. This has forced some recentralization of investment decisions, along with partial rationing of loans by quota. Moreover, since mandatory plan constraints on firms have been relaxed, while most controlled prices remain below equilibrium levels, shortages of goods are widespread. Many opportunities have arisen to raise prices illegally and to divert funds to unauthorized uses, including rewards in cash or in kind (notably housing) for managers and workers. Some unauthorized uses have been perceived as corruption or as examples of "unhealthy tendencies," and most of the diverted income should have gone to the state as taxes, at a time of budget deficits. These developments have provided ammunition for reform opponents and have even shocked some reform advocates (whose views should not be confused with those of Western liberals).

Finally, over most of the period of Communist rule, the state budget has had the task of channelling funds from light industry and agriculture to heavy industry, which has enjoyed priority access to investment. During the 1950s, about 75 percent of the savings used to finance investment were squeezed out of agriculture; since then, around 90 percent have come from profits and sales taxes on light industry. There is also a program of regional income redistribution. Wealthier cities and provinces, such as Shanghai and Liaoning, remit well over half their tax revenues to the central government, while the latter's subsidies to poorer regions, such as Tibet and Ningxia, have covered more than half the expenditures of these provincial-level governments.[11] Between 1949 and 1985, in fact, Shanghai had to contribute 88 percent of its revenues to the national budget—which prevented it from meeting its own needs—and it still remits over 75 percent.

D. Rationing and Job Assignment

Planning in China has been supported by widespread job assignment, which has largely replaced the free labor market. Although reformers are reviving the latter, it still plays a smaller role in China than in the USSR or Eastern Europe—a reflection of the stricter control over individual life in China. Workers have usually been assigned to a work unit for life, to which membership has been virtually a second citizenship. Transfers have been almost impossible to obtain, unless one goes to a clearly less desirable job or location. Even within a work unit, transfers to a completely different type of work from one's initial assignment are unusual. Each unit controls the travel rights of its employees and will often provide housing, medical care, and/or schooling for their children. In principle, an individual cannot obtain a home without a job in the same area. Until the recent reforms, enterprises could not legally recruit workers directly. Instead, they obtained labor through local employment bureaus, which manage the job assignment system in each area. This is still frequently the case, although times are changing.

Job assignment has helped to suppress inflationary pressures that might have resulted from shortages of skilled labor. However, China's present leaders have also criticized it as slow, rigid, bureaucratic, and generally producing a bad match between labor supply and demand. Partly to reduce unemployment and to ensure jobs for the large numbers of school leavers over the next few years, they have been promoting expansion of urban cooperatives and small private enterprises, which also produce goods and services in short supply. Such firms accounted for more than half the roughly 40 percent increase in urban employment over 1978–84. As a consequence of radical policies, the individual (small private) economy had almost disappeared by 1978, but nine years later, it was employing over 20 million people. Around 80 percent of all retail stores, service shops, and restaurants established in recent years are in private hands, and private enterprises accounted for a fourth of retail sales in 1986. Until 1988, a private business was allowed no more than seven employees, who were not family members of the owner. This ceiling was widely violated, however—some factories employing over one hundred workers—and these larger private firms have now been legalized by a 1988 constitutional amendment. Current plans are to continue expanding the private and small cooperative sector, which reduces shortages of consumer products and increases employment, with only a fraction of the investment required by state firms.

Yet, the basic job assignment system is likely to remain, although it should become more flexible and better take into account variations in the aptitudes of potential employees. Direct recruiting by state enterprises will probably continue to expand as well, and efforts are under way to tie wages more closely to job performance. In this context, the government wants to end the ''iron rice bowl'' commitment, according to which workers in the state sector cannot be fired or demoted (and are rarely promoted) and can pass on their jobs to their children.

Officially, the iron rice bowl has been "smashed." A small, but growing percentage of workers is now employed on fixed-term contracts, and a few workers have been laid off when their contracts expired. However, the practice of effective lifetime employment is likely to die slowly and not at all in some industries and locations (where it may be efficient, owing to the importance of on-the-job training). The government is expanding vocational training and has introduced a new pay system, under which each employee's earnings will consist of four parts: a basic subsistence wage; a component based on position or type of work; a seniority component; and a bonus tied to performance.

Expansion of the private and cooperative sector, as well as of China's ties with foreign countries and the loosening of job assignment, has improved career prospects for many Chinese—especially those able to acquire skills badly needed in the current drive to modernize. Earlier, we said that a command economy potentially provides the economic base for more enduring control by a single political party than does a market economy. In particular, career advancement requires party approval, and alternative career paths are circumscribed. Loyalty to one's superiors in the party hierarchy is a key ingredient in career success, and the Chinese party has often stressed ideological and political factors (or "redness") over expertise in promotions to administrative and managerial posts. However, the reforms are eroding this monopoly over career alternatives, one reason behind the "anti-corruption" drive (in the summer of 1989) to get relatives of party officials to drop their business interests.

Moreover, although Chinese university students are still constrained by the job assignment system, they now speak of three different career paths. First, the *black* path arises from successful completion of an advanced degree in a Western country. So far, this has meant a good job for most returnees, and China especially needs scientists, technicians, computer and information specialists, and managers. These areas are expanding. Second, the *gold* path arises from becoming a successful businessman, usually in the growing market sector. Here there is often a large pent-up demand, owing to past suppression via the rationing system (described below), but it is also important to make money fairly quickly and to acquire friends with good political credentials. Business horizons still tend to be short in socialist countries because the political winds have often shifted in the past. Finally, the *red* path of advancement through the party and state bureaucracy is still the surest, most stable route in many parts of China, although its reputation is lower than in the past. The emphasis on managerial or administrative expertise vs. redness is now greater, although dedication to the party and its goals is still important.

Price ceilings for consumer goods are supported by rationing of some staple foodstuffs and other daily necessities, as well as of a number of consumer durables. Ration coupons have often been distributed through the work place, and permission of one's work unit plus coupons have been necessary to buy light industrial goods, although this is less frequently true now than formerly. Housing is allocated by local housing offices, as well as by work units. Rents are especially low, amounting, on average, to 1–2 percent of a household's disposable income, and the shortage of housing in urban areas is acute. More generally, as in other socialist countries, consumer goods and services are in excess demand at official prices, and households hold surplus savings, on balance, because of difficulties of transforming money into goods. Historically, Chinese rationing of consumer products has been more formal and severe than in the Soviet Union or Eastern Europe, although the present régime has had success in expanding supplies. This has permitted a relaxation of rationing. By 1984, officials were claiming that 80 percent of light industrial products were no longer in short supply, and the same is now true of some basic foodstuffs. Yet, per capita savings deposits were about 13 times as great at end-1987 as at end-1978. Much of the 285 billion yuan increase represented funds that would have been spent, had supplies of desired consumer goods been available. Potentially, these accounts, plus savings of unknown magnitude being held in individual homes, represent fuel for inflation and/or work disincentives. Because of the threat of inflation, the effort to replace rationing with flexible prices that respond to supply and demand is portrayed by the Chinese as the most difficult and sensitive part of their current reform program.

Rationing supports family planning—since families receive food ration coupons for no more than two children—as well as the system of job assignment, since food ration coupons are only good in one location. In addition, each Chinese needs an internal passport or *hukou* (family register), in order to obtain housing, employment, ration coupons for grain or cooking oil, and also to get married or enroll his or her children in the local school. Each *hukou* is valid for just one area and is the main means of population control, although it is possible to survive illegally in China's cities (e.g., as a private businessman). Families sometimes receive more ration coupons than they can use, and rationed goods are often available in state stores without coupons, although at higher prices. At still higher prices, they are available on the free market, which is supplied by individual peasants, as well as by other individual and cooperative enterprises. Supplies here have greatly expanded in recent years. This weakens the internal passport system, although free-market prices of scarce items can easily be several times official levels.

E. Allocation of Raw Materials and Intermediate Goods

In the 1950s, when China was copying the Soviet Union, it also tried to ration key producer goods formally, from the apex of the planning hierarchy, although this system was never as extensive or comprehensive as in the USSR or Eastern Europe. In the 1957 decentralization, much of the rationing of scarce industrial inputs devolved onto the provinces, although part of this was subsequently recentralized, and lower government levels are also involved in allocation. Formally, producer goods are classified into three categories. The State Planning and Economic Commission distributes category I products, considered most important, while industrial ministries allocate goods in category II. The State Price Commission sets prices for these products, which in the past have covered 70–80 percent of all producer goods by value. Local governments, at the county level and below, handle the distribution and pricing of category III products, considered of lesser importance. In most cases, producer-goods prices have been set below equilibrium levels, and relative prices have reflected neither relative marginal costs of supply nor relative marginal values to users or to planners. In this sense, they are irrational.

To obtain quotas of category I or II inputs, an enterprise must submit requests to its superior government agency. Thus, a county-level firm would state its needs to the county administration, which would pass them up through the regional chain of command, eventually to Beijing. As in other command economies, the supply system works poorly, shortages and bottlenecks going hand-in-hand with overstocked warehouses and hoarding of all kinds of inputs. As a rule, state agencies prevent direct ties between producers and users. Firms produce to meet plan targets rather than users' needs, causing quality problems and supply-demand mismatches. Moreover, each planning unit from the enterprise on up tries to make sure it will have the inputs it needs to fulfill its plan targets, plus a margin of insurance. Each tends to overstate its needs and to treat requirements of other planning jurisdictions as residual. (A county, for example, will try to get local cement factories to supply local users before those in other counties.)

Consequently, firms, ministries, provinces, counties, etc. try to integrate backward to produce their own inputs. It becomes common for ministries to control enterprises producing goods that have been formally assigned to other ministries. Each planning unit turns out too wide a variety of products, often on an inefficiently small scale, and self-sufficiency, rather than specialization according to comparative advantage, tends to become the rule. The categorization of producer goods implies the existence of three separate state supply networks in any area. This raises the level of inventories, along with the likelihood that a supply bottleneck in one input will coexist with a surplus of a substitute good. Only by going through administrative channels can firms substitute the surplus input for the one in deficit, and this is hard or impossible to do if the two are in different categories and, thus, in different supply networks. What sometimes saves the day is a network of black markets on which firms exchange producer goods directly and, as a rule, illegally. Audrey Donnithorne writes that ". . . enterprises have sometimes to dispatch staff or agents to scour the country to get some wanted item. In May, 1958, a report told of a Shanghai teahouse, which, in the old days, had been a center for rice dealers . . . , but now was an acknowledged mart for metals and machinery, with patrons coming from all over China."[12] These markets are dominated, not by salesmen, but by "pushers" or purchasing agents (analogous to the Soviet *tolkachi*), who have developed a talent for obtaining scarce supplies, generally for bribes or other favors. Frequently, such exchanges involve barter.

In such conditions, the current reform seeks to expand the role of legal producer goods markets, as well as to increase regional specialization according to comparative advantage and to separate economic management from government administration, so that goods move more freely across political boundaries. The reformers want not only to expand direct ties between producers and users, but also to promote competition on both sides of the market and to end the persistent excess demand. While mandatory planning and administrative allocation will continue for basic means of production and consumption, even here the role of the plan is to contract. Firms are to receive production targets within their capabilities, which will also be limits on the amounts of their outputs that the state will automatically buy. At the same time, claims on resulting profits are supposed to motivate them to expand beyond target levels and sell the excess directly to users. They will also be able to appeal targets or quotas that appear to be out of line with demand, although it is not clear whether they will be motivated to do this.

Once again, the question of pricing poses an acute danger to the reform effort. Prices must move closer to equilibrium levels, requiring large increases for many basic inputs, whose users may already be unable to survive without persistent subsidies. Eventually, prices must respond flexibly to supply and demand, which will generally require pricing to become the responsibility of producers. All this is foreseen as part of the reforms, but the major steps remain to be taken, as of mid-1989. Many large firms still lack autonomy, and their managements are used to having finance, marketing, and supply carried out for them by the state. Within many enterprises, the power of the party secretary remains considerable, even though he usually does not understand management or the technical aspects of production. The reforms have increased the leverage of municipalities and county-level governments over production and resource allocation, with some good results. But if further increases in enterprise independence are not forthcoming, the long-term impact of this change may be negative, since it will then increase local self-sufficiency and empire-building.

Similar reforms were tried in the early 1960s. Then, the government, headed by Liu Shaoqi and Deng Xiaoping, launched a drive to get enterprises to specialize more completely in their main product lines and to promote closer supplier-user relations.

> Face-to-face contact between suppliers and customers was an important aspect of this campaign. Employees of a Shanghai pneumatic tool factory . . . were dispatched to the mines to observe at first hand the damage wrought by their own shoddy workmanship. Within three years, successful reforms catapulted the same unit to national prominence as a cost and quality leader. . . .[13]

Where the need for flexible supply relations was great, the planners began to organize materials allocation conferences (MACs). These bring together producers and users of particular types of goods from within a given county or province or even from all over China. The basic purpose of the MAC is to sign contracts and establish supply relations, but also to find users for new products and producers for firms with new input requirements. A related type of meeting, the materials exchange conference (MEC), is called to arrange for the sale of overstocked inventories. To paraphrase a Chinese professor,

> central planning in China since the 1957–58 administrative decentralization has been mainly procurement planning, based on inter-provincial transfers. . . . Under this system, in industries which are subject to central allocation, each province proposes to the center a figure for provincial output and a second figure for shipments to other provinces. . . . Materials allocation conferences . . . are used, after these total provincial surpluses or deficits have been decided, to allocate interprovincial flows among factories, and also to specify more clearly the quality and variety to be produced. . . .[14]

MACs and MECs have added an element of flexibility to Chinese planning, but there is still no shortage of horror stories about overcentralization, rigidity, bureaucratic foul-ups or red tape, and administrative delays. Most of the 1961–66 reform initiatives were reversed during the Cultural Revolution, and reformers were denounced as "capitalist-roaders," subsequently to be beaten, humiliated, sentenced to prison or hard labor, tortured, and even killed—generally without receiving a formal trial.

7-3. Approach to Planning and Development

Nearly all socialist countries are oriented toward economic growth, featuring priority expansion of heavy industry, and China has been no exception. Shortly before his death in early 1976, Premier Zhou Enlai outlined a two-stage plan, by which China would "accomplish the modernization of agriculture, industry, national defense, and science and technology by the end of the century." It now appears that Zhou was overoptimistic, although his long-range modernization goals have become the centerpiece of long-run economic planning and policy. Moreover, the share of GNP devoted to saving and investment has averaged over 25 percent since 1952 vs. 5 percent in 1933 (the latter being typical of developing nations). More than half of all investment went into heavy industry until the 1979 readjustment of priorities.

However, it is also true that Mao Zedong—China's leader from 1949 until his death in 1976—wanted to build a classless society of selfless, altruistic citizens, who would be dedicated to one another, to the socialist revolution, and to China. In a sense, Mao sought the transformation of human nature desired by conventional Marxists, but without preceding this by the achievement of material superabundance. In the Chinese context, the end of scarcity appears especially remote. To a degree, the goals of economic development and of "building the new man" worked hand-in-hand, and the radicals claimed many achievements in this regard. These include the ten-mile long bridge across the Yangtze River at Nanjing and the Red Flag Canal in Northwestern Henan Province—which is over 1,500 miles long, with its trunk canals and auxiliary channels. It was built entirely by hand and carved through 1,250 hilltops over a ten-year period to irrigate nearly 100,000 acres of previously parched land in Linxian county.

From being a nation with no oil, completely dependent on imports, China has risen to thirteenth place in world crude-oil production. It leads the world in coal output, ranks tenth in production of natural gas, is fourth in overall energy output, and third in energy consumption, after the U.S. and USSR. It also ranks first in grain and cotton production and in the outputs of seventeen rare metals, including tungsten, molybdenum, and titanium. It is fifth in total mineral production. Between 1965 and 1978, it raised grain output by over 55 percent, thanks to massive, labor-intensive efforts at water control plus a sixfold rise in fertilizer output. Growth rates in heavy industry and electric power have been dramatic. The transport network now hauls more than ten times as much freight as it did before 1950. The utilization of rural labor in local, small-scale industry provides a model for other developing nations.

Yet, the cost of its achievements has also been staggering, and colossal errors have been committed in economic management. Not long ago, it was common to point to China as a model developing country, and a worldwide cult formed around the "Maoist road" to development. Part of China's appeal stemmed from her apparent ability to provide the basic necessities of life and more to every citizen. In 1970, John Gurley, a former editor of the *American Economic Review*, wrote,

> the basic, overriding economic fact about China is that for twenty years, it has fed, clothed and housed everyone, has kept them healthy, and has educated most. Millions have not starved; sidewalks and streets have not been covered with multitudes of sleeping, begging, hungry, and illiterate human beings; millions are not disease-ridden. To find such deplorable conditions, one does not look to China these days, but to India.[15]

Now, it is clear that China mainly succeeded in hiding the suffering caused by disastrous mistakes of her leaders, largely in the radical wing of the party. In 1971, Emperor Hailé Selassie of Ethiopia toured China and came to admire the accomplishments of the régime. He asked Mao what had been the cost in human life since 1949 of these "victories of socialism." "Fifty million dead," replied Mao. A little flabbergasted, Selassie noted that this represented twice the population of Ethiopia.[16] "But only a small percentage of that of China," replied Mao. On a more mundane note, the average real wage in state industry, the most favored sector of the economy, fell by about a fourth over 1957–77, according to official statistics.

Mao's ideal man was an all-rounder rather than a specialist. "With hammer in hand he will be able to do factory work; with hoe, plough, or harrow he will be able to farm; with the gun he will be able to fight the enemy, and with the pen he will be able to express himself in writing," he wrote to Lin Biao at the start of the Cultural Revolution in 1966. In particular, managers would ideally be both "red" and "expert," i.e., selfless, ideologically pure, dedicated to the pursuit of a classless society, and also brilliant entrepreneurs and administrators. Unfortunately, China has been unable to generate a class of new men and women that combine all these qualities sufficiently—nor, for that matter, has any other nation been able to do so.

During the latter part of his life, Mao's idealism was subverted by radical elements in the party for their own ends.

In terms of political control, China has oscillated between reliance on moral incentives and ideological fervor, on the one hand, vs. expertise and material incentives, on the other, as catalysts of development. This is summarized in the phrase, "Red vs. Expert." Favorable economic performance—under the control of administrative and technical experts—has generated concern about "revisionism" in ideology and about the reemergence of "capitalist" property relations, including income and status differentials. Subsequently, a slogan such as "politics takes command" would become the theme of an intensive ideological campaign stressing correct political thought as the key to improving socialist relations and building the Maoist version of a communist society. Equality was to be the hallmark of this society, and its cornerstone was to be the "new Communist man," who had learned to work solely in order to contribute to the good of all people and to the state.

Thus, during periods of ideological fervor,

> campaigns were organized to eliminate significant differences in the roles, status, privileges, material benefits, and types of work of leaders, followers, managers, workers, the poorly and well-educated, the skilled and unskilled, the generalists and the specialists, and so forth. Moral incentives tended to replace material incentives as the principal work motivators, and more working hours were lost in political meetings, ideological indoctrination, and study sessions.

Mobilization of labor, often on a mass scale for highly visible construction projects, was a theme of these periods, as was "self-reliance" (and self-sufficiency), in which everyone was encouraged to rely on his own efforts. Professional managers and planners often lost control to political cadres, and political pressures on the People's Bank to expand loans and relax financial surveillance increased. In some cases, professionals were "shipped off to the countryside for a time to learn their proper place by lifting rocks and shovelling manure."[17] Subsequently, economic growth would come to a halt or reverse itself. Eventually, this would regenerate concern over performance, leading to a return of the experts and to a renewed emphasis on professionalism and discipline, as well as on the use of material incentives, to stimulate growth.

There have been two periods of intense ideological fervor—the Great Leap Forward and its aftermath (1958–61) and the height of the Cultural Revolution (1966–69). Each followed a period of good to outstanding economic performance and each caused economic chaos, which resulted in widespread suffering. In particular, at least 20 million are believed to have starved over 1959–62, as a result of the collapse of the Great Leap Forward. Industrial output fell by one-third in 1961, although this was partly due to the 1960 Sino-Soviet split. The years 1974–76, leading up to the death of Mao, witnessed further ideological and political struggle between radical and moderate factions in the party. The radicals assigned highest priority to ideological factors and to having a "correct" political attitude.

Most radicals were from poor peasant backgrounds and were more poorly educated than the moderates. Thus, they often lacked technical competence and tended to distrust people with expertise, toward which they acquired a degree of contempt. The radical leaders, however, were Shanghai urban sophisticates—the "Gang of Four," including Mao's wife, Jiang Quing, and Zhang Chungqiao, a deputy prime minister and first political commissar of the Shanghai district. (All four members of the "Gang" were also Politburo members.)

In October 1976, just one month after Mao's death, the members of the Gang of Four were arrested, but only in December 1978 did the moderates and decentralizers gain control of the top echelons of party and government. In doing so, they probably put an end to the oscillation between Red and expert, since the radicals have been thoroughly discredited, and most radical leaders have been purged. Today, the emphasis is on modernization, improved management and planning, and higher living standards, instead of mobilization, equality, and class struggle. A drive has begun to push China into the front rank of industrial nations by the end of the first third of the twenty-first century. China's present leaders hold the radical approach to development at least partly responsible for China's industries being fifteen to thirty years behind technological levels in the West. Radical reliance on moral incentives, or collectivization of material rewards, is now criticized as "everyone eating from the same big pot."

Conflict over economic organization has assumed the more conventional format of a struggle between centralizers and decentralizers. The former favor the Soviet model, along with priority expansion of heavy industry and high rates of investment. The latter want economic development more oriented to demand, pointing out that rapid growth in the past has not led to commensurate welfare improvement or to innovation, because production has been too much for its own sake rather than to meet the needs of users. Thus, the decentralizers have launched the reform program outlined above, which includes greater enterprise independence, performance-based incentives, more responsibility and authority for professional managers, more control by employees over the selection of lower level decision makers, and a more tolerant attitude toward cooperative and small private firms.

The decentralizers also assign a major part of the blame for China's technological backwardness to over-reliance on Soviet-style command planning. Thus, one official has advocated production targets "of a guiding nature . . . instead of rigid quotas . . . as regards the majority of enterprises and their products."[18] Zhao Ziyang, former General Secretary of China's Communist party, believes that socialism has just three basic requirements: payment according to labor input, public ownership of the material means of production, and some form of central planning.[19] The first of these reaffirms income differentials based on differences in mental or manual labor input and is a rebuff to radical efforts to collectivize material rewards.

On balance, we can identify eight periods in the evolution of the Chinese economy since the Communists came to power in 1949. The first, 1949–52, was an interval of reconstruction, during which the party consolidated its control following victory in the civil war. The second, 1952–57, comprises the First Five-Year Plan, also the period of most rapid economic growth. The Great Leap Forward, 1958–61, was followed by a period of economic recovery, 1961–66, identified with Liu Shaoqi, who was then disgraced during the Cultural Revolution and rehabilitated posthumously in 1980. It featured a return to material incentives, restoration of authority to managerial and technical experts, and reimposition of financial controls, whose disappearance had helped to fuel many of the GLF excesses. During the Liu Shaoqi period, many firms had to seek customers for their products, and competition was by no means unknown—a kind of "breakthrough of the future into the present."

Then followed the height of the Proletarian Cultural Revolution (1966–69), after which a brief period of renewed moderation and growth set in, only to be interrupted by the political campaigns and struggles of 1974–76. These were partly over which faction in the party would inherit Mao's mantle, but also over the question of egalitarianism vs. growth, moral vs. material incentives, and Red vs. Expert. Within the context of the latter, China's willingness to borrow foreign ideas and technology—as well as the nature and strength of her commercial and trade relations with other countries—was a particularly burning issue. After "smashing" the Gang of Four, China's leaders set out to expand these ties via the present open door policy. There followed efforts by the centralizers, over 1976–78, to establish control, using Hua's modernization program as their catalyst. This failed, and the present period began at end-1978. It is not yet clear whether the events of May and June 1989 will mark a new watershed. In 1981 and 1986, China also launched new five-year plans—respectively, her sixth and seventh. These were not very important over 1957–80, but their significance now appears to have increased.

In the Great Leap Forward, Mao had also tried to decentralize command planning. This movement was preceded by the 1957–58 administrative decentralization described earlier. In addition, over 1956–57, Communist party cadres had taken over much of the authority previously exercised by enterprise directors and government administrators. An "anti-rightist" purge of political moderates, experts, intellectuals, and officials suspected of overly strong regional loyalties made these moves feasible, and to a degree, necessary. The party cadres who remained or were newly promoted often identified their own welfares or career prospects with the central will, as expressed through the party's radical wing. This made it possible to control enterprises by means of broad guidelines and directives sent down through the party hierarchy, in addition to the smaller number of production-related targets that remained. The net result was greater formal decentralization than before, but more rigid ideological control. Strict adherence to ideological norms and to "correct political thought" was partly substituted for adherence to detailed production targets. Enthusiasm and loyalty also became more important in assessing managers, and bonuses were reduced or eliminated.

Given the régime's desire for nearly miraculous growth in 1957–58, the merging of party and government roles and the takeover of enterprises by party cadres represented an effort to centralize power that was actually viewed as a prerequisite to economic decentralization. Only when politically reliable men were in control of firms, farms, and government organs could the leadership substitute broad directives for detailed controls. The thrust of these directives was to initiate a hoped-for shortcut to economic development through a massive mobilization of labor. However, the use value of production declined, because party cadres in charge tended to maximize output without paying attention to demand, quality control, cost considerations, or even basic technical aspects of production. As a result of farm mismanagement, coupled with bad weather, grain output plummeted over 1960–61, and famine stalked the land. The Sino-Soviet rift and Soviet pull-out in August 1960 became the final blow, and the Great Leap Forward collapsed in disaster.

During the First Five-Year Plan, China had copied the Soviet approach to development, stressing construction of large-scale, capital-intensive industry in the cities. Because of rising industrial wages and falling living standards in the countryside (since the peasants were supplying most of the forced saving needed to finance industrial growth), a rural-to-urban migration took place. Unfortunately, the heavy industries being set up had a low labor absorption capacity, and male urban unemployment had probably reached 20 percent or more by 1957. During the same period, wage and salary differentials were widening within industry to a degree that was unacceptable, at least to Mao and the party's radical wing, and China's economic dependence on the USSR was viewed with growing concern. Moreover, despite rapid economic growth, China's leaders believed the ministries were restraining the economy below its potential, and a goal of decentralization was to remove this constraint.

However, the effect of removal was to increase mismanagement and to worsen economic coordination, as noted above. Nevertheless, several elements of the new approach to development in 1958 have survived, although in altered form. These include the policy of "walking on two legs"—or building small-scale, labor-intensive industry, in addition to large-scale factories—and that of "self-reliance." The latter still means relying on one's own efforts, but it no longer connotes extreme self-sufficiency or rejection of contacts or technology from abroad (the "closed-door" policy), as it did when the radicals were in control.

7-4. Growth and Distribution

A. Distribution

We close this chapter with a brief statistical profile of the Chinese economy. In principle, China is an egalitarian society. Before 1949, 20–25 percent of national income went to landlords, merchants, moneylenders, and the like, who were largely a consuming class. By eliminating this class, appropriating much of their income for investment, and redistributing the rest, the Communist régime both reduced wealth differentials and raised economic growth. Nevertheless, large income differences exist today, especially between urban and rural areas, and also between different geographical regions. Reform efforts to tie rewards more closely to individual performance appear to have reduced urban-rural differences, although they are raising inequality within localities and, possibly, between different regions. The absence of a personal income tax on Chinese citizens limits redistribution via the revenue side of the budget.

One source estimates a real income difference between urban and rural areas on the order of 5-to-1 in 1980, in favor of the cities, vs. about 2-to-1 in the 1930s.[20] Peasant incomes rose rapidly over 1980–87, under the rural responsibility system, perhaps doubling in real terms (although this is difficult to say, since official price indexes understate inflation). Urban incomes also rose, and the ratio between the two remained far above 2-to-1. Getting a city residence permit for an offspring is still the dream of many farm households. Growth of the urban-rural gap over 1950–80 resulted from the high priority for industrial growth—which has held down investment in rural areas—in combination with diminishing returns to labor on land plus the limit on migration out of agriculture and the exclusion of nearly all rural families from state-financed welfare benefits and schooling. Thus, the out-migration from agriculture during the 1980s, generally motivated by the lure of higher earnings, may be the biggest step to date toward reducing differences in living standards. In 1980, a Chinese source wrote that "in the poorest production teams, some peasants cannot even be sure of enough food or clothing," while in Shanghai, the wealthiest city, there were at least two TV sets for every three families as early as 1981.[21]

Nevertheless, because of the comparative attraction of city life, as well as the high birthrates of the 1950s and 1960s, and the disruptions of the Cultural Revolution, China has also faced serious urban unemployment. During the late 1970s, 20 million young people were reported to be "waiting for work." Most of these were not heads of households, but rather school leavers, who had not yet been assigned a job in state industry. Yet, they represented about 4.5 percent of China's labor force, and some had been waiting for up to ten years. By early 1982, the State Labor Bureau was claiming that most of the unemployment had been eliminated, although it subsequently rose again, to about 15 million in 1988.[22] Unemployment reductions have been achieved mainly by starting and expanding urban cooperatives and small private businesses, rather than through growth of the state sector.

Mao once said that, before China could pass from socialism to communism, three important differences would have to be eliminated—between town and country, worker and peasant, and manual and mental labor. This elimination has a long way to go. Where progress has been made, moreover, it has come through policies such as the rural responsibility system and the relaxation of barriers to mobility, coupled with expansion of cooperative and private enterprise, which reverse the radical utopian line of the Great Helmsman.

B. Urban Budgets and Benefits

Although China is a poor country, the basic necessities of life are free or extremely inexpensive in urban areas. Thus, education and medical care are free, and housing is subsidized, so that rent usually claims under 5 percent of a household's income. According to an official sample survey in 1985, rent came to just 1.08 percent of total expenditure, water and electricity to 1.03 percent, and fuel to 1.38 percent. Transportation took another 8.4 percent. The major items of expense were food (53.31 percent vs. 58.43 percent in 1957), clothing (15.34 percent), other articles for daily use (11.14 percent), "articles for cultural life and recreation" (7.5 percent), and "tobacco, liquors, and tea" (5.2 percent). Cloth is rationed, along with grain products and some other foodstuffs. Western observers believe that official samples have upward biases in terms of income, and it is known, for example, that transport is quite expensive for some commuters, taking up to 20 percent of household income.

In China, as in other socialist nations, steep sales or turnover taxes plus large markups of producer prices over costs greatly increase the prices of durable consumer goods, which sometimes cost far more than in the United States. The retail price of a Chinese watch can be ten times its production cost, to cite an extreme case, and markups of 100 percent are not unusual. Together, profits and sales taxes account for 85–90 percent of government revenue and finance most of China's high rate of investment (averaging 25–30 percent of GNP), although the role of enterprise and household savings has been growing. Even at the high prices indicated, most consumer durables are in short supply, and Chinese families save more than they want to because of shortages of goods to buy. In addition, the absence of consumer credit requires accumulation of savings before purchases can be made. When deposited, personal savings have earned interest at a rate slightly above the rate of inflation in most years. Typical objects of voluntary savings have been a bicycle, a TV set, a radio, some furniture, a tape recorder, a sewing machine, an electric fan, a watch, a camera, and even a washing machine.

Workers in industry receive comprehensive welfare benefits. In general, those awarded army combat heroes and model workers have been more liberal than the benefits available to others, but the most important difference is between state employees and other members of the work force, who are largely excluded from the state-financed welfare system. Thus, the latter covers no more than 20–25 percent of the labor force. In the state sector, sick-leave benefits come to 60–100 percent of monthly salary or wages for the first 6 months, depending on length of service, and 40–60 percent thereafter. Disability benefits include free medical and nursing care plus payment of living expenses and regular wages while individuals are undergoing treatment. State maternity benefits include a cash payment at birth plus 50–70 days off with pay before and after confinement. State retirement benefits are especially generous, although only 10 million retirees were receiving them in 1984 (and another 3 million elderly were living in "Homes of Respect for the Aged''). Thus, men can retire from the state sector at age 60 and women at age 50 with 75 percent of last preretirement salary, provided they have worked 20 years or more. If they become disabled, this rises to 80–90 percent. Retired men often find another job, so that their total income actually rises. If they are willing to move to the country, they receive a grant toward construction of a house. If they stay in the city, their children will often live with them, because of low salaries for young workers and a severe housing shortage.

C. Growth, Structure, and Inflation

Table 7.1 describes the global evolution of the Chinese economy over 1952–86 in terms of income and production, taking 1952, the first year in which national income surpassed the pre–civil war peak, as a base. Until recently, China published few data on economic performance, allowing Western scholars to develop their own growth industry, estimating Chinese development. The latter 1970s saw an upsurge of official data. Nevertheless, the figures for GNP, industry, and agriculture are Western estimates, although the GNP figures are consistent with the official growth of national income, calculated according to the Marxist definition.

According to the table, GNP per head grew by an annual average of 4.3 percent, while agricultural and industrial output per capita rose, respectively, by 2.3 percent and 8.5 percent annually. Per capita GNP growth exceeded the medians for both socialist and developing nations and was well above mid-range for Western economies. It was slightly above most Western growth estimates for the Soviet economy over the same period. The main growth generator was the high rate of investment, in addition to which 5–10 percent of GNP has gone for defense and 60–65 percent for public plus private consumption. As in other socialist countries, the average return on investment has fallen. Industrial output per worker rose by over 50 percent during the First Five-Year Plan (1952–57), and then slightly more than doubled between 1957 and 1985, according to official statistics. However, these gains were largely due to increases in capital per worker. In addition, construction times doubled over 1955–80, inventory-to-sales ratios rose by more than 80 percent in state industry, and consumption of energy per unit of national income was over twice as high in 1980 as in 1955.

Thus, while China has generated rapid industrial growth, this has been mainly extensive as in other socialist economies. Because of mistakes in planning, as well as the high priority of heavy industry and a lack of initiative or cost consciousness on the part of state enterprises, living standards have failed to keep pace with the growth of output. A 17 percent decrease in the average real wage in state industry over 1957–77 was followed by an 41 percent rise during 1977–85. Per capita real income of families of state industrial workers climbed by more than 75 percent over 1957–85, but this was mainly due to increased labor-force participation, largely by females. State workers are the most favored socioeconomic group, aside from party officials. Moreover, official statistics understate the rate of inflation,

Table 7.1

Evolution of Selected Output Indexes for China Per Capita of Population (1952-86) (1952 = 100)

Index	1952	1957	1965	1970	1975	1978	1980	1986
GNP	100	120	137	166	204	242	272	423
Agriculture	100	106	95	104	109	120	130	210*
Industry	100	186	329	457	650	817	942	1,592
Grain	100	106	94	102	108	111	114	129
Steel	100	354	719	915	1,100	1,401	1,599	2,084
Electric power	100	236	735	1,102	1,666	2,092	2394	3,292
Coal	100	177	279	372	454	557	546	711
Crude oil	100	296	2,040	4,837	10,878	14,076	14,000	16,066
Metal-cutting machine tools	100	182	229	704	793	796	565	624
Chemical fertilizer	100	346	3,512	4,356	8,356	13,268	18,368	17,055
Cement	100	214	453	625	1,005	1,358	1,623	3,047
Bicycles	100	900	1,823	3,201	4,838	6,354	9,465	22,049*

Sources: State Statistical Bureau, *Statistical Yearbook of China, 1986* (Oxford: Oxford University Press, 1986). Arthur G. Ashbrook, Jr. "Economic Modernization and Long-Term Performance," in U.S. Congress, Joint Economic Committee, *China Under the Four Modernizations, Part I* (Washington, D.C.: U.S. Government Printing Office, 1982) Table 2, p. 104; Directorate of Intelligence, *Handbook of Economic Statistics, 1987* (Washington, D.C.: U.S. Government Printing Office, 1987).
* 1985

Table 7.2

The Evolving Breakdown of Chinese Net Domestic Product and Employment by Sector of Origin

Sector	Shares of NDP (1980 prices)		
	1957 (%)	1958 (%)	1982 (%)
Agriculture	58.7	37.9	38.8
Industry	16.8	41.7	43.9
Services	24.5	20.4	17.3

Sector	Employment Shares		
	1957 (%)	1978 (%)	1982 (%)
Agriculture	81.2	73.8	70.2
Industry	7.6	15.5	16.3
Services	11.1	10.7	13.5

Sector	Relative Productivity (= Sectoral Output/Worker ÷ Total Output/Worker)		
	1957	1978	1982
Agriculture	0.7	0.5	0.6
Industry	2.2	2.7	2.7
Services	2.2	1.9	1.3

Source: K. C. Yeh, "Macroeconomic changes in the Chinese Economy During Readjustment," *China Quarterly*, December 1984.

and therefore understate real wage declines, while overstating increases.

Table 7.2 complements 7.1 by showing how the structure of the economy changed over 1957–82. The basic transformation was a decline of agriculture, services, and light industry, relative to heavy industry. Investment priorities are also reflected by a decline of labor productivity in services, as well as by the comparatively low productivity of labor in farming, although pricing policy and controls on labor mobility played major roles in the latter. Not only did farm output grow more slowly than industrial production over 1952–80, but food output per capita was probably below the peak reached during the 1930s, and diet composition—with 75 percent of all protein intake coming from grain—remained about the same.[23] The rural population was more severely affected by this than were urban residents. Over the country as a whole, the average daily intake of calories was no more than 2,100 in 1980, close to what is considered minimal by Asian standards. Agriculture has had a higher priority since 1979 than before, and harvest increases after 1980 were especially welcome. The share of services in NDP has also begun to rise since 1982.

Finally, the low rate of inflation is remarkable, although it does not mean an absence of inflationary pressures. (Moreover, as in Hungary, the reform has quickened the pace of price increase.) Officially, consumer prices rose by an annual average of 1.7 percent over 1950–85. The increase exceeded 5 percent only in 1950, 1951, 1960, 1961, 1980, and 1985 (as well as in 1986, 1987, and 1988), although the official index understates the burden of inflation on consumers, by failing to take account of price increases in the growing free market sector. The Communists came to power amid a hyperinflation. If we set the official wholesale price index equal to 100 in 1937, this had risen to 1,258 by 1941; 158,362 by 1945; 2,617,781 by 1947; and 287,700,000 by mid-1948. In 1948, the price level rose by 60 to 65 times and in 1949, by another 70 times. Then, the increase was reduced to 93 percent in 1950 and to about 12 percent in 1951.[24] In 1955, the Communists issued a new currency, the *renminbi* (people's money), generally called the yuan, and exchanged it for the old yuan at a ratio of one new = 10,000 old. The chief cause of inflation was resort to the printing press, especially by the Kuomintang, when its machinery for collecting taxes broke down amid the wartime conditions then prevailing.

Thus, the Communists were able to end inflation and stabilize the currency, once they had established administrative control over the country and put their own tax-collecting machinery in place. Their ability to contain price increases was an important factor in their acceptance by the people. In the short run, it is possible to control inflation by tighter rationing of goods and/or by increasing the pressure on households and firms to save their earnings. China has also used rationing to keep down the prices of staples, such as rice, flour, and cloth over long periods, achieving "a low standard equal distribution" in the process. But for the whole economy, inflation can only be controlled over the long run by not allowing the money supply to grow faster than real net national product.

To this end, the central government balanced its budget in most years over 1951–78, although there were serious deficits during the Great Leap Forward. Then, 1979 brought a record deficit, equal to 15.5 percent of total revenue, resulting from increased subsidies to hold down retail food prices (when prices paid to farmers were raised) plus a rise in defense spending and large wage increases for the lowest-paid workers in state industry. (The latter reduced profits of state enterprises, a major source of state revenue.) Subsequently, the economic reforms allowed firms and regional governments to divert funds from the central government to unauthorized investment, wage increases, and bonuses. Price subsidies plus aid to loss-making farms have remained high, and there have been job creation programs, as well as rehabilitation payments to purge victims of the radicals. The center has run a deficit in every year since 1979, and annual money supply growth exceeded 30 percent over 1984–88. By 1988, official consumer price inflation was 20 percent per year in urban areas. Inflationary (demand) pressures implicit in present excess savings and probable future deficits are potentially strong enough to sidetrack the current reforms—a problem to which we shall return in chapter 9.

Notes

1. Zhu Weiwen, "Energetically Organize the Exchange Between Industrial and Agricultural Products," *Chinese Economic Studies*, Spring 1980, p. 85.

2. A. L. Erisman, "China: Agricultural Development, 1949–71," in U.S. Congress, Joint Economic Committee, *People's Republic of China: An Economic Assessment.* (Washington, D.C.: U.S. Government Printing Office, 1972).

Because most of China's rainfall occurs during the summer monsoon and flooding of major rivers is always a threat, water conservation has been of prime importance throughout China's history.

3. Dwight Perkins, "Plans and Their Implementation in the People's Republic of China," *American Economic Review*, May 1973, p. 225.

4. For example, although theoretically managers had to get ministerial permission for investment in fixed assets costing as little as 200 yuan, investment sometimes exceeded approved totals. "A photochemical plant in Swatow . . . grew in 8 or 9 years from a small laboratory to a modern plant with an annual output of 70 million yuan in 1960; in the 5 years before 1960, the state had invested only 1.2 million yuan in this firm." See Audrey Donnithorne *China's Economic System* (London: Allen & Unwin, 1967), p. 168.

5. In the USSR, 105 regional economic councils or *sovnarkhozy* (later reduced to 47) replaced 44 ministries that had managed the Soviet economy from Moscow. One goal was to bring management closer to production, and another was to break up the empire-building tendencies of the ministries, who had succeeded in eroding *Gosplan*'s authority. Another aim was to strengthen then Premier Krushchev's control by putting his own men in positions of authority. The Soviet reorganization was not really a decentralization; most enterprises were probably more tightly controlled from above than they had been. It was reversed after Krushchev's fall from power in late 1964.

6. Tibet did not become an autonomous region until 1965.

7. T. G. Rawski, "Chinese Economic Planning," *Current Scene*, April 1976, p. 2.

8. In August 1978, it was possible to travel thousands of miles through China's best rice-growing regions and rarely see anything in the fields except peasants and water buffalo.

9. Li Chaochen, "Joys and Headaches of a Factory Manager," *China Reconstructs*, May 1982, p. 29. The quote below comes from Gao Yangliu, "Signs of Capitalism in China? The Shenyang Experiment," *China Reconstructs*, March 1987, p. 40.

10. The discussion below relies on two works by Katherine H.Y Huang Hsiao: *Money and Monetary Policy in Communist China* (New York: Columbia University Press, 1971) and "Recent Developments in Money and Banking," *China Quarterly*, September 1982. See, as well, Carl E. Walter, "Dual Leadership and the 1956 Credit Reforms of the People's Bank of China," *China Quarterly*, June 1985.

11. See Nicholas Lardy, "Economic Planning and Income Distribution in China,"

Current Scene, November 1976, Table 3, p. 9. See, as well, Lardy's article, "Centralization and Decentralization in China's Fiscal Management," *China Quarterly,* March 1975. For a contrary view, see Audrey Donnithorne, *The Budget and the Plan in China: Central-Local Economic Relations* (Canberra: Australian National University Press, 1972). For Lardy vs. Donnithorne, see pp. 328–54 of the *China Quarterly,* June 1976.

12. Donnithorne, *China's Economic System,* p. 290. See, as well, E. C. Koziara and Chiou-shuang Yan, "The Distribution System for Producers' Goods in China," *China Quarterly,* December 1983.

13. Rawski, "Chinese Economic Planning," p. 2.

14. The above is as related by Bruce Reynolds, "Central Planning in China: The Significance of the Materials Allocation Conferences," ACES *Bulletin,* Summer 1975. These conferences are also described in Barry Richman, *Industrial Society in Communist China* (New York: Vintage Books, 1972), pp. 712–18; 727–37. The professor in question is Zhang Zhun of Nankai University, Tianjin.

15. John W. Gurley, "Maoist Economic Development: The New Man in the New China," *The Center Magazine,* May 1970, p. 31.

16. This is recounted by Jacques and Claudie Broyelle in their article, "Mao," *L'Express,* Nov. 1, 1980, p. 101.

17. The quotes in this and the preceding paragraph are from Dwight Perkins, "Plans and Their Implementation in the People's Republic of China," *American Economic Review,* May 1973, and Barry Richman, "Ideology and Management: The Chinese Oscillate," *Columbia Journal of World Business,* January–February 1971.

18. He Jianzhang, "Basic Forms in the Socialist Economy," *China Reconstructs,* January 1982, p. 44. At the time, He was deputy chief of the Economic Research Bureau of the State Planning Commission.

19. In the property-rights sense, the first two of these requirements are redundant, as indicated in section 1-1.

20. See Fox Butterfield, *China: Alive in the Bitter Sea* (New York: Times Books, 1982), pp. 245–47ff, as well as Lardy, "Consumption and Living Standards in China, 1978–83." By contrast, Adelman and Sunding find a much smaller gap between urban and rural areas and conclude that income inequality has been less in China than in virtually any other country. Arguably, however, the data they use understate this gap. See Irma Adelman and David Sunding, "Economic Policy and Income Distribution in China," *Journal of Comparative Economics,* September 1987.

21. Qian Jiaju, "Is China 'Going Backward'?" *China Reconstructs,* March 1981, p. 8.

22. *Beijing Review,* April 19, 1982, pp. 20–21.

23. For example, food grain output over 1929–37 averaged somewhere between 170 and 180 million tons per year in what is now China. The population averaged under 450 million. In 1980, food-grain production was 320 million tons, but the population had more than doubled. See John L. Buck, "Food Grain Production in Mainland China Before and During the Communist Regime," in J. L. Buck, O. L. Dawson, Yuan-li Wu, *Food and Agriculture in Communist China* (New York: Praeger, 1966). See, as well, Buck's classic *Land Utilization in China* (Chicago: University of Chicago Press, 1937). Finally, see Lardy, "Food Consumption in the People's Republic of China," and Butterfield, *China: Alive in the Bitter Sea.*

24. See C. D. Campbell and G. Tullock, "Hyperinflation in China, 1937–1949," *Journal of Political Economy,* June 1954. See also Luo Gengmo, "Socialism and Inflation," *Beijing Review,* November 1, 1982.

Questions for Review, Discussion, Examination

1. Recalling the discussion of property rights in section 1-1, why would a ban on buying, selling, and leasing of land, as well as on secondary markets in stocks

and bonds, be a socialism-preserving feature of the current reforms? Do you think these bans are likely to be successful or will they increasingly be circumvented? Discuss. (In China, several features of the current reforms have been initiated from below, and rules or laws have then been changed to conform to practice.)

Give one other socialism-preserving feature of the reforms.

2. During the 1950s, China copied the Soviet planning model. However, by 1957 a *de facto* administrative decentralization was already under way, which was then formally ratified. Why was it impossible for China to centralize control over her economy to the same degree as in most other socialist countries? What was the nature of the 1957–58 decentralization?

3. Why has China tended to oscillate between centralization and decentralization?

4. What caused the modernization program of Hua Guo-feng, Mao's immediate successor, to falter? What was questionable about its goals?

5. When the reformers took power in late 1978, they began a fourfold reform program. What were its four elements and what is the "open door" policy (which was already under way, but then became the fifth component of the reform program)?

6. Why might reformers compare a command economy to a system of "arranged marriages," while a market economy is likened to "freedom to choose a marriage partner"?

Why haven't Chinese managers run their factories as though they owned them?

7. What is the nature of the dual approach to reform of the domestic economy being followed by China?

*8. What have been the two main goals of the budget and banking system in China (as in other Soviet-type economies)? Describe the problems that have arisen in meeting these goals and explain why they have arisen.

Which sectors of the economy have had a high priority and which have had a low priority and how could we verify this from financial flows?

9. Explain how the Chinese banking system was changed in 1984.

*10. How has the "soft budget constraint" prevented China from shifting to a workable system of loan-financed investment?

More generally, how does the soft budget constraint prevent the establishment of any system that requires firms to accept business risk?

11. Describe the Chinese job assignment system. How efficiently has it worked? What have been the problems with it?

12. What is the "iron rice bowl" and why do Chinese reformers want to "smash" it? Are all its features necessarily inefficient?

13. How have the reforms eroded the Communist party's control over career alternatives? How have they weakened the internal passport system? How may the party be trying to reassert its control over career alternatives of party officials following the June 1989 crackdown on prodemocracy elements?

14. Ideologically, private and small cooperative firms are the lowest form of

enterprise organization in countries professing to follow the teachings of Marx and Lenin. Yet, this sector has expanded explosively since 1978 in China. What immediate practical problems has this sector helped to solve, which have helped it to grow despite its ideological stigma?

15. Distribution of producer goods in China is sometimes described as bureaucratic and cumbersome. Briefly indicate why this may be true. How do "pushers" or purchasing agents help to improve matters, on occasion? What has been the role of MACs and MECs in this regard?

*16. In terms of political control, China has oscillated between "Red" and "Expert." What does this mean? Is this oscillation likely to continue? What distinct periods in the evolution of China's economy since 1949 can we identify? Briefly describe each. What were some identifying features of periods in which ideologues ("Reds") were in control?

*17. Why did decentralization during the Great Leap Forward increase mismanagement and waste, ultimately leading to famine (in combination with bad weather during that period)?

18. Although Maoists are usually regarded as egalitarian, Maoist policies in China may well have increased inequality, especially between urban and rural areas. What policies were responsible for this increase and why did they lead to greater differences in living standards?

19. Why has open inflation been rising in China in recent years?

* = more difficult or basic

8

THE CHINESE ECONOMY: SPECIAL TOPICS

8-1. The Organization of Agriculture

As in all command economies except Poland, China has collectivized agriculture, in the sense that rural economic cooperatives legally own 95 percent of the farm land, and state farms occupy most of the rest. Each rural cooperative also owns the buildings, much of the farm machinery and equipment, and the capital of small enterprises on its land. Thus, collective property is a legal category separate from state-owned property, and most Chinese peasant families belong either to a rural cooperative or to a state farm. In principle, and to a degree in practice, members have a voice in running the cooperatives, although cooperative leaders must be approved by the party. Most individuals will remain all their lives in the region where they are born and rarely be allowed to leave. Although many will leave farming for industry, services, and construction, this will be done by bringing industry, etc., into the region, and strict controls on urbanization will remain.

Most collectively owned land was also farmed collectively until the early 1980s. Collectivization took place in 1956, more than six years after the Communists first came to power, but the growth in farm output which many party members expected to result never materialized. Thus, it is likewise in rural areas that the current reform movement has scored its greatest success, in large measure by restoring individual use and income rights to the land. Since 1959, the tendency has been to decentralize control over farming—following centralization over 1952–59—most recently down to the household level under the rural responsibility system. Even before these reforms, a portion of the land, generally averaging 5–15 percent of the total, was set aside to serve as private plots of peasant households, on which they may grow crops, keep a few pigs and chickens, tend fruit trees, etc. Legally, household plots are collective land and may not be bought or sold, although they are normally inherited by a family's offspring. Excluding rice, a significant share of China's farm exports comes from them. Peasants also engage in other sideline activities, such as making pottery, footwear, and clothing, doing repair work, and producing tools. In recent years, many peasants have begun to specialize full-time in what were formerly sideline occupations, as part of reform efforts to reduce the numbers of people working the land and to increase the role of the market in rural areas.

Ideologically, private farming and household subsidiary production are the lowest forms of rural production. Although encouraged today, the party's radical wing has sought in the past to cut them back and even to eliminate them. The cost of these campaigns, in terms of lost output and peasant discontent, has been high, and the 1982 Constitution guarantees the right to own private plots, as well as to engage in sideline activities on an individual or household basis. According to a recent Chinese source, "[peasants'] private plots, household sideline production, and the country fairs [or rural markets] are a necessary supplement to the socialist economy and should not be interfered with by anyone."[1] Today, production imperatives dominate ideological considerations, after much struggle and disruption.

As noted, collectivization originally took place over the course of 1956, according to the Soviet model. As a rough approximation, there was, on average, one collective farm for each village, and the radical wing of the party hoped to raise production by joining small, individual plots under unified management. These gains did not materialize, both because the farms were too large for effective management and because the managers were often chosen for their redness, rather than for their expertise. They tended to be egalitarian in awarding work points (or credit for collective farm labor input), which had the effect of partially divorcing reward from performance at the household level. Administrative and bookkeeping skills were also in short supply, and there was frequent conflict with the peasants, many of whom resented having their land taken away and who often found the marginal reward for working their private plots to be far above that for working the collective fields. The latter 1950s were a period when radical power was growing, however, and when the collectives failed to provide hoped-for results, the radical solution was to merge farms again, in the commune movement of 1958.

Thus, in 1958, China established a three-level organization—commune, brigade, and production team—to manage collective work in the countryside. Originally, the commune was to become the basic unit of rural consumption, as well as of production, and it also took over the functions of local government at the township level. The members of each commune were to rear their children to an extent in common, to eat in communal mess halls, to sleep in communal dormitories, and so forth. But this aspect never got off the ground, and before long, most communes were not basic units of farm management or of income distribution either, although they did retain an important role here until the recent reforms. Up to 1984, they were basic units of local government below the county, although they have since lost this function to the resurrected township governments (*xiang*). The communes thus merged the functions of economic management and government administration, which the present régime has been seeking to separate. Since 1984, the communes have either been dissolved or converted to economic cooperatives, with no formal political role.

Over 1958–84, the communes were responsible for procuring grain, for drawing up plans for subordinate units (the production brigades and teams), and for managing water and pest control, afforestation, and transportation projects. They also cooperated in building roads, hydroelectric stations, and large water control projects. As rural cooperatives, they continue to operate facilities for marketing crops, as well as stores where consumer goods, seed, fertilizer, implements, and other farm inputs are sold. Finally, they managed local factories, mines, and construction projects. Although the communes quickly lost much of their direct control over farming—since they magnified the management problems of the former collective farms—the rapid growth of rural small-scale industry after 1964 enhanced their financial strength and power. These firms supply important inputs for farming, including fertilizers, tools and machinery, building supplies, and electric power. In addition, farm machinery produced outside the commune was usually sold to the communes or to agricultural machinery stations operated by the central government, which rented their services to the communes.

Below the commune level came the production brigades, which were approximately the same size as the former collective farms and thus usually coincided with the rural village. In the early 1980s, China had about 54,000 communes, averaging 16,000 members and 16 brigades each. When the commune proved to be too large a unit for the direct management of farm production, the brigade became the basic unit of accounting and management in 1959, less than a year after the communes were formed. However, the brigades also proved to be too large in most cases. They continued to be units of village-level government, as well as social and cultural centers, and they managed a variety of undertakings—in small-scale industry, forestry, fish farming, rearing of pigs and other animals, repair shops, and local supply, marketing, and credit cooperatives. Under the rural responsibility system, many of the brigades' economic activities were contracted out to individual peasants or small groups after 1978. In addition, the brigades provided basic health services, and an effort is still made to assign at least one "barefoot doctor" (lady paraprofessional trained to deliver babies, treat minor illnesses, and detect major ones) to each village. Finally, the brigades undertook small water control and construction projects, fought forest fires, and reclaimed land. The village is usually the lowest level at which the Communist party is organized.

Since the brigade also merged the functions of economic management and government administration, it too became a target of reformers. In most places, its economic and political roles have now been split—the latter being assigned to a village-level government and the former to one or more economic cooperatives. The brigade was also a link between the commune and the production team. When the brigade proved too large a management unit for agriculture, the team became the basic unit of accounting and control in 1961–62. The team owned small farm equipment and tools, although these increasingly became the property of individual households and small groups of peasants after 1978. Now, most of the teams have also been converted to economic cooperatives or dissolved. Thus, in a given area, each peasant household will belong to one or more cooperatives, which replace the former commune, brigade, and/or team. Units of local government and party are now the township and the village.

From 1961 until the early 1980s, production teams usually took the final decisions about which crops to grow and which production methods to use in most places, although subject to state delivery targets, which were constraining, and to considerable interference from the commune and brigade levels. (In particular, most teams had to devote more land to grain than they would have done voluntarily, given existing prices.) The team also determined the distribution of its income among member families, based on the work-point system, with the constraint that every family was guaranteed a basic food-grain allotment—which in poor teams, meant an extremely egalitarian distribution. For performing each task, a team member would receive a certain number of work points, based on quantity and quality of work effort, but with a bias toward compressing differences between households. Subject to every family receiving its food-grain allotment, each member's share of team earnings was determined by the percentage of team work points he or she was able to accumulate. Earnings above the allotment were usually paid in cash.

Peasants did not earn guaranteed wages like workers in state industry, even when they worked in a factory managed by the commune or brigade. Instead, they were paid in work points through the team, and the factory paid the team, in turn, for their services. The team decided how much of this money to pay back to individual workers. (The latter often leave their jobs to help in the fields at the height of the harvesting and planting seasons.) Neither did team members have guaranteed pensions. In most cases, a retired peasant still relies on his or her working offspring (the extended family system). Only in the absence of a son or daughter capable of working will the village pay a small pension.

Most of the income received by each team was a residual, or what remained of the proceeds from selling its crops, mainly to the state, after making required deductions. In this sense, the team was the basic unit of ownership in the country-side—a position now occupied, in most places, by the household—even though the commune legally owned the land. Required deductions were, first of all, taxes and other obligations to the state, then contributions to the team's investment and welfare funds, and, finally, medical and educational fees for team members. The rest belonged to individual households. This residual depended on team output, along with state taxes, prices, and farm procurement policies.

The team's obligation to the state was, first of all, to pay a tax in kind (grain) that, by 1980, averaged less than 5 percent of the grain crop across China as a whole. This was fixed in 1952 at 10 percent of total grain output and remained more-or-less constant until 1979, when a significant reduction took place. In addition, the team had to sell targeted amounts of crops to the state—the "fixed quota" purchase—at state procurement prices. These targets were set in the planning process; on average, procurement prices were by 1981 about 2.5 times levels originally set in 1949. The team could also sell stipulated additional quantities to the state at higher prices. The above-quota purchase, described as "obligatory," but not "compulsory" (since there were, in principle, no penalties for failure to comply), was sold to the state at prices 50 percent higher than procurement prices. Over and above this, the government could make a "discussion" purchase at negotiated prices. The latter could not be more than twice the corresponding procurement prices.[2]

By the late 1970s, the members of a representative team sold about a third of all produce from the collective land to the state or on the rural market. The latter was a free alternative, at least to the discussion purchase. Slightly over half of all earnings from work on the collective land went as income in cash or kind to team members. Another 10 percent to 20 percent was invested, and the rest was spent on welfare, health care, and education. In bad years, a team might be forgiven part of its delivery obligations and even receive a food subsidy, although in normal years virtually all teams would be expected to at least be self-sufficient in food. Following increases over 1979–81 in prices paid to farmers, the average cost of food to the state rose above the average revenue it was receiving from sales to urban consumers. During the record 1984 harvest, the state was paying higher average prices in many areas than the free-market price. Thus, agriculture has been receiving large subsidies since 1979 (which go, more specifically, to keep urban food prices below prices paid to farmers), in contrast to the Soviet development model, which stresses taxing agriculture to finance investment in large-scale industry. "The change in the grain situation is captured by a former peasant from Anhui province, who said, 'it used to be the case of having "to go through the back door" [i.e., having to use connections or bribes] to buy grain, but starting about 1980 it was necessary to "go through the back door" to sell grain.' "[3] However, by 1985, state prices for grain were again well below those on the free market.

Prior to 1980, the purchasing power of most peasant households was quite low.[4] Per-capita consumption of grain in the countryside actually fell over 1956–78, even though it was rising by nearly 16 percent in urban areas. According to a Chinese estimate, the real compensation for an average day of farm labor dropped by a third. In this way, peasants were squeezed for savings to finance investment in heavy industry. The present leadership has criticized and reversed these policies, raising farm purchase prices and instituting the household responsibility system, while lowering the agricultural tax and the share of the fixed-quota purchase in total farm output. Plans to raise agriculture's share of state investment have been dropped, however, probably because food price subsidies have helped to cause budget deficits. Instead, the share of state investment going to agriculture is even lower in the 1980s than in the 1960s or 1970s.

The average production team had a membership of 20 to 30 families, and there were over 100 teams in an average commune. While each team elected its own leaders (as do the successor cooperatives), these had to be approved at the village level, and rural party cadres also controlled the marketing of grain in many areas. Nevertheless, because of their small size, radical party members considered the teams to be a form of quasi-private ownership that they wanted to abolish, along with private plots and rural markets. They failed to do this, however, and current policy goes in the opposite direction. The radicals wanted to centralize decisions and responsibilities up to the brigade level and, ultimately, up to the commune level. But the effect of their intervention was to reduce peasant motivation, farm output, and even the reproductive power of the soil, since they frequently practiced bad soil and water management, devastating millions of acres of usable farmland in the process.

It was, in part, to solve problems of low motivation and bad management that the present régime decided to decentralize further, and the party was also pushed along by the peasants themselves faster than it wanted to go. Some Western authors describe this as a "decollectivization," although the official Chinese view holds that it is rather a case of allowing individual and collective management to coexist, with each specializing in its area of comparative advantage. In farming, the basic idea is that the producer and manager should be one and the same. Under the rural responsibility system, the collective fields allotted to a team (and, subsequently, to its successor cooperative) have been divided among its members. The team has assigned land to each household which is in addition to its private plot; across China, the average farm household received about 1.2 acres. Each household now signs a contract with the state detailing its delivery targets for grain and other crops, based on the quantity and quality of its land. Primary responsibility for meeting contracted delivery targets and paying the grain tax now rests with the household in most places. Contract prices are averages of former procurement and above-quota prices, with the latter weighted at 70 percent.

Each contract also stipulates how much money the household owes for collective investment projects, welfare, and other expenses. "Leadership and planning [are still] done in a unified way ..., and draft animals and large farm implements, like the land, still belong to the collective."[5] Each family pays for the use of collectively owned tractors or water buffalo, as well as for irrigation and other services, and each must still contribute labor to collective water conservation and other investment projects. Nevertheless, investment in agriculture and in water control (which is critical in China) appears to have fallen since 1978. Since the demise of the communes in 1984, water control facilities and management have deteriorated in many areas. The same is true of social welfare expenditure and the delivery of rural social services, such as education and health care, which were generally not at satisfactory levels before.[6]

Contracts are also signed for raising pigs, chickens, or ducks; tending fruit trees; breeding animals; fish farming; and for other specialized activities, which used to be managed more directly by production teams and brigades. In each case, "individuals, households, or small groups assume clear-cut production responsibilities, and earnings are linked to fulfillment of these tasks."[7] The drive to increase specialization among production units (and, consequently, the role of market exchange) has become a major theme of reform, even in areas where decentralization has not gone down to the household level. Once a household or other group has met its contractual obligations to the state, it is free to dispose of whatever additional output it has produced, as it wishes. Thus, the household is now the residual claimant to income from work on the collective land in most places, and the work-point system has been abolished in most of Chinese agriculture.

The household now has more freedom than the team did between 1962 and 1978 to decide how to produce (types of seeds, fertilizers, labor input, etc.), as well as what assortments of crops to grow. However, effective acreage quotas still exist in many places, and the state can use its leverage in negotiating contracts, as well as discrimination in the prices or availabilities of inputs under its control, to get peasants to alter their output profiles—usually in favor of more grain or cotton. Some households have acquired use rights over well-defined sections of the collective land for up to thirty years, although fifteen years appears to be the usual length of lease (which should be long enough to give farmers an incentive to maintain and improve the productivity of their plots). Increasingly, peasants are investing in their own farm implements, including small tractors, which are enjoying a sales boom—although this only partly offsets the decline in state investment in agriculture. A peasant may use his tractor to plow for a neighbor, provided he does not charge more than the local state farm machinery station, and this has become another way in which households may specialize. The demand for technical information about crop and livestock production has been high, and government extension services have been strained.

In China, as in other socialist nations, household private plots have historically contributed a disproportionate share of farm output. In the late 1970s, nearly 25 percent of all produce, by value, sold to the state commercial network came from household production, and families also sold food from their private plots on rural free markets. (At the time, these plots averaged well under 10 percent of total commune property.) Most of the animal products, poultry, fresh eggs, and medicinal herbs came from household plots. In 1981, peasant income from sideline production, including the private plots, came to 70 percent or more of total earnings from collective agriculture. Prior to the responsibility system, households were allocating their labor inefficiently, spending too much time working their own plots and not enough on the collective land. The marginal product of labor was potentially higher on the collective land, but additional work on the private plots brought in more disposable income for most households. The state has solved this problem, at least in part, by raising procurement prices for grain, which is mainly grown on the collective land, and by making the incentives for working the collective fields more like those for working the private plots.

One result of the new system was a 34 percent rise in grain production over 1978–84 to a record 407 million tons, despite a shift of land and other resources out of grain and into other crops and the reduction of state investment in agriculture noted above. The bumper harvest of that year overwhelmed storage facilities and the transport system, so that some produce spoiled. In areas with histories of famine and privation, granaries overflowed. Partly to reduce its large price subsidies, the state has reduced its role as buyer and seller of farm produce, although officials acknowledge that government participation on a smaller scale is likely to remain indefinitely. In 1985, the state abolished formal procurement quotas. However the system of delivery contracts with peasant households remains, and the state continues to try to hold down urban retail prices for basic commodities (staples), such as grain, cotton, oilseeds, tobacco, pork, and jute. Prices of nonstaple goods were largely decontrolled, although new restraints were applied in the fall of 1988, following a resurgence of inflation.

Since peasants must sign delivery contracts or lose their rights to collective land, *de facto* state procurement of grain and other staple crops continues, and at contract prices well below those on the free market, even though the state is selling grain to urban consumers at lower prices still. Prices of key farm inputs have also risen rapidly since 1979, and some have been in critically short supply. Together with the continuing low marginal product of farm labor, these factors have caused some peasants to leave agriculture for employment in small industrial, service, and commercial enterprises, which have been mushrooming in rural areas. Many of those who have left agriculture have effectively sold their use and income rights to the collective land to those who remain, and efforts have been underway to increase the size of farms, in order to allow more efficient use of machinery. In some areas, this may mean a new expansion of collective or cooperative farming, and controls over agriculture have tended to increase during 1988–89.

According to one study, Chinese agriculture achieved a 28 percent increase in total factor productivity (output per unit of combined labor, capital, and land input) over 1978–84. About a fourth of this was due to higher prices paid for farm produce and three-fourths to changes in property rights and incentives.[8] Official estimates suggest that real, per-capita income of peasant households doubled over 1978–84— although this is probably an exaggeration—and more than 30 percent of them built new homes. Most peasants are now working more productively than before 1979, with less supervision or interference. They also enjoy higher living standards. However, the period since 1974 has witnessed grain output increases in many parts of the world, and percentage increases in some nations, including India, Thailand, and Argentina, have exceeded those in China. After 1984, grain output fell in China and has remained below the record harvest—partly because free-market prices of vegetables, fruit, cotton, and other crops have made producing these more attractive. In addition, per acre rice yields are still below Japan, South Korea, and Taiwan, although above those in India. However, the first three nations also use more chemical fertilizer per acre. Potential gains from the Green Revolution may now be greater in China, although their realization is apt to depend on agriculture receiving a higher investment priority.

China's rural responsibility system may emerge as the most successful decentralization ever carried out by a socialist country, especially given the numbers affected (13–14 percent of the world's population), but such reforms do have a history of being reversed. They have also begun to highlight a basic contradiction between the state's desire for near self-sufficiency in food and its income distribution priorities. If all prices were to become rational, under the food self-sufficiency constraint, the scarcity of land would cause land rents to soar, which would be reflected in soaring prices of staple foods, notably grain. But this would put an unacceptable burden on urban households. Historically, collectivization redistributed income from rural to urban areas, and the state is still keeping procurement prices for grain and other staples below free-market levels. (In addition, over 1988–89, the state has been forced to pay for part of the crop with IOUs rather than cash.) As a result, peasants lack sufficient incentive to produce grain and pork, but urban households are complaining about high retail prices of food, even though subsidies to keep these down are a burden on the state budget.

Moreover, while rural incomes have risen relative to those in the cities, income differentials within many rural areas have widened. The collective land was originally divided on an egalitarian basis, but some peasants have nearly gotten rich from farming or sideline activities, while others have found it hard to adjust to the new system. A further complication is that more children now mean more labor power to a rural family and, thus, extra income or food for many parents, as well as greater security in old age and other traditional joys of large families. (Demand for the latter is often income elastic.) This threatens the success of China's birth-control policy, which mandates just one child per couple. To keep down family size, the state has implemented a "double contracting" system. "Along with contracts for output quotas, contracts on family planning are also signed between production teams and peasant households."[9] These provide financial incentives for small families—including large fines for above-plan babies—in addition to which there is a threat of discrimination against second children, in terms of medical benefits, schooling, and access to jobs. The threat of eventual reform reversal is another reason why peasants invest in children, as well as in new homes. At least these, they feel, will not be taken away. Thus, the rural birthrate has returned to levels characteristic of the mid-1970s.

Finally, in China as in other socialist countries, the approximately 2,100 state farms are more highly mechanized, on average, than is the rest of agriculture. Altogether, state farms account for about 4 percent of the total cultivated area and 1.4 percent of China's peasant population, but they have at least 20 percent of its tractor power, as well as half of its combine harvesters and heavy-duty motor vehicles.[10] State farms play an important role in research and development and are widely used as experimental farms, as well as to reclaim wasteland. Many have heroic histories, since they were originally settled by PLA soldiers, who turned wasteland into productive cropland in wartime under the harshest conditions imaginable. They also serve as penal institutions. Most common criminals go to state "reeducation through labor" farms, after which only 8 percent become repeat offenders. In some cases, political as well as ordinary prisoners have labored to bring remote regions into production. The régime wants to speed up land reclamation over the last fifteen years of this century, which may lead to an expansion of state farms.

Historically, state farms, as "factories in the fields," have been managed like state industrial enterprises. While each farm has been divided into production teams, the farm, rather than the team, has been the basic unit of accounting and control. State farm workers have received wages and fringe benefits like those of state industry. During the 1960s and 1970s, most state farms operated at a loss, and total losses were as high as one billion yuan annually. Since then procurement prices have gone up, and many state farm operations have been decentralized down to the household level, under the contract responsibility system. About 80 percent of state farmland was divided into 925,000 small family farms. In this way, state farms resemble collective agriculture, although state farm households are still more constrained by state planning. By the early 1980s, this sector had become profitable and was enjoying good harvests, along with the rest of the country. It has also received a substantial amount of foreign investment.

8-2. Foreign Economic Relations

A. Foreign Trade

Command planning covers foreign trade, as well as the domestic economy. It is still true that foreign trade corporations, which are effectively departments of the Foreign Trade Ministry, conduct the bulk of trade and trade-related negotiations. There were only eight such corporations in 1970, but with the expansion of trade after 1976, their number rose to over thirty. In contrast to market economies, centrally-planned systems are usually import rather than export oriented, and this is still true of China. They trade primarily to obtain goods, deemed essential, that they cannot produce in sufficient quantities at home, and they try to export lower priority goods in exchange for these. Because of the uncertainties that world price fluctuations, changes in product availability, and political changes introduce into planning, most command economies also try to keep down the level of foreign trade, as a way of making planning less complex. They plan the bulk of their trade in advance at prearranged prices.

For many years, China's promotion of "self reliance" (interpreted as self-sufficiency) reduced trade even further. In 1983, exports plus imports were still just 23 percent of GNP, despite a doubling of trade volume over 1973–83. China's two-way trade was still less than that of Singapore, Hong Kong, or Taiwan, although each of these countries had a tiny fraction of China's population. Over 1983–86, trade volume soared by another 80–90 percent to reach 27–28 percent of GNP, and large balance-of-payments deficits appeared for the first time since 1950. In part, they resulted from a loosening of controls over imports, which were subsequently retightened. China's trade isolation has ended, but it will have to keep tighter quota restrictions on imports or foreign exchange than are usual in a Western nation, to ensure both that import priorities are respected and that the balance-of-payments deficit does not remain too high.

Like the currencies of other command economies, the Chinese renminbi (or yuan) is not convertible, and it is still overvalued. One cannot freely buy and sell it in exchange for other national currencies at official exchange rates or prices. In mid-1988, the black market was exchanging 6.3 yuan for one U.S. dollar vs. an official rate of 3.72 (or about 40 percent lower). Historically, China's producers have been largely shielded from foreign price fluctuations, and available foreign currencies have been rationed among alternative uses according to national priority. This insulation from world market demand and supply has removed the material interest that firms might have in taking advantage of export opportunities or in economizing on imports. Excess demand and guaranteed domestic markets, as well as the tendency to tax away nearly all profit, have reinforced this lack of interest. In line with current reforms, efforts were made to reawaken it, beginning in 1979. Provinces received foreign-exchange allocations, based on their exports and, along with some large enterprises and other government bodies, were allowed to export and even to import on their own.

As a result, these entities began competing with each other for foreign business, which may have worsened China's terms of trade with other countries. In the six months after September, 1984, its reserves of foreign currencies nosedived from $17 billion to $11 billion, and the trade deficit soared, as noted above. Consequently, the Foreign Trade Ministry recentralized control over international trade and payments, although some powers remained with regional governments. In 1988, a further reform measure transformed the foreign trade corporations into independent business enterprises responsible for their own profits and losses. They lost the power to set domestic prices of exports or imports, and exporting firms have also received more decision-making authority. As a rule, these enterprises are assigned retention quotas, or percentages of their proceeds from export sales to convertible-currency areas, which they are allowed to keep or to convert to yuan at exchange rates close to those prevailing on the black market. (The latter right is to help them maintain cost competitiveness with foreign producers.) For most firms, the retention quota is 50 percent or less, but for electronics and armaments producers, it is often 100 percent, which gives a strong incentive to export weapons.

China is also the only socialist nation which counts no other socialist countries among its top five trading partners. During the 1950s, most of China's trade was with the socialist bloc, including about 50 percent with the USSR, and most of its imports consisted of machinery, tools, and plants and equipment, with a high percentage of complete plants. The Chinese First Five-Year Plan (1952–57) was built around Soviet shipments. Then came the Sino-Soviet rift in August, 1960. Today, the share of China's total two-way trade accounted for by Japan or Hong Kong is over twice as great as the combined share of all socialist countries. (The latter has been running under 10 percent.) After paying off the last Soviet loan in 1964, China boasted for over a decade that it had no external or internal debts. However, extreme unwillingness to use Western credits is now identified with the discredited radical approach to development (the closed-door policy). Western loans have helped to finance several major projects since 1978, and China's gross foreign debt had reportedly risen to about $35 billion by end-1988. This is manageable, but could become troublesome if the persistent trade deficit continues.

Although China's trade grew rapidly during the 1950s, it plummeted after the Sino-Soviet rift and showed almost no net growth over 1959–72, during which time it was reoriented toward Japan and the West (with whom China now has the bulk of its trade deficit). The composition of imports also changed. In place of a heavy concentration on plants and machinery, foodstuffs began to absorb a much larger share of imports, and complete plants nearly vanished until the early 1970s. In part, this was a consequence of the Sino-Soviet split in 1960 and the disastrous fall in farm output during and just after the Great Leap Forward. Over 1972–74, China resumed importing complete production facilities, largely from Japan, West Germany, and France. In 1978, about 60 percent of all imports were industrial raw materials, while 25 percent were industrial plants and equipment, and 15 percent were foodstuffs and other consumer goods.[11] By value, over half the production facilities being imported were to manufacture fertilizers, petrochemicals, and synthetic fibers. However, following the abrupt change in priorities in 1979, imports of complete plants again declined. In their place has come heightened interest in machinery embodying advanced technology. Computers are a current craze, and manufactures plus machinery and transport equipment accounted for nearly 75 percent of imports in 1985 vs. about 10 percent for consumer goods.

Almost half of China's exports are now manufactures or chemicals, and textiles and clothing together account for more than half of this category, with much output coming from small firms. China has become a leading textile exporter, and its ability to provide good quality at low prices has led to import barriers against its products in the West. About 40 percent of export earnings come from light industry, and farm goods account for another 20 percent. Remaining exports include armaments and minerals—notably crude oil, which earns more foreign exchange than any other single product. (Crude oil accounted for 10 percent of all imports in the 1950s.) China has also become a major exporter of rare strategic metals—tungsten, titanium, chromium, and molybdenum—and it gives some development aid, mainly to Burundi, Madagascar, Zaire, Sudan, Nicaragua, and Nepal, in recent years.

B. The Open Door

Until 1977, China held aloof from joint venture or cooperation agreements with Western firms and even forbade foreign companies to lease property in China. Rarely were foreign technicians allowed on Chinese territory between the Sino-Soviet split in 1960 and the late 1970s. By then, most socialist nations were taking advantage of cooperation agreements and joint ventures as ways of acquiring Western technology. Typically, the Western party to such a contract builds a plant embodying the desired technology in its partner socialist country. In the case of a joint venture, the Western partner receives an ownership share of the project, including a claim on its profit or output. In the case of a more usual cooperation agreement, the Western partner receives no equity, but does get a guaranteed return on its investment. Instead of signing such agreements, China drastically limited its copying of foreign technology and relied on "prototype buying"—i.e., importing a few samples of a capital good, copying the technology embodied in it, and producing a similar product at home, without paying royalties to the foreign supplier.

In the meantime, China became more and more technologically backward vis-à-vis the West—a cost the radicals were willing to bear. Once the moderates were in power after Mao's death, however, modernization became a priority, and China reversed its policy. Over 1977–78, China signed its first cooperation agreements, and a new law on joint ventures went into effect, which has since been extended and elaborated, although the basic legal framework remains less well-defined than foreign investors would like. Today, China welcomes foreign investment, as part of the Open-Door policy, and has even allowed a few companies with majority or 100 percent foreign ownership to locate on its soil. In 1980, China set up four "special economic zones" in Guangdong and Fujian provinces, within which foreign equity investors receive tax and tariff advantages. The most important of these is Shenzhen, next to Hong Kong. Formerly a rural area, Shenzhen had over 1,000 enterprises by end-1986. (Hong Kong, itself, one of the world's bastions of laissez faire capitalism, reverts to China in 1997.) In 1984, China added new zones in fourteen cities along her eastern seaboard and on Hainan island, within which policies toward foreign investors resemble those in the original zones. It added a final three zones (near Canton, Shanghai, and Xiamen, respectively) in February 1985.[12] Many foreign ventures have also been established outside the twenty-two zones, and 58,000 square miles of offshore waters are open to exploration by invited foreign oil companies.

The Open-Door policy has four major components—the creation of special investment zones, the attraction and efficient investment of foreign capital, the increase of foreign trade, and the import of modern technology and management techniques.[13] Over the long run, the last is most important and indicates the current thrust of China's self-reliance policy, in contrast to the self-sufficiency and isolation of the radical years. According to a West German newspaper, China approved direct investment projects from 7,775 foreign companies over 1979–86, involving total investment outlays (from Chinese and foreign sources) of $16.2 billion.[14] About $6 billion of this was from Western companies. According to a Chinese source, "In the eight years since the open policy was initiated, some U.S. $20 billion has been invested from abroad, and over 10,000 items of advanced technology introduced. Sino-foreign joint ventures now number 7,000. . . . China has also set up 277 joint ventures or solely Chinese ventures abroad, and 50 Chinese companies now undertake construction and other projects for customers in foreign countries."[15] Total foreign investment in China now appears to exceed that in all other socialist countries combined, and by end-1988, the number of joint ventures had climbed to about 10,000. In addition, China has been readmitted to the World Bank and International Monetary Fund—which has raised its access to foreign loans and technology—and it has signed long-term trade agreements with Japan and the European Economic Community.

Foreign sources have been financing 5–10 percent of China's fixed productive investment, but there has been less investment from abroad than reformers had hoped for. As a rule, foreign firms invest in China to take advantage of cheap labor or other inputs, to gain access to the Chinese market, or to participate in the energy sector (oil, natural gas, or coal)—these being the three main ways of earning a profit on such investments. A major difficulty has been the need to deal with the state bureaucracy plus the lack of infrastructure in the special economic zones, although upgrading of infrastructure has been a priority in recent years. Other headaches for foreign investors have included difficulties in repatriating profits and lack of guaranteed access to supplies, credit, or the domestic market. A number of joint ventures have been unprofitable, but the most serious problem may be ill-defined property rights surrounding foreign equity participation.

Not only are existing rules less clear than they might be—even though China has over 160 laws and regulations on foreign economic ventures—but major uncertainties about China's political future reduce the attractiveness to foreign investors of expected returns several years down the road and raise their current profit requirements for investing. The events of May and June 1989 have heightened these anxieties. This also increases the cost of infrastructural and bureaucratic delays, and the eventual reversion of most joint ventures to 100 percent Chinese ownership reinforces the current profit requirement. Should reformers lose control over party and government, foreign equity participations would probably encounter new restrictions, increased taxation, and possibly, even direct harassment, which would reduce or eliminate foreign access to profit. Nationalization would likely be speeded up. During the 1950s, Chinese-owned private companies suffered a similar fate, despite earlier promises by the state not to take them over. Finally, foreign equity investment is restricted by China's exclusive interest in gaining access to advance technology and in learning to produce goods it cannot now turn out. It also wants to expand exports, although some firms with foreign equity participation are allowed to supply mainly the domestic market.

Tables 8.1(a) and 8.1(b) give a summary picture of China's trade. Table 8.1(a) gives its commodity composition in 1975, 1980, and 1985. Table 8.1(b) gives total

Table 8.1a

Composition of Trade by Commodity for the People's Republic of China (in millions of U.S. dollars)

Export commodity	Exports 1975	Exports 1980	Exports 1985	Import commodity	Imports 1975	Imports 1980	Imports 1985
Total	7,130	18,925	31,325	Total	6,830	19,305	39,480
Food and live animals	2,045	3,210	3,925	Food and live animals	815	2,860	1,635
Live animals	215	340	330	Cereal and cereal preparation	540	2,225	1,050
Meat and meat preparations	240	385	510	Sugar, sugar preparations, & honey	155	300	215
Fish and fish preparations	190	400	405				
Cereals and cereal preparations	615	485	780	Crude materials, excluding fuels	730	2,325	3,330
Vegetables and fruit	435	935	985	Rubber, crude (including synthetic and reclaimed)	165	430	315
Beverages and tobacco	80	120	135				
Crude materials, excluding fuel	840	1,820	2,930	Textile fibers and their waste	395	2,065	1,575
Oilseeds, oil nuts, and oil kernels	160	185	500	Minerals fuels, lubricants, and related materials	130	175	500
Textile fibers and wastes	245	545	1,165	Petroleum and petroleum products	40	30	310
Crude animal and vegetable materials	225	540	495	Animal and vegetable fats and oil	40	180	100

Table 8.1a (*continued*)

Mineral fuels, lubricants, and related materials	1,025	4,415	7,215
Petroleum and petroleum products	865	4,165	6,630
Animal and vegetable oils and fats	55	85	1,300
Chemicals	350	180	1600
Chemical elements and compounds	100	480	685
Manufactured goods	2,450	7,420	12,880
Textile yarn, fabrics, made-up articles	1,035	2,765	4,380
Nonmetallic mineral manufactures	170	415	400
Manufactures of metal	110	390	570
Clothing	355	1,665	3,375
Miscellaneous	445	1,345	2,910
Machinery and transport equipment	260	610	1,185
Other	25	65	1,325

Chemicals	815	2,185	3,655
Chemical elements & compounds	250	545	825
Fertilizers, manufactured	390	980	885
Manufactured goods	2,265	5,060	13,290
Textile yarn, fabrics, made-up articles, and products	90	845	2,100
Iron and steel	1,475	2,235	5,865
Nonferrous metals	395	420	1,315
Miscellaneous	75	485	2,445
Machinery and transport equipment	2,010	5,350	16,375
Machinery, other than electric	985	2,790	6,825
Electric machinery	190	1,070	4,715
Transport equipment	835	1,490	4,835
Other	25	170	600

Source: Directorate of Intelligence *Handbook of Economic Statistics, 1987* (Washington, D.C.: U.S. Government Printing Office, 1987), pp. 108-19.

Table 8.1b

Total Two-way Trade Between the People's Republic and Its Main Trading Partners

Country	Total trade (millions of U.S. dollars)			Rank		
	1973	1978	1985	1973	1978	1985
Japan	2,021	5,022	21,144	1	1	1
Hong Kong	796	2,312	12,003	3	2	2
West Germany	487	1,314	3,141	4	3	4
France	231	395	937	11	10	12
Malaysia and Singapore	460	705	2,711	5	6	5
United States	876	1,189	7,442	2	4	3
Romania	265	789	855	9	5	13
Canada	409	525	1,394	6	8	8
Australia	247	588	1,321	10	7	9
United Kingdom	340	362	1,100	7	11/12	11
Soviet Union	272	499	1,978	8	9	6
Italy	196	362	1,204	12	11/12	10

Sources: 1985: State Statistical Bureau, *Statistical Yearbook of China, 1986* (Oxford: Oxford University Press, 1986), pp. 484–486; 1978: John L. Davie, Dean W. Carver, "China's International Trade and Finance," in U.S. Congress, Joint Economic Committee, *China Under the Four Modernizations*, Part 2 (Washington, D.C.: U.S. Government Printing Office, 1982), Tables A-2, A-3, pp. 41–42; 1973: Editor, "China's Foreign Trade, 1973–74," *Current Scene*, December 1974, Table 5, p. 9.

two-way trade between China and its main trading partners in 1973, 1978, and 1985.

8-3. Sino-Soviet Economic Cooperation During the 1950s

During the 1950s, China tried to pursue forced industrialization according to the formula pioneered by Stalin in the Soviet Union. This meant favoring investment and defense spending over consumption, along with rationing of most producer and some consumer goods in both rural and urban areas. During the First Five-Year Plan (1953–57), investment in industry was over four times that in agriculture plus water conservation, and investment in heavy industry was several times as great as in light industry. Steel, machinery, electric power, coal, nonferrous metallurgy, cement, and the transport sector were all investment priorities, and many large, capital intensive factories were built, mainly in the cities. As well, a campaign was begun to stamp out illiteracy and to establish the technical schools needed to produce competent workers for expanding industry. By the end of the First Five-Year Plan, the number of university graduates was about three times as great as in 1949 (63,000 vs. 21,000).

There was a pronounced transfer of resources toward heavy industry. One author writes: "As in the Soviet Union, the big enterprises were supposed to produce and not worry about accumulation [or about making profits]; that would be taken care of by the rest of society. Since heavy industry was given priority, these enterprises were allowed to engage in waste as long as they came up with the goods."[16] The purpose of controls over the lower priority sectors was to generate savings for investment in heavy industry. The Soviet formula for economic development—when applied to a country with a large farm sector and a small, backward industrial sector—requires heavy taxation of agriculture to finance industrial expansion. Agriculture is also supposed to supply a large, steady flow of industrial raw materials, and a rural-to-urban migration is to provide workers for the growing industrial complex.

The Soviet Union pursued such a strategy ruthlessly during the 1930s and 1950s, and agriculture also financed the bulk of industrial investment in China over 1950–57. However, China did not squeeze her peasantry hard enough to generate the rapid industrial growth that was achieved then. In addition, a massive flow of material support from the Soviet Union, including the largest and most comprehensive transfer of technology in history, magnified the growth-generating power of farm savings. The USSR played a major role in constructing 260 large capital- and technology-intensive enterprises, including delivery of 156 complete plants, around which the First Five-Year Plan essentially revolved. "Without inputs from the Soviet Union, there would have been no Chinese Five-Year Plan" is a statement needing qualification, but is probably not too strong. By 1957, "Some 57 percent of Chinese steel production and 50 percent of her coal came from Soviet-constructed enterprises, which absorbed over half of China's investment during the first plan. . . . To put it simply, the Chinese put up the buildings with the aid of Russian engineers, and the Russians sent in and installed most of the machinery."[17]

According to a Soviet source, "The shipment of whole complexes of equipment for large industrial enterprises greatly eased for China the process of industrial construction, for it secured the introduction within a very brief time span of industrial establishments of great capacity employing the most advanced technology. It is particularly important that the equipment was supplemented with technical assistance by the suppliers. . . ." All in all, "during her First Five-Year Plan, China imported about half of all the machinery and equipment it put into place and practically all of the heavy and complicated equipment." "The location and scheduling of the plants was designed to keep the supplies of raw materials and components in balance with the requirements of users. Thus, the completion of an electric power plant was followed by completion of an aluminum [or steel] plant and, in turn, by an aircraft [or machinery] plant. . . ."[18] Furthermore, regular Soviet shipments of raw materials helped to keep the factories going. Table 8.2 documents the Soviet contribution.

Qualification of the above claims is necessary, because China did pay quickly for the equipment and materials that the Soviets provided. (Stalin had refused to grant her long-term credits on a large scale.) The entire trade deficit with the USSR during the 1950s amounted to less than $400 million and was completely paid off by 1965. Although Soviet exports were probably undervalued, and massive technical assistance plus widespread training for Chinese specialists was provided at nominal expense, the value of the net outflow from the USSR to China over the decade was still below the $2 billion worth of equipment dismantled and removed by the Red Army from Manchuria at the end of World War II. However, China exported mainly foodstuffs, textiles, and manufactured consumer goods. In exchange, it received the sinews of heavy industry on a scale and in a package form unprecedented in trading relations between any two nations in peacetime. The Soviets supplied China with whole factories virtually intact, together with the technical expertise needed to operate them. According to Premier Zhou Enlai, 10,800 Soviet experts plus 1,500 from other socialist countries worked in China over 1949–59. Nearly 40,000 Chinese were educated or trained in the USSR.

Without a fund of accumulated knowledge and experience in chemicals, metallurgy, and other modern engineering industries, plus access to the associated technology and the ability to reproduce it, no nation can hope to achieve a rapid expansion in these areas. China had no such base in 1953. Consequently, Soviet assistance took China far beyond the production possibilities it could have achieved simply by shifting resources into heavy industry and out of agriculture, light industry, and services. It effectively transformed goods such as rice, soybeans and sandals into steel, chemical, and metallurgical plants at a pace several times as rapid as it could have hoped for otherwise. Not only did it achieve greater industrial growth for its sacrifice of present consumption, it also received the technological basis for future growth—e.g., as embodied in technical training and

Table 8.2

The Dimensions of Soviet Assistance to Industrial Projects Initiated under China's First Five-Year Plan
(Capacity in thousands of metric tons, except for trucks)

Product	Total increase in annual productive capacity	Increase owing to 156 Soviet aid projects (%)
Pig iron	5,750	92.1%
Steel	6,100	82.8%
Rolled steel	4,440	90.4%
Coal	93,100	22.7%
Crude oil	3,500	51.4%
Metallurgical equipment	190	50.3%
Electrical generating equipment	800	45.0%
Chemical fertilizers	910	28.5%
Trucks (units)	9,000	100.0%

Source: Choh-Ming Li, *Economic Development of Communist China* (Berkeley: University of California Press, 1959), Table 2, p. 10.

in over 21,000 sets of technical documents received by China from the Soviet Union and Eastern Europe.

Chinese industrial growth averaged nearly 16 percent per year during the First Five-Year Plan, while GNP averaged just under 6 percent. The output of steel was nearly four times as high in 1957 as in 1952. The USSR did not do as well during its own First Five-Year Plan (1928–32), largely because the Soviets did not have so much outside assistance. The Soviet consumer got a break from large Chinese exports of consumer goods, but the USSR's own official growth rate of industrial output over 1952–57 fell by around one percent (from 12.6 percent to 11.6 percent) owing to its contributions to Chinese growth. While this does not seem like much, Soviet planners were intensely growth oriented during this era, and Nikita Krushchev, then Soviet Premier, was obsessed with overtaking the U.S. in industrial output. Thus, the Soviet authorities probably raised more than an eyebrow at Chinese requirements, and these demands subsequently escalated, as China sought to industrialize overnight during the Great Leap Forward. Although initially astonished at and then increasingly skeptical of GLF, the Soviets at first cooperated and stepped up their trade with China. Chinese imports from the USSR rose by 16.5 percent in 1958 and by another 50.5 percent in 1959, when they reached over $950 million. China exported even more to the Soviet Union ($1.1 billion in 1960), but at least two-thirds of the exports were consumer goods or textiles, while, in 1959, two-thirds of the Soviet exports consisted of machinery and equipment, including $400 million worth of complete plants.

As indicated, the USSR was being forced to substitute consumer goods for industrial growth against its planners' preferences, while China was able to do the opposite on attractive terms. According to a Chinese source, "prices on various machinery items imported from the Soviet Union were 20 percent to 30 percent lower and sometimes even 30 percent to 60 percent lower than prices of analogous equipment on British and American markets."[19] Soviet deliveries were usually ahead of schedule, and it was during this period that some of China's best-known plants were imported, such as the first tractor factory at Loyang and the iron and steel combine at Wuhan, both of which began production in 1958.

But this was also a period of rising tension and growing ideological hostility between the two countries. China made a primary claim to an Alaska-sized portion of the USSR (580,000 square miles) on her northern and western borders, which Chinese emperors had ceded to the Russian czars during the nineteenth century. The territory in question now has a population of over 25 million. China also questioned the status of the Mongolian People's Republic and laid a secondary claim to another million square miles of the Soviet Union. In foreign affairs, the "peaceful coexistence" policies of Nikita Khrushchev, the Soviet leader, were anathema to the Chinese. Mao continued to call for violent class conflict until a "genuine" socialist order would come to prevail throughout the world. Thus, the Chinese were more favorable to wars of national liberation and more insistent on the inevitability of world revolution.

Moreover, when China claimed to have achieved as much growth in 1958 as during the entire First Five-Year Plan, the Soviets were aware that this was an exaggeration and that valuable materials, tools, and equipment, much of which came from the Soviet Union, were being wasted. One Soviet specialist noted that "According to the official figure, 4 million tons of iron were processed in small local blast furnaces, but of this amount, hardly more than one per cent was useable, the remaining 99 percent being slag, unwashed ore, or . . . a pure invention of the statisticians."[20] To many Soviet leaders, it seemed that their investment was going down the drain. Krushchev warned that the USSR had tried communes during her period of war communism (1918–21) and that they did not work. By 1960, the Chinese were trying to indoctrinate visiting Soviets in their point of view and subjecting the latter to closer surveillance and greater harassment, even while raising their demands for technical and material assistance.[21]

The identity of the final straw remains unknown, but in August 1960, most Soviet specialists left abruptly, taking some of their blueprints with them and leaving some construction projects incomplete. Nearly 260 projects of scientific and technical cooperation were abandoned. In a number of cases, the Chinese were unable to complete these enterprises, to operate them, or to troubleshoot them for several years. During his 1966 visit, Barry Richman observed that the Wuhan Iron and Steel plant, the Loyang Tractor factory, and the Beijing Steel Wire factory were all plagued with low productivity. The latter enterprise was "in near chaos," although the growing power of the radicals over professional management (with the approach of the Cultural Revolution) was probably a contributing factor in all three cases.[22] Overall, the cost to China of the pull-out is inestimable, but if the Soviets wished to teach China a lesson, the effect was instead to increase its determination to stand alone, if need be.

Arthur Ashbrook notes that the USSR had agreed to supply China with 300 modern industrial plants over 1953–67, worth about $3.25 billion, of which around half were finished when the withdrawal occurred. If the entire package had been put into place and efficient operation and maintenance by Chinese specialists assured, he argues, China would have had the nucleus of a powerful, self-sufficient industrial base. "If Peking had . . . waited 7 more years, the whole integrated group of 300 Soviet aid plants would have been onstream; as it was, great new industrial plants were left without customer . . . or supplier plants [and without ready access to replacement parts] or experienced troubleshooters."[23] However, the extent to which China could have continued to follow an independent path in foreign and domestic affairs while continuing to receive Soviet assistance is unclear.

8-4. Small-Scale Enterprise

Sometimes, the Chinese describe the First Five-Year Plan as a period of "leaning to one side." Specifically, this refers to trade orientation toward the Soviet Union, but because of the nature of this trade, it also refers to economic development based on construction of large, capital-intensive plant complexes, mainly in heavy industry. Beginning in 1958, the Chinese would start to "walk on two legs"—that is, to build many small-scale, labor-intensive firms, while continuing to expand the large-scale capital-intensive sector. Walking on two legs also includes efforts to educate the population, to provide health care and sanitation, and to improve their livelihood through local initiative. Development of small-scale enterprise is scarcely a new phenomenon in China. Household subsidiary activities—in the form of artisan work, handicrafts, repair, and the like—have existed for centuries in Chinese villages. The peasants deliberately plan their work to fill in time left over from farming. Seasonal variations in household subsidiary production have been the opposite of those in agriculture. Failure to realize this caused China's leaders to underestimate the opportunity cost of mobilizing millions of peasants for water conservation and road-building projects, along with work in backyard steel furnaces, coal mines, and other small enterprises during the Great Leap Forward.

Nevertheless, household-scale firms are not always good vehicles for spreading technological progress, and they were not producing an optimal mix of goods and services from the leaders' point of view. There were also potential gains from scale economies and division of labor that could be realized in factories much smaller than those originally sent in by the Soviets, but several times larger than the individual household. This is, in fact, the kind of firm promoted in rural areas since 1958, although household subsidiary production continues to be important. During the Great Leap Forward, the policy of promoting small-scale industry was disastrous, but during the 1960s, it was put on a sounder basis. Even so, losses of state-run small firms in 1978 came to over half of all losses in state industry, and today, further efforts are underway to improve the performance of this sector (on which more below).[24]

Rural industry has grown rapidly in recent years. Total output value shot up by 35 percent in 1985, by 21 percent in 1986, and by 28 percent in 1987. It now exceeds the output value of agriculture (although value added is still greater in farming) and comes to over 30 percent of the output value of industry as a whole. Altogether, more than 17 million small industrial, service, and commercial enterprises employed around 20 percent of the labor force by early 1989, and there are many more small firms in the cities. Over half of all chemical fertilizer, 75 percent of the bricks, tiles, lime, sand, and stone used in construction, nearly all small farm tools and machinery, about a fourth of the outputs of coal and pig iron, and nearly a third of all hydroelectric power are now produced in small firms. Generally speaking, output increases of several times occurred between 1965 and 1988.[25]

Small firms also produce significant amounts of steel, machinery, machine and hand tools, mining and irrigation equipment, cement and various construction materials, small diesel and electric motors, trucks, buses, boats, pesticides and herbicides, pharmaceuticals, and a wide variety of consumer goods. A major role of small-scale industry is to assist agriculture. Historically, this has been done through the "five small industries" of chemical fertilizers, farm machinery, cement, hydroelectricity, and iron and steel. Because China has consciously located small plants throughout the countryside, their operations can be tailored to complement the labor requirements of farming. The cities also have their share of small-scale industry. In 1971, a visitor observed that "It is common on the back streets of cities as far apart as Canton, Xian, and Beijing to come across small workshops, where workers, most of them housewives, work at tasks that range from making body parts for cars to assembling electric welding machines or transistors."[26] In recent years, efforts to reduce unemployment and to provide jobs for urban school leavers have focused on creating and expanding cooperatives in light industry, construction, and services.

In China's circumstances, a major advantage of small-scale industry is that it uses more labor per unit of invested capital than do large-scale factories and mines. This is crucial in a country where the ratio of labor to every other productive input is higher than virtually anywhere else in the world. The difference between small- and large-scale industry can be striking. For example, Jon Sigurdson once calculated that producing 3 million tons of synthetic ammonia in small plants would provide 250,000 jobs vs. 2,000 in large factories, which are much more capital intensive.[27] To an extent, this is also a question of light vs. heavy industry, since light industry is more labor intensive and sacrifices fewer scale economies when plant capacity is restricted. According to a Chinese labor expert, a million yuan invested in heavy industry creates only 94 jobs, on average, whereas the same investment creates 257 jobs in light industry and even more in services.[28] Thus, China's industrial priorities

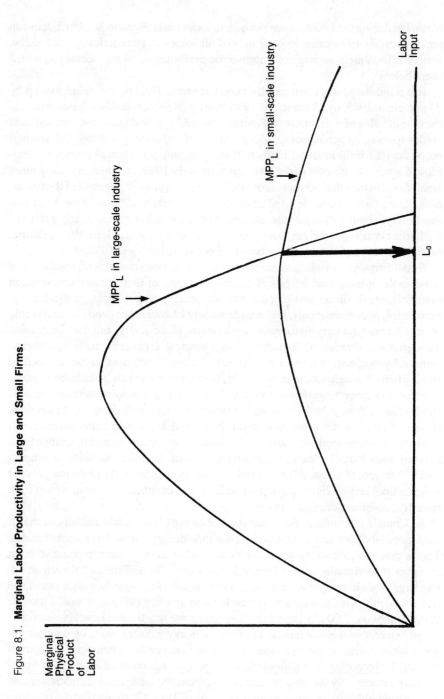

Figure 8.1. **Marginal Labor Productivity in Large and Small Firms.**

have been unfavorable to job creation.

In this context, consider Figure 8.1. Labor is more productive in large-scale industry, in the sense that output per unit of labor input is higher there. Indeed output per unit of capital input may also be higher than in small firms, depending on the industry, and large enterprises often turn out a higher quality of product.[29] However, let us say that the *marginal* physical product of labor (MPP$_L$) is the additional output per unit of additional labor input that results from an expansion of the labor force. The size of MPP$_L$ will depend on how much capital labor has to work with. Figure 8.1 compares the behavior of labor's MPP$_L$ in large vs. small factories, for a given amount of capital invested in each kind of production facility. We may think of this capital as being invested either in one large or in many small plants.

In the former case, MPP$_L$ rises rapidly, as labor input expands toward the minimum needed to man all the factory's assembly lines, materials handling processes, and so forth. But after this minimum is reached, MPP$_L$ will eventually start to fall, if labor input keeps on growing, since additional workers become harder and harder to accommodate productively within the enterprise. Eventually, adding more workers will no longer raise output, which is to say that MPP$_L$ will be zero. By contrast, let us divide the same capital input into small chunks—each constituting a small factory with a small labor force—and expand employment by bringing more of these factories into production. Now, we shall get smaller initial increases in MPP$_L$, because production runs are shorter, production processes are less mechanized, and the level of technology is not so high. But neither will we get much of a decline in MPP$_L$ as employment continues to rise, assuming that the small factories are all similar. The same amount of capital can now be spread over more workers, all of whom are productively employed in the sense that MPP$_L$ is positive.

More generally, suppose we have a developing nation, initially composed of a large agricultural and a tiny industrial sector. This country's leaders want rapid industrial growth, and the optimal capital-to-labor ratio is much higher in modern industry than in agriculture. Moreover, modern industry cannot productively employ nearly as much labor per unit of capital as can agriculture or handicrafts. Large-scale industrial enterprises in China are much more labor intensive than in North America or Western Europe, but the extent to which labor can be substituted for capital within them is still limited, and such limits are a key constraint on many developing economies. The greater the ratio of industrial to agricultural output, the greater the size of the capital stock required to keep a labor force of any given size fully employed.[30]

This is basically how the process of development has led to unemployment or to underemployment in a number of developing countries. The heavy industrial production facilities whose growth is being promoted do not generate enough jobs because they are capital intensive, with limited possibilities of substituting labor for capital. More labor-intensive sectors (light industry, agriculture, and services) do not generate enough jobs because there is not enough investment in them. Industrial growth also attracts a rural-to-urban migration, which converts some rural underemployment into urban unemployment. Thus, a contradiction often arises between full employment and rapid industrial growth, and China faced such a dilemma by the end of the 1950s. There is no ideal resolution without sacrificing some growth, especially when the leadership places a high priority on heavy industry, where capital intensity and economies of large scale are greatest. In these conditions, the ''walking on two legs'' policy may represent the best compromise China could hope for.

Within the context of our example, walking on two legs means promoting both small-scale, labor-intensive industry and large-scale, capital-intensive production. By operating several technologies at once—some with high and some with low labor-to-capital ratios—the planners can hope to raise the ratio of industrial to farm output that is compatible with low unemployment. As indicated, capital can be invested more divisibly in small enterprises, although the average yield on investment is higher in large-scale industry. However, this return does not take into account the social benefit of a higher capacity to absorb labor. The latter suggests a higher investment priority for small-scale production—and also for light industry, agriculture, and services vis-à-vis heavy industry—than is traditionally accorded in a Soviet-type economy.

The employment-generating capacity of small-scale industry extends beyond the number of jobs which it directly provides. In China, most of the labor force still works in agriculture and directly related occupations, such as water control. About 60 percent of China's total employment increase between the late 1950s and the late 1970s was in agriculture.[31] Small-scale industry facilitated this rise in farm labor input, with virtually no net increase in the amount of land under cultivation. Many of its products—chemical fertilizers, irrigation equipment, farm tools and small machines, building materials, electric power, and others—raise the marginal productivity of farm labor. They allow productive use of more labor on each plot of land, while helping to expand the food supply. In addition, the outputs of small firms have allowed crop diversification into fruits, vegetables, meat, and dairy products, whose production is more labor intensive than grain, as well as ''a marked increase in the labor time devoted to infrastructure: roads; water control and irrigation systems; land terracing; reforestation; [and] building of schools, hospitals, public buildings, and housing.''[32] Nevertheless, by 1980 at least 90 million of China's farmers were underemployed, and rural infrastructure has suffered comparative neglect during the 1980s. Thus, the main employment-generating effect of the millions of rural enterprises established since 1980 has been their direct provision of jobs to peasants leaving agriculture.

In China's circumstances, small firms can also utilize ''scattered, low-quality resources,'' along with surplus, scrap, and waste materials and components scrounged from every possible source. China is well endowed with natural resources, including oil, iron ore, hydroelectric potential, and a third of the world's coal reserves. But these resources are often scattered in small deposits throughout the country. China's hydroelectric potential is the world's largest. Yet it utilizes less than 6 percent of it (to generate about 18 percent of its total electricity output). One reason is that much of the potential lies in many small sites, and China now has nearly 90,000 small hydro and thermal power-generating stations scattered throughout the countryside. According to one author: "... medium and small hydropower stations can use scattered waterpower resources, cost only thousands or even a few hundred yuan, take a short time to build, and some generate electricity in the first year or so. In this way, power can be obtained from a head drop of only a few meters or even less than a meter. ... In the frontier province of Yunnan, for instance, the people's communes have used their own efforts and methods to build over 5,000 small power stations [ranging] from a score of kilowatts to 2,000. ... Small power stations ... have ... enabled three-fourths of the communes to use electricity today."[33]

China's overburdened transport facilities greatly raise the costs of all kinds of construction materials and intermediate goods, whenever they have to be carried very far. A large cement plant in Shanghai may be able to make a higher quality product for a much lower cost than a small county-run factory in neighboring Jiangsu province. But by the time the Shanghai cement has reached the county in Jiangsu, its price will be higher, and the additional quality will not be too important on many local construction projects. Given China's circumstances, it makes sense to scatter small firms throughout the country that use mainly local resources and supply mainly local needs. Small firms can often use machinery cast off by the modern sector, and in many cases, workers in small-scale industry are expected to show self-reliance by making their own tools and machinery. Together with households, small firms also provide local repair facilities and spare-parts servicing. Because most small enterprises are under local control, those supplying agriculture or processing agricultural raw materials can be flexible enough to tailor their production to local needs. In many cases, local industries can also get by without skills, materials, components, or machinery that have become bottlenecks in large-scale industry.[34]

Other benefits from small-scale industry are more intangible. By relieving unemployment in the cities, they reduce a potential source of frustration, embitterment, and disillusion with the régime. Moreover, dispersion of small-scale industry has brought people all over the country face-to-face with the process of development, thereby familiarizing them with basic industrial skills. Many of these firms start out as pilot plants, training workers and acclimatizing them to industrial technology. Larger enterprises also help to train workers and technicians for small-scale industry, and medium-sized firms located in intermediate-sized cities—which are often seats of county or township governments—have played an active role in disseminating skills, know-how, and familiarity with industrial design and technology to the more numerous small enterprises. According to a Chinese official:

> Industrialization cannot be grafted onto a country like a foreign body. It must grow within the country at the grass roots level—managed by the local communities and

geared to the satisfaction of local needs. .... It is only through the creation of small workshops at the local level that the people will understand machinery. .... During the First Five-Year Plan, the tendency was to direct everything from Beijing. Today, we feel that as much industry as possible should be managed locally, by the people on the spot. By doing so, we not only encourage the creative forces among the people, we also show the people that we trust them.[35]

Visitors to China during the 1970s stressed that local industrial networks were closely and carefully coordinated, that local needs were studied (for example, through household surveys), and that the quantity and quality of raw materials were assured before starting production. However, these assessments were too optimistic. Because light industrial products are a major revenue source for counties and communes, the profit motive is important in founding firms to produce these goods. This reinforces the drive to control costs and to turn out products in demand. But the record of some small-scale heavy industries is not nearly so good. Many of these firms started in the late 1960s had to close 10–12 years later, including over half the small iron and steel mills and a number of plants making farm machines and tools. They "were technically backward, and the goods they produced were of low quality or even unsaleable."[36] Many also consumed raw materials and fuel wastefully, and local farm machinery plants often produced goods in quantities beyond any conceivable local demand, which then piled up in warehouses. (They became classic examples of production to meet plan targets rather than market demand.) Efforts to rescue such firms have focused on technical help from larger, more efficient enterprises, which take on workers and managers from backward units as apprentices and help to reorganize the latter.

Within a highly centralized economy, many benefits of small-scale industry would go unrealized. The proliferation of such plants under central management would turn command planning into an informational nightmare, probably leading to a rigid, counterproductive control over this sector, as well as to underinvestment in it. However, decentralized control in China has also created problems of its own. For example, the local reinvestment of profit has raised regional inequality. Moreover, the past emphasis on regional self-sufficiency plus the lack of coordination between different planning jurisdictions has led to excess capacity in some industries (notably farm machinery). As a result, many firms operate at low levels, owing to shortages of raw materials or power, or because of market saturation of their products.

Regional duplication has also meant failure to realize some scale and experience economies, which are achievable within small firms, as well as irrational location patterns. The latter actually raise the burden on the transport network (since, e.g., a small pig iron plant may be far from its raw material sources). To combat this, authorities are trying to enforce the principle of the "three locals," according to which local small enterprises are to use local resources to produce for a local market. More generally, the present régime wants to raise the efficiency of small-scale industry, and the obvious recommendation is to tie the success or failure of such firms more closely to profitability, based on actual sales of their products. If profitability is to be a good index of efficiency, regional monopolies in both heavy and light industry will have to be broken. This will require small firms to specialize more and to expand their markets beyond township or county borders. The separation of economic from political management is designed to make this easier.

Today, China is promoting small-scale industry even more enthusiastically than during the 1960s and 1970s, although subject as well to more stringent cost-effectiveness requirements, as part of the general drive toward marketization. (Thus, about a million rural enterprises went out of business over 1986–88, although many more were started during the same period.) In line with cost-effectiveness and the earlier-noted readjustment of priorities, a larger percentage of new small firms is in light industry and services, where direct labor absorption capacity is greater, cost disadvantages resulting from small size are less, and product demand is potentially high in many places.[37] Small- and medium-sized firms also have the task of ensuring full employment in the cities and of providing jobs for most of the 25 percent or more of the labor force that has left farming or will do so over the next twenty years. In the process, they will hopefully improve the flow of goods and services and enrich the daily lives of the many millions of Chinese who look forward to a more prosperous future.

Notes

1. Chen Rinong, Bian Hui, "China's Agriculture and its Future," *China Reconstructs*, August 1979, p. 22.

2. N. Maxwell and P. Nolan, "The Procurement of Grain," *China Quarterly*, June 1980.

3. Jean C. Oi, "Peasant Grain Marketing and State Procurement: China's Grain Contracting System," *China Quarterly*, June 1986, p. 278.

4. See Nicholas Lardy, "Consumption and Living Standards in China, 1978–83," *China Quarterly*, December 1984, and "Food Consumption in the People's Republic of China," ch. 10 of R. Barker, R. Sinha, B. Rose, eds., *The Chinese Agricultural Economy* (London: Croom Helm, 1982), especially Table 10.6, p. 158. Regarding the discussion below, see Peter Nolan, "De-Collectivisation of Agriculture in China, 1979–82: A Long-Term Perspective." *Cambridge Journal of Economics*, September–December 1983, p. 390, and Jan Prybyla, "On Some Questions Concerning Price Reform in the People's Republic of China," working paper no. 9–87–16, Dept. of Economics, Pennsylvania State University, University Park, Penn., September 1987.

5. Peng Xianchu, "Greater Responsibility on the Farm," *China Reconstructs*, October 1981, p. 24.

6. Nicholas Lardy, "Overview: Agricultural Reform and the Rural Economy," in U.S. Congress, Joint Economic Committee, *China's Economy Looks Toward the Year 2000* (Washington, D.C.: U.S. Government Printing Office 1986).

7. Peng Xianchu, "The Collective is Alive and Well at Wanyu Commune," *China Reconstructs*, September 1982.

8. See J. McMillan, J. Whalley, and Li Jing Zhu, "Incentive Effects of Price Rises and Payment System Changes on Chinese Agricultural Productivity Growth," London, Ontario, Canada, University of Western Ontario, Department of Economics, Working Paper No. 8701C, January 1987.

9. *Beijing Review*, November 1, 1982, p. 3.

10. See Lei Yuzin, "State Farms Today," *China Reconstructs*, January 1985, and "Reform and Development of State Farms," *China Reconstructs*, April 1988.

11. See W. Klatt, "China's New Economic Policy: A Statistical Appraisal," *China Quarterly*, December 1979, p. 726. Foodstuffs were under one per cent of total imports in 1959, but nearly 40 percent by 1964. Since 1961, the People's Republic has imported several million tons of grain per year, mainly from Canada, Australia, and the United States. Complete production facilities were 20 percent of all imports in 1959, but just 2 percent of a lower import total in 1964.

12. This statement was true as of late 1988. Following a recentralization in 1985, however, only four of the newer zones retained the right to sign contracts for foreign investment without central approval.

13. He Chulin, "Eight Years of the Open Policy," *China Reconstructs*, November 1987, p. 12.

14. See *The German Tribune*, April 19, 1987.

15. Bian Fa, "Reform—China's Second Revolution," *China Reconstructs*, October 1987, p. 19. See, as well, Zhang Quan, Fan Zhilong, "Foreign Capital Speeds Modernization," *China Reconstructs*, June 1985, and Huang Wenjun, "Developments in China's Foreign Economic Relations and Trade," *China Reconstructs*, March 1985.

16. Franz Schurmann, *Ideology and Organization in Communist China* (Berkeley: University of California Press, 1966), p. 333. Enterprise profits deducted into the state budget were a major source of investment finance.

17. Walter Galenson, "Economic Relations between the Soviet Union and Communist China," in *Study of the Soviet Economy*, Russian and East European Series, vol. 25 (1961), p. 39. The next two quotes are from the same source, pp. 38 and 39.

18. Arthur Ashbrook, "China: Economic Policy and Economic Results, 1949–71," in U.S. Congress, Joint Economic Committee, *People's Republic of China: An Economic Assessment* (Washington, D.C.: U.S. Government Printing Office, 1972), p. 17.

19. Galenson, "Economic Relations between the Soviet Union and Communist China," p. 44.

20. Mikhail Klochko, *Soviet Scientist in Red China* (New York: Praeger, 1964), p. 81. See, as well, chs. 5, 6, 10, and 11 of this book for further discussion of the Great Leap Forward by an eye-witness. Klochko's impressions were by no means all negative. At one point, he notes (p. 159) "The quality of building construction is higher in Peking than in Moscow and, unlike Moscow, the collapse of walls in buildings under construction is not common."

21. As a Communist party member, Prof. Klochko attended Soviet Ambassador Chernenko's explanation of the Sino-Soviet rift to Soviet party members resident in China on August 6, 1960 (described in *Soviet Scientist in Red China*, ch. 13), and was on the last train carrying Soviet citizens out of Beijing.

22. Barry Richman, "Capitalists and Managers in Communist China," *Harvard Business Review*, February 1967, pp. 76–77.

23. Ashbrook, "China: Economic Policy and Economic Results 1949–71," p. 22.

24. As an example, see Huo Bolin, "Shanghai Helps Backward Small Industries," *China Reconstructs*, December 1980.

25. Regarding rural small-scale industry in China, see Carl Riskin, "Small Industry and the Chinese Model of Development," *China Quarterly*, April–June 1971; Jon Sigurdson, "Rural Industry—A Traveller's View," *China Quarterly*, April–June 1972, and "Rural Industrialization in China," in U.S. Congress, Joint Economic Committee, *China: A Reassessment of the Economy* (Washington, D.C.: U.S. Government Printing Office, 1975); Christine Wong, "Rural Industrialization in the People's Republic of China—Lessons from the Cultural Revolution Decade," in U.S. Congress, Joint Economic Committee, *China Under the Four Modernizations* (Washington, D.C.: U.S. Government. Printing Office,

1982), and "Rural Enterprises in China: Too Many, Too Soon?" *China News Analysis*, no. 1380, March 1, 1989.

26. Alexander Casella, "Mao's China, 1972: A Nostalgia for Yenan, 1935," *New York Times Magazine*, February 22, 1972, p. 37.

27. Sigurdson, "Rural Industrialization in China," p. 423.

28. "Employment and Unemployment," *China Reconstructs*, February 1981, p. 25. This article is an interview with Kang Yonghe, Director of the State Labor Bureau of China. He is the expert in question.

29. Rawski writes that "we find identical models of machine tools being manufactured in Shenyang and in small, self-equipped plants in rural areas." (See Thomas Rawski, "Chinese Economic Planning," *Current Scene*, April 1976, p. 9). But as a rule, the quality of heavy industrial products from small-scale plants is lower than from large-scale, modern plants.

30. The situation can be made worse by substituting capital for labor in agriculture, as many developing countries have tried to do. Then, "the eviction of tenant farmers and other measures of land consolidation create a new agricultural proletariat that roams the country-side." (Irma Adelman, "Strategies for Equitable Growth," *Challenge*, May/June 1974, p. 39). For a more general discussion of the problems of equitable growth, largely in developing countries usually considered to be outside the "socialist bloc," see Irma Adelman and Cynthia Taft-Morris, *Economic Growth and Social Equity in Developing Countries* (Stanford: Stanford University Press, 1973).

31. See Thomas Rawski, *Economic Growth and Employment in China* (New York: Oxford University Press, 1979), especially chs. 1, 2, 4.

32. Lloyd Reynolds, "China as a Less-Developed Economy," *American Economic Review*, June 1974, p. 424.

33. Bian Hui, "The Role of China's Medium and Small Industries," *China Reconstructs*, July 1977.

34. The above points are made by Riskin, "Small Industry and the Chinese Model or Development." However, see as well his later article, "China's Rural Industries: Self-Reliant Systems or Independent Kingdoms?" *China Quarterly*, March 1978, as well as Wong, "Rural Industrialization in the People's Republic of China. . . ."

35. Casella, "Mao's China, 1972: a Nostalgia for Yenan, 1935," p. 37.

36. Huo Bolin, "Shanghai Helps Backward Small Industries," p. 34.

37. Current priorities in development of rural industry, as of 1987, appear to include food processing; textiles, clothing, and footwear; farm tools, machinery, and parts; other types of machinery; electrical products; traditional and modern medicines, and wine-making.

Questions for Review, Discussion, Examination

*1. China was able to collectivize agriculture in just one year (1956), whereas it had taken Stalin seven years (1929–36) and caused far greater loss of property and lives in the USSR. Yet, the gains from collectivization expected by the party's radical wing failed to materialize in China. Give and briefly discuss at least three reasons for this.

2. Describe the three-level organization set up by China to manage farm production over 1958–78. Roughly how large was each level, on average? What functions did each perform? Did this organization help to promote rural prosperity in China? Discuss briefly.

*3. What is the "responsibility system," as applied to rural areas of China? Why did it le ad to a large initial increase in farm output? What other factors have contributed to the rise in output? Have there been any negative consequences of the rural responsibility system? Explain.

What further organizational changes are now occurring in Chinese agriculture? Do these threaten the constitutional ban on sales of land?

4. What does rising specialization in China's rural areas suggest about the role of the market there? Are peasants free to decide what crops to grow in response to expected market prices? What do you think explains the persistence of some *de facto* state targets and quotas?

*5. Give at least four concrete ways in which the organization and conduct of foreign trade in China depart from standard practice in Western market economies.

Is the Chinese currency undervalued or overvalued vis-à-vis Western currencies at official exchange rates? How is this practice consistent with domestic exchange? What constraint does it put on decentralization of control over foreign trade?

Finally, how have the reforms affected Chinese foreign trade?

6. What are the main components of the "open door" policy? How does it depart from earlier practice? What evidence do we have of China's expanding economic ties with other nations?

7. What are China's special economic zones? Why has there been less investment from abroad than China's reformers had hoped for (even though foreign investment in China has been substantial)?

8. Why was Soviet assistance to China during the 1950s essential to rapid industrial growth during that decade? What was the nature of this assistance?

*9. Outline the role of small-scale industry within the Chinese economy. What problems of economic development does small-scale industry help to solve, particularly in the Chinese context, and what is the cost to China of investing in small-scale rather than in large-scale industry?

10. What can you say about the desirability of centralizing or decentralizing the administration of small-scale industry? What limits the growth of small-scale industry?

11. Both radicals and reformers have promoted small-scale industry in China, but with a difference. How does the current emphasis on expansion of small-scale industrial and service enterprises depart from expansions under past periods of radical control (such as 1958–60, during the Great Leap Forward and 1966–69, during the Cultural Revolution)?

12. Why is expansion of small firms in rural areas a crucial part of efforts to raise rural living standards without further overcrowding of large cities?

* = more difficult.

Suggested Further Readings

Note: Chinese authors are translated in the journal, *Chinese Economic Studies*. A pictorial, *China Reconstructs*, also contains articles on China of interest to economists, as does the *Beijing Review* and *Xinhua* weekly. All three are published in Beijing. In addition, the journal, *China Quarterly*, publishes articles by Western scholars representing all points of view in a variety of disciplines, including economics. *China News Analysis*, a newsletter published in Hong Kong, has been extremely informative on the progress of economic reform in recent years. Finally, the September 1987 issue of the *Journal of Comparative Economics* (Vol. 11) is entirely devoted to the Chinese reforms.

American Rural Industry Delegation. *Rural Small-scale Industry in the Peoples' Republic of China.* Berkeley: University of California Press, 1977.

Ash, Robert F. "The Evolution of Agricultural Policy." *China Quarterly* 116 (December 1988): 529–555.

Baark, Erik. "Commercialized Techology Transfer in China, 1981–86: The Impact of Science and Technology Policy Reforms." *China Quarterly* 111 (September 1987): 390–406.

Bian, Fa. "Reform—China's Second Revolution." *China Reconstructs* 36 (October 1987): 16–20.

Bian, Hui. "The Role of China's Medium and Small Industries." *China Reconstructs* 26 (July 1977): 19–21.

Bunge, F., and Rinn-Sup Chinn, eds. *China: A Country Study.* Washington, D.C.: U.S. Government Printing Office, 1981.

Butterfield, Fox. *China: Alive in the Bitter Sea.* New York: Times Books, 1982.

Chamberlain, H. B. "Party-Management Relations in Chinese Industries: Some Political Dimensions of Economic Reform." *China Quarterly* 112 (December 1987): 631–661.

Chen, Nai-Ruenn, and Walter Galenson, *The Chinese Economy Under Communism.* Chicago: Aldine, 1969.

"China's Special Economic Zones." *Beijing Review* 27 (January 23, 1984): 24–31.

Cheng, Chu-Yuan. "Industrial Modernization in China." *Current History.* New Series 79 (September 1980): 24–28.

———. *China's Economic Development: Growth and Structural Change.* Boulder, Colo.: Westview, 1982.

Dong, Fureng. "Some Problems Concerning the Chinese Economy." *China Quarterly* 84 (December 1980): 727–736.

Donnithorne, Audrey. *China's Economic System.* London: Allen & Unwin 1967.

———. *The Budget and the Plan in China: Central-Local Economic Relations.* Canberra: Australian National University 1972a.

———. "China's Cellular Economy: Some Economic Trends Since the Cultural Revolution." *China Quarterly* 52 (October–December 1972b): 605–619.

Du, Runsheng. "China's Countryside Under Reform." *Beijing Review* 27 (August 13, 1984): 16–21.

Eckstein, Alexander, Walter Galenson, and Ta-Chung Liu, eds. *Economic Trends in Communist China.* Chicago: Aldine 1968.

Emerson, John Philip. "Urban School-leavers and Unemployment in China." *China Quarterly* 93 (March 1983): 1–16.

Field, Robert Michael. "Slow Growth of Labour Productivity in Chinese Industry, 1952–81." *China Quarterly* 96 (December 1983): 641–664.

———. "Changes in Chinese Industry Since 1978." *China Quarterly* 100 (December 1984): 742–761.

Galenson, Walter. "Economic Relations Between the Soviet Union and Communist China." *Study of the Soviet Economy.* Soviet and East European Series 25 (1961): 32–56.

Gao, Yangliu. "Signs of Capitalism in China? The Shenyang Experiment." *China Reconstructs* 36 (March 1987): 40–42.

Gold, T. B. "Back to the City: The Return of Shanghai's Educated Youth." *China Quarterly* 84 (December 1980): 755–770.

Guo, Zhongyi. "Combatting Price Rises." *China Reconstructs* 37 (May 1988): 8–10.

He, Chulin. "Eight Years of the Open Policy." *China Reconstructs* 36 (November 1987): 12–15.

He, Jianzhang. "Basic Forms in the Socialist Economy." *China Reconstructs* 31 (January 1982): 42–44.

He, Kang, and Liu Jianjun. "Minister He Kang on China's Agriculture." *Beijing* 32 (May 1–7 1989): 20–24.

He, Xiaopei. "An Investigation Into the Current Compensation System for Mental and Manual Labor." *Chinese Economic Studies* 18 (Fall 1984): 77–95.

Hoffman, Charles. *The Chinese Worker*. Albany: State University of New York Press, 1974.

Huo, Bolin. "Shanghai Helps Backward Small Industries." *China Reconstructs* 29 (December 1980): 34–35.

Huang Hsiao, Katheryn H. Y. *Money and Monetary Policy in Communist China*. New York: Columbia University Press, 1971.

———. "Money and Banking in the People's Republic of China: Recent Developments." *China Quarterly* 91 (September 1982): 462–477.

Jackson, Sukhan. "Reform of State Enterprise Management in China." *China Quarterly* 107 (September 1986): 405–432.

Kambara, Tatsu. "China's Energy Development During the Readjustment and Prospects for the Future." *China Quarterly* 100 (December 1984): 762–782.

Kang, Yonghe, and Qiu Jian. "Employment and Unemployment." *China Reconstructs* 30 (February 1981): 25–27.

Klatt, W. "China's New Economic Policy: A Statistical Appraisal." *China Quarterly* 80 (December 1979): 716–733.

Klochko, Mikhail. *Soviet Scientist in Red China*. New York: Praeger, 1964.

Kojima, Reeitsu. "Agricultural Organization: New Forms, New Contradictions." *China Quarterly* 116 (December 1988): 706–735.

Koziara, Edward C., and Chiou-Shuang Yan. "The Distribution System for Producers' Goods in China." *China Quarterly* 96 (December 1983): 689–702.

Kueh, Y. Y. "Economic Reform in China at the *Xian* Level." *China Quarterly* 96 (December 1983): 665–688.

———. "Food Consumption and Peasant Incomes in the Post-Mao Era." *China Quarterly* 116 (December 1988): 634–670.

Kueh, Y. Y., and Christopher Howe. "China's International Trade: Policy and Organizational Change and Their Place in the 'Economic Development.' " *China Quarterly* 100 (December 1984): 813–848.

Lardy, Nicholas. "Centralization and Decentralization in China's Fiscal Management." *China Quarterly* 61 (March 1975): 25–60.

———. "Food Consumption in the Peoples' Republic of China." In Barker, R., R. Sinha, and B. Rose, eds. *The Chinese Agricultural Economy* (London: Croom Helm, 1982), pp. 147–162.

———. "Consumption and Living Standards in China, 1978–83." *China Quarterly* 100 (December 1984): 849–865.

Lee, Yok-shiu F. "The Urban Housing Problem in China." *China Quarterly* 115 (September 1988): 387–407.

Lei, Yuxin. "Reform and Development of State Farms." *China Reconstructs* 37 (April 1988): 14–16.

Li, Chaochen, and Li Lailai. "Smashing the 'Iron Rice Bowl' and 'One Big Pot.' " *China Reconstructs* 32 (May 1983): 9–15.

Li, Haibo. "Bu Xinsheng, a Bold Reformer." *Beijing Review* 27 (July 16, 1984): 19–23.

Liao, Jili. "Reforming Economic Management." *China Reconstructs* 30 (March 1981): 4–7.
Liu, Chenlie. "How a Free Market Operates." *China Reconstructs* 31 (May 1982): 42–43.
———. "Business: The Private Sector." *China Reconstructs* 36 (December 1987a): 8–10.
———. "The Crisis of Farmland Alienation." *China Reconstructs* 36 (December 1987b): 24–26.
———. "Consolidating Farmland for Greater Efficiency." *China Reconstructs* 38 (May 1989): 25–27.
Liu, Yimlin, and Zheng Zeyu. "Official Spells Out Investment Laws." *Beijing Review* 28 (January 21, 1985): 16–19.
Luo, Gengmo. "Socialism and Inflation." *Beijing Review* 27 (November 1, 1984).
Lu, Dong. "Reforms Invigorate 1984 Economy." *Beijing Review* 28 (March 11, 1985): 15–17; 24.
Lu, Peijian, and Li Haibo. "Banking Reform Favours Centralization." *Beijing Review* 27 (April 9, 1984): 16–18.
Lu, Yun. "Peasants' Initiative Unleashed by Contracts." *Beijing Review* 27 (October 29, 1984a): 18–21; 29.
———. "Specialized Households Emerge." *Beijing Review* 27 (December 3, 1984b): 23–27.
Nolan, Peter. "De-Collectivization of Agriculture in China, 1979–82: A Long-Term Perspective." *Cambridge Journal of Economics* 7 (September–December 1983): 381–403.
Oi, Jean C. "Peasant Grain Marketing and State Procurement: China's Grain Contracting System." *China Quarterly* 106 (June 1986): 272–290.
Peng, Xianchu. "Greater Responsibility on the Farm." *China Reconstructs* 30 (October 1981): 23–30.
———. "What Happened in the Countryside." *China Reconstructs* 30 (October 1981): 21–22.
Perkins, Dwight. *Market Control and Planning in Communist China*. Cambridge: Harvard University Press 1966.
———. "Plans and Their Implementation in the Peoples' Republic of China." *American Economic Review* 63 (May 1973): 224–231.
Prybyla, Jan. *The Chinese Economy: Problems and Policies*. Columbia: University of South Carolina Press, 1978.
———. "On Some Questions Concerning Price Reform in the People's Republic of China." Working paper no. 9–87–16, Dept. of Economics, Pennsylvania State University, University Park, Pennsylvania (September 1987).
Rawski, Thomas. *China's Transition to Industrialism*. Ann Arbor: University of Michigan Press, 1980.
Reeder, John A. "Entrepreneurship in the People's Republic of China." *Columbia Jounral of World Business* 19 (Fall 1984): 43–50.
Renmin Ribao Commentator. "Institute on Economic Planning System Better Suited to China's Conditions." *Beijing Review* 25 (October 11, 1982): 21–23; 26; 28.
Reynolds, Lloyd. "China as a Less Developed Economy." *American Economic Review* 65 (June 1975): 418–428.
Richman, Barry. "Capitalists and Managers in Communist China." *Harvard Business Review* 45 (January–February 1967): 57–78.
———. "Ideology and Management: The Chinese Oscillate." *Columbia Journal of World Business* 6 (January–February 1971): 23–33.
———. *Industrial Society in Communist China*. New York: Vintage Books 1972.
Riskin, Carl. "Small Industry and the Chinese Model of Development." *China Quarterly* 46 (April–June 1971): 245–273.
———. "China's Rural Industries: Self-Reliant Systems or Independent Kingdoms?" *China Quarterly* 73 (March 1978): 77–98.
Rosen, Stanley, ed. "The Private Economy, Part I." *Chinese Economic Studies* 21 (Fall 1987).

———. "The Private Economy, Part II." *Chinese Economic Studies* 21 (Winter 1987–88).

Schram, S. R., ed. *Authority, Participation, and Cultural Change in China.* Cambridge: Cambridge University Press, 1973.

Schurmann, Franz. "Economic Policy and Political Power in Communist China." *Annals of the American Academy of Political and Social Science* 349 (September 1963): 49–69.

———. *Ideology and Oganization in Communist China.* Berkeley: University of California Press, 1966.

Shirk, Susan L. "Recent Chinese Labour Policies and the Transformation of Industrial Organization in China." *China Quarterly* 88 (December 1981): 575–593.

Sigurdson, Jon. "Rural Industry—A Traveller's View." *China Quarterly* 50 (April–June 1972): 315–332.

———. *Rural Industrialization in China.* (Cambridge: Harvard University Press, 1977).

"Summary of Panel Discussion on Price Theory by the Chinese Price Institute." *Chinese Economic Studies* 18 (Spring 1985): 20–34.

Sun, Ping. "Individual Economy Under Socialism." *Beijing Review* 27 (August 13, 1984): 25–30.

Tian, Jiyun. "Problems in the 'Substitution of Taxes for Profits' in State-Run Enterprises." *Chinese Economic Studies* 17 (Winter 1983–84): 68–77.

———. "Price System Due for Reform." *Beijing Review* 28 (January 28, 1985): 16–19, 24.

Travers, Lee. "Post-1978 Rural Economic Policy and Peasant Income in China." *China Quarterly* 98 (June 1984): 241–259.

U.S. Congress, Joint Economic Committee. *An Economic Profile of Mainland China* (2 vols). Washington, D.C.: U.S. Government Printing Office, 1967.

———. *China: A Reassessment of the Economy.* Washington, D.C.: U.S. Government Printing Office, 1975.

———. *China Under the Four Modernizations* (2 vols). Washington, D.C.: U.S. Government Printing Office, 1982.

———. *China's Economy Looks Toward the Year 2000* (2 vols). Washington, D.C.: U.S. Government Printing Office, 1986.

Walder, A. G. "Wage Reform and the Web of Factory Interests." *China Quarterly* 109 (March 1987): 22–41.

———. "Factory and Manager in an Era of Reform." *China Quarterly* 118 (June 1989): 242–264.

Walker, K. R. "China's Grain Production, 1975–80 and 1952–57: Some Basic Statistics." *China Quarterly* 86 (June 1981): 783–811.

———. "Chinese Agriculture During the Period of Readjustment, 1978–83." *China Quarterly* 100 (December 1984): 783–812.

Wang, Chuanlun. "Some Notes on Tax Reform in China." *China Quarterly* 97 (March 1984): 53–67.

Wang, George C., ed. "China's Special Economic Zones." *Chinese Economic Studies* 19 (Winter 1985–86).

———. *Economic Reform in the PRC.* Boulder, Colo.: Westview Press, 1982.

White, Gordon. "The Politics of Reform in Chinese Industry: The Introduction of the Labour Contract System." *China Quarterly* 111 (September 1987): 365–389.

Wu, Junyang. "Current Economic Conditions and Reform of the Price System." *Chinese Economic Studies* 18 (Spring 1985): 55–76.

Xue, Muqiao. *Current Economic Problems in China.* Boulder, Colo.: Westview Press, 1982.

———. *China's Socialist Economy.* Rev. ed. Beijing: Foreign Languages Press, 1986.

Yan, Kalin. "How to Deal With Losing Enterprises." *Beijing Review* 28 (March 11, 1985): 25–26.

Yang, Peixin. "On Building a Socialist Capital Market in China." *Chinese Economic Studies* 20 (Winter 1986–87): 67–74.

Yang, Shengming. "Earnings, Prices, and Lives." *Chinese Economic Studies* 17 (Winter 1983–84): 31–36.
Ye, Rutang. "Providing Shelter for a Billion People." *China Reconstructs* 36 (July 1987): 33–39.
Yeh, K. C. "Macroeconomic Changes in the Chinese Economy During the Readjustment." *China Quarterly* 100 (December 1984): 691–716.
Zhang, Chunsheng, and Song Dahan. "Separation of Government Administration From Commune Management." *Chinese Economic Studies* 17 (Spring 1984): 76–83.
Zhang, Zeyu. "A Mirror For Urban Economic Reforms." *Beijing Review* 27 (December 3, 1984): 19–22. Zhao, Ziyang, "Advance Along the Road of Socialism with Chinese Characteristics." *Beijing Review* 30 (November 9–15 1987): 23–49.
Zheng, Tuobin. "The Problem of Reforming China's Foreign Trade System." *Chinese Economic Studies* 20 (Summer 1987): 27–49.
Zhou, Yongkang. "Developing a Responsibility System in Industry." *China Reconstructs* 29 (December 1980): 19–20; 26.
Zou, Erkang. "Special Economic Zone Typifies Open Policy." *Beijing Review* 27 (November 26, 1984): 19–22.

9

REFORMS IN HUNGARY
AND IN CHINA

9-1. Introduction: The Transition to a Market Economy

Before exploring further the comparatively extensive reform efforts in Hungary and China, we shall give an idealized version of the transition from command to market planning, written in 1968 by a Czech economist, who at the time was outlining the expected transformation of his own country.[1] He listed four basic changes that reform was to bring:

> (a) A fundamental change in the role of prices. . . . Instead of the system of fixed prices—which served above all as an instrument of measuring costs and the volume of output—prices and profitability become fundamental guides for enterprises in deciding what and how much ought to be produced. Price thus becomes a basic element of the system. It becomes flexible as a function of supply and demand, including foreign trade.
> (b) The incomes of enterprises . . . become fully dependent on the financial situation of the enterprise, i.e., on the degree of success of entrepreneurial activity. The enterprise therefore acquires complete jurisdiction over decisions concerning the utilization of its income, the allocation of this income between investment and compensation of employees, and the direction of its investment and wage policies.
> (c) In this connection the entire nature of the activity of enterprises is changed. Whereas in the past the management of enterprises aimed only at fulfilling output targets . . . [and] while supply, sales, and investment policy were handled on behalf of the enterprises by central organs, . . . under the new system, enterprises are

forced to engage in entrepreneurial activity in the fullest sense of the word, i.e., including marketing, project-designing activity, technical research, foreign markets, etc. Industrial enterprises are organizations engaged in many-sided productive and commercial activities.

(d) The role of the plan is changing; and by the same token, the central organs of management of the economy must completely revise their methods of directing the economy. In place of a set of directive indicators and orders, arises the role of instruments of economic policy, such as the state budget, credit policy, tariff policy, tax policy, and other indirect instruments. From the point of view of planning, there occurs a transition from a monocentric to a polycentric system, i.e., in place of a single central plan—in which the plans of enterprises were merely a detailed breakdown of centrally established targets—we shall have a spectrum of enterprises planning on their own. Vis-à-vis the enterprises, the central planning body performs two functions:

(1) Supplying information concerning future development, which is to serve the enterprises as a basis for their own development and planning decisions;

(2) Formulating basic objectives of central economic policy and determining the role of economic instruments with whose aid these objectives are to be attained and which also influence very strongly the plans of enterprises.

According to this view, the transition from command to market planning identifies closely with expanded roles for prices, profitability, enterprise management, and use of indirect, financial incentives, or "economic regulators," to steer the economy. Thus,

> under the regulative system, the financial interest of the enterprise is connected not with the annual plan indicators handed down from above, but with profitability . . . . By means of inducements and penalties that affect prices, interest rates, and so forth, the enterprise is encouraged to fulfill government aims through the profit incentive, not by avoiding it.[2]

Expanded enterprise independence also creates competition, as new firms arise and existing firms invade new markets in search of profits. Such competition is the keystone of efficiency in a market economy. Without it, some goods that people are willing and able to pay for will never be produced, and firms will have an incentive to keep output too low and prices too high (or quality too low). What is profitable to an enterprise may not be beneficial to society. Competition plays a major role in promoting an efficient allocation of resources between firms and in motivating enterprises to make good use of the resources at their disposal. In order for competition to work, firms must be free to introduce new products and technologies and to capture part of the resulting benefit to society in the form of (at least temporarily) higher profit. They must also be able to enter industries where excess profits are being earned, because this is the force that ensures output expansion in response to increases in demand.

But competition has a dark side, as well. With a few exceptions, efficiency requires firms to exit from industries in which they can only produce at a loss. The possibility of bankruptcy, as the ultimate penalty for inefficiency, must be a real one. While this by no means precludes measures to soften the impact on the workers affected, and to find new work for them, job security is lower in a market economy, as some of the underemployment of a Soviet-type economy is transformed into open unemployment by pressures to produce in a cost-effective manner. The transition will also be traumatic for many enterprise managers, who are unable to adjust to a wider range of responsibilities or to deal with business risk. This has been a major cause of reform reversal.

9-2. The Reform in Hungary

A. The Aftermath of NEM

Hungary did not stop compiling annual or five-year plans when its reform—also known as the New Economic Mechanism (NEM)—was originally launched on January 1, 1968. Later on, Hungarian officials would argue that the main goal of the 1968 changes was to improve planning by allowing the central planners and the ministries to focus on the strategy of economic development, while leaving many details of production and exchange to be worked out by firms, under government and local party supervision. Formally, the plans drawn up in the National Planning Office are now broken down by branch of industry, but not by individual firm. However, statements by top planning officials suggesting that it would be unthinkable for enterprises to ignore these plans imply that at least an implicit breakdown does exist. In principle, firms now make up their own plans, guided by considerations of profitability. In practice, enterprises are vulnerable to ministerial pressure, based on the central plan, which is still binding for the ministries.

During the first years of NEM, a bonus system went into effect that tried to link managerial, and to a lesser extent, worker incomes to enterprise profitability. The planners introduced bonuses based on profits and graded them in such a way that top managers—with the greatest decision-making responsibility—could raise their basic salaries by up to 80 percent, middle managers could raise theirs by a maximum of 50 percent, but workers could only increase theirs by up to 15 percent. The discovery of this scheme, and its apparent inequities, by workers and the press led to an outcry that caused it to be dropped. Subsequently, the ministries received the right to set top management bonuses on a firm-by-firm basis. All other bonuses are now determined within the enterprise, and profitability has remained a success indicator of secondary importance in the official economy. The ministries already had primary responsibility for determining base salaries and for hiring, firing, and promoting managers. As it turned out, centralization of the bonus system was an omen. ''A considerable [part] of the functions which were returned to firms in fact (or only formally, as resolutions) [in] 1968, slipped back into the hands of hierarchic control within a few years (e.g., company planning, developmental policy, the credit system, pricing, wages management, etc.)."[3]

Hungarian enterprises have never been completely without decision-making autonomy. Even during the early 1950s, a vast flow of quantitative information went up the chain of command, in the form of enterprise requests for materials, financing, additional production capacity, and other inputs. In return, firms were often told, in effect, that they had to produce their output with less input. Yet, central plans were ultimately based on a juxtaposition of enterprise requests and target-setting from the achieved level with basic demands on the economy by the political leadership. Given the high information cost of central planning and the shortage of equipment for gathering, processing, and disseminating information, this was probably the best way of deriving useful plans. Similarly, by allowing enterprises to play a role in determining the assortments of products to be exchanged between them after 1968, as well as delivery dates and other details, and by intervening informally to constrain these choices, the planners have been able to increase flexibility, while reducing the volume of vertical information flow and saving paperwork at all levels. In addition, for most medium sized and small enterprises, ministerial or local government supervision has been reduced to a minimum, and something close to a genuine market prevails. The autonomy of collective and state farms has also risen.

The most dramatic actions taken by NEM during the late 1960s were the abandonment of formal centralized rationing of most scarce materials, the abolition, in principle, of production targets handed down to the enterprises; an expansion of loans (as opposed to budget grants) for investment; a rise in direct ordering of inputs by enterprises, and a reduction by over one-third in ministerial personnel (most of whom went to the enterprises). However, NEM has resulted in no overall saving of administrative personnel. Indeed, by the mid-1970s, "the volume of administrative work [had] grown out of proportion because of weaknesses in enterprise management, the fast increasing supply requirements of local and central [planning] organs, and extensive bureaucracy."[4] In 1975, the authorities had to ban the hiring of administrative personnel. Subsequently, this was relaxed to permit hiring of replacements, but the number of administrators and managers has continued to rise relative to total employment. Firms still behave as if their activities were geared to plan targets. The phenomenon of "storming" continues, and managers continue to be judged on performance improvement (in terms of output, value added, profitability, etc.) from year to year.[5] As a consequence, they continue to hoard scarce inputs, and there is still a second-economy market on which enterprises exchange scarce supplies of raw materials and industrial goods.

When central rationing of scarce materials ended, informal rationing arose to replace this. If a firm had traditionally supplied a certain good to various users, it continued to be responsible for doing this. This "responsibility for supply" obligation became a key element of planning. In 1975, an Inter-ministerial Committee for Pricing and Marketing received power to formally allocate some producer goods, and, in effect, to set some output targets. This committee was subsequently abolished, as part of the "New Direction" of 1979–80. However, it was replaced by the State Economic Commission (SEC), with responsibility for maintaining "economic equilibrium," in connection with which it can take over direct management of supply, if necessary. The National Prices and Materials Board (PMB) also has responsibilities in this area. Formal and informal quotas have continued to play a major role in the allocation of producer goods into the mid-1980s. Writing in 1979, one Hungarian economist even argued that ministerial intervention in enterprise decision making, including preparation of the enterprise plan, was greater than before 1968 (although this statement was probably no longer true by 1988).[6]

A thorough-going price reform preceded NEM, which brought relative official prices of different goods more into line with relative costs. Yet, once set, many prices were frozen or subject to ceilings that maintained the general state of excess demand.[7] Today, prices of most goods are classed as "free." As a rule, however, these prices do not respond freely to supply and demand because price increases frequently require some form of justification. Here, the burden of proof is on the firm. Not only are large profits subject to heavy taxation when used to raise personal incomes, they are also frowned upon. A firm taking advantage of excess demand to raise its prices may find investment credits, subsidies, or other assistance harder to come by. It could even face prosecution for making excess profits. This plus the stigma involved is enough to deter most managers.

One consequence of price control has been a tendency for prices to rise in a few, relatively large discrete jumps—usually as a result of central initiatives—rather than in a smooth progression. Another consequence was a reversal during the 1970s of the usual two-tier socialist pricing system—in which retail consumer prices are much higher than wholesale prices of the same goods, with the state collecting the difference in the form of sales or turnover taxes.[8] Instead, wholesale prices had risen above retail prices, on average, owing to more stringent controls over the latter. The situation was further complicated by heavily subsidized prices of raw materials and fuel, which shielded the domestic economy from the effects of the energy crisis until near the end of that decade.

Thus, the government did a major revision of producer prices over 1979–80. It sought to restore a "normal" socialist pricing structure, as well as to end subsidies on consumption of fuel and raw materials and to establish a more uniform rate of turnover tax. Most producer goods prices were cut slightly, but raw materials prices were raised by an average 15 percent, including a 30 percent rise in fuel prices. At the same time, the tax on wages was cut from 35 percent to 17 percent, and the 5 percent tax on undepreciated capital was eliminated. Nevertheless, costs rose, on balance, for most firms, and the average rate of profit fell by 60 percent. Officially, consumer prices jumped by 19 percent between 1978 and 1980, including a 25 percent rise in food prices, and by an average 6.8 percent per year over 1980–87.

(Unofficially, the increase has been greater.) Since 1978, financial constraints have grown more important for many Hungarian households. The 1979–80 reform also laid down the principle that changes in domestic prices of traded goods should follow price changes on the world market, instead of changes in domestic costs. Prices of nontraded goods are still marked up from domestic costs to provide "reasonable" or "fair" profits, and firms in the Price Club (described above in section 5-4) may set their own prices, provided they stick to the pricing policy they agreed to follow, as a condition for admission to the Club.

From the advent of NEM until 1981, Hungary's industrial structure grew more concentrated rather than more competitive. Despite the net turnaround since then, most markets for industrial goods are dominated by a tiny handful of domestic suppliers, and import competition is next to nonexistent.[9] In most instances, large Hungarian enterprises are amalgamations of small plants producing similar products and usually fail to realize significant scale economies. Indeed, mergers have tended to lower efficiency, and there are many instances of relatively inefficient firms swallowing up efficient ones, only to become even more inefficient after the fusion. Conversely, when the huge Csepel Iron and Metalworks was split into fifteen separate firms in 1983, the new enterprises began to perform more efficiently as separate units than they had as one. The main reasons for mergers have been enterprise efforts to increase their bargaining power with the central authorities responsible for allocating scarce resources and efforts by the latter to simplify their control functions.

At the same time, a major barrier to increased competition has been the difficulty which enterprises encounter in trying to invest in new lines of production. Until 1982, a firm could not move into a new market without approval from its superior (a ministry or local government authority), nor could it found a new enterprise. Since 1982, one firm may found another, known as a "subsidiary" enterprise, and the parent enjoys a claim on the profits of its offspring. This should increase the opportunity to exploit foreign or domestic markets where excess profits are feasible, but thus far not much advantage has been taken of it, suggesting that firms are unable or unwilling to use such an avenue to promote competition. Yields on investment vary widely from industry to industry, which may be a sign of major resource misallocation, although this evidence is tainted by the persistence of irrational prices (which would be poor guides to investment choices). Earlier, we noted that inefficient firms, especially large ones, have often been able to count on subsidies, which can be given on more than fifty different grounds.[10] Many enterprises threatened by exposure to market forces have been far more effective on the political market, lobbying to reverse the reform and to gain sustenance from the state budget.

Following the introduction of NEM in 1968, the performance of the Hungarian economy improved for awhile, according to official statistics, but then deteriorated sharply in the latter 1970s, under the impact of the energy crises. The price of Soviet oil shot up 130 percent in 1975, following a change in the COMECON pricing formula, and by 1985, was above the world market level.[11] Between 1976 and 1979, only 70 percent of Hungary's imports from the West were covered by exports, and Hungarian industry increased its consumption of imported oil rapidly following the increase in oil prices. At first, enterprises were largely shielded from this increase by subsidies, but even when domestic energy prices did go up, firms sometimes used more energy in consequence. Faced with excess demand for their products and cost-plus pricing, they had little incentive to practice conservation. (Indeed, their output values rose with increases in production costs.) Since 1980, progress has been made in conserving energy, but the growth slowdown persists. Given the need to expand exports, it has only been possible to maintain living standards in the short term by drastically cutting the investment share of national income. This also reduces growth.

When Hungary launched NEM, it also ushered in the Third Three-Year Plan (1968–70), intended to cover a transition period before the reform would become complete. A feature of the transition was the presence of brakes, including wage and price controls, insulation of domestic producers from the world market, and a proliferation of highly differentiated taxes and subsidies. Some of the latter were originally justified on grounds that enterprises had not had time to build up their reserve funds and therefore needed some insurance against future liabilities, in order to motivate them to take risks. These brakes were supposed to subside by the start of the Fourth Five-Year Plan in 1971. Instead, they were strengthened and have persisted, although without producing any apparent upsurge in risk-taking. In 1973, the 50 largest industrial enterprises, employing nearly 40 percent of all industrial workers and producing half of industrial output, came under direct "guidance" from the National Planning Office, which proved to be a major step toward recentralization. Most of these firms were in financial difficulty, and their workers had expressed discontent and fear for the future.

Since the mid-1970s, the proportion of investment directly controlled by the central authorities has tended to rise, both because of the nature of the capital projects undertaken and, more recently, as a consequence of the fall in the investment share of national income. Following the energy crisis, the emphasis was on large infrastructural projects designed to improve Hungary's energy supplies. In addition, Hungary has had to cooperate with the Soviet Union on projects designed to maintain a satisfactory flow of imported energy from the USSR. Control over such investments rests with the central authorities, who retained responsibility for infrastructure under the ground rules of NEM. This is how the energy crisis helped to undermine reform, although the main steps to recentralize were taken before the crisis set in.

Over the 1970s, Hungary suffered an average 20 percent decline in terms of trade with other nations, according to official statistics. Hunary's net debt in convertible currencies had reached $7 billion by end-1980 (and almost $15.5 billion by end-1987). As conditions worsened, the economy was unable to adapt to changes in world market demand or to take advantage of opportunities to increase export market shares. As with other COMECON nations, Hungary was being out-competed in low-technology manufactures by the newly emerging industrial nations, and it was still not competitive with advanced Western nations or with Japan at the high-technology end. More than 80 percent of Hungary's exports to the West were raw-materials intensive, and many of these raw materials had to be imported. Investment expansion was out of control, but it did little to raise the flow of convertible-currency exports, although it did increase the demand for imported goods.

B. The New Direction Since 1979

Because of the balance-of-payments crisis, the government was forced to virtually halt growth, which allowed it to stop the expansion of imports. Real net material product in 1986 was just 7 percent higher than in 1980 and real GNP was less than 5 percent higher.[12] Beginning in 1979, the planners renewed their commitment to decentralization and became more concerned about comparative advantage, cost effectiveness, and flexibility in adapting to changes in world market demand and supply. In the process, they became more willing to dismiss managers unable to adapt to the wider responsibilities that go with decentralization. They also split up a number of large enterprises and trusts, at least on paper. As well, they have reorganized a few technologically obsolete firms, discharged some workers from enterprises with surplus labor, closed several backward factories, and made it easier for private companies to get started and grow. Efforts have been made to relocate employees discharged by state enterprises, and open unemployment remains minuscule by Western standards. Authorities still remember the early 1970s, when uncertainty and fear of job or income loss among industrial workers helped to turn many of them against reform. Several architects of NEM, who had been purged or demoted during the period of recentralization, subsequently made comebacks, including the chief architect, Rezso Nyers. More generally, the New Direction includes the following measures, in addition to the 1979–80 price reform described above:

(a) Hungary has taken steps to liberalize foreign trade and has introduced uniform exchange rates between the forint and each convertible currency. Although the forint is still overvalued, these rates are quasi-flexible over time, as noted earlier. On January 1, 1988, nearly every Hungarian firm became eligible to apply for foreign trading rights and, thus, to compete with the foreign trade companies of the Ministry of Foreign Trade. However, with interest payments on the external debt taking about 20 percent of Hungary's convertible currency receipts in 1987 and possibly more in future years, imports are tightly controlled, and Hungarian users are constrained by informal quotas based on use in a base period. Thus, "liberalization" is mainly an effort to expand exports.

(b) The rapid expansion of East-West trade during the 1970s, in which Hungary shared, served as a limited substitute for reform, because it gave COMECON nations better access to advanced technology. The same is true of cooperation agreements and joint ventures between Western countries and Eastern Europe, which usually result in new production facilities in the East (where wages are relatively low), based on technology developed by the Western partner. Hungary is a partner in over 1,000 of these agreements, more than any other East European country has signed. Although they have accounted for a small share of its trade with the West, they have been qualitatively important.[13]

With the souring of East-West relations in the late 1970s, and growing insistence by the Western partner on equity participation as a precondition to technology transfer, Hungary's access to Western technology declined. To revive this, it has set up duty-free zones inside its borders, in order to attract more Western investment in the form of joint ventures—or companies jointly established and owned by a Western firm and its Hungarian partner (and, ultimately, the Hungarian government). Joint ventures in these zones may import goods without paying tariffs and export without clearance from customs. However, sales in Hungary by joint ventures will normally require clearance, and along with purchases from Hungarian firms, must generally be made in convertible currencies. As a rule, joint ventures must pay all expenses in convertible currencies from their convertible-currency receipts. At the same time, because these enterprises are viewed as foreign legal entities, Hungary will make concessions to the foreign partners on wage regulation, management, accounting, and taxation. By the end of 1988, around 25 joint ventures had been formed, and many more new ones are taking shape in 1989, although total Western investment has been disappointing.

Hungary is also building six nuclear power generating stations near the town of Pecs, about sixty miles south of Budapest, in cooperation with other COMECON nations, mainly the USSR, which is supplying technology and fuel. Four stations were on line by end-1987 and could supply up to half of Hungary's total electricity, while the largest two will be built during the 1990s.[14] These projects have absorbed more than 40 percent of Hungary's industrial investment in recent years and continue the policy of emphasizing supply expansion, rather than conservation, in dealing with the energy shortage.

(c) One can argue that making the best use of imported technology requires demand-oriented development, which can only be brought about by decentralization. In this context, a 1980 reorganization abolished the Ministry of Labor and replaced it with a smaller State Office for Wages and Labor, which is supposed to give less detailed regulation of wages and salaries. As we saw earlier, new rules now link increases in earnings more explicitly to productivity. In addition, workers in loss-making enterprises are supposed to be allowed virtually no increases, although this provision is applied sparingly. (For example, in 1986, out of sixty-six loss-making firms and one hundred with low profitability, just eight were forbidden to raise employee earnings.) There has also been a reallocation of labor toward relatively efficient sectors, including a decline in the share of the work force in industry over 1974–85, that went against the trend of previous years of socialist rule. The share in services, which were long neglected, has risen to an all-time high (20–25 percent in 1985), although it is still below levels common in Western Europe, while that in agriculture (21 percent), where Hungary enjoys a comparative advantage, is higher than in the West.

A second reorganization amalgamated the three remaining industrial ministries into a single Ministry of Industry, with about half the total staff of its predecessors. It is supposed to give less direct supervision and to interfere less in the affairs of subordinate firms. The former industrial ministries had been the main allies of large enterprises, when the latter sought preferential treatment.[15]

(d) To complement (c), the government is trying to reduce the dependence of enterprise managements on the planning hierarchy.[16] To this end, supervisory councils have been established in each state firm with powers to evaluate management in a comprehensive way and to assess the long-term plans of the enterprise. These councils have gained the power to hire and fire enterprise directors, and at least 50 percent of their members must be elected by the employees (and must be employees themselves), although others represent the unions, the party, and outside experts. Where firms have several different plants or several firms are still organized as a trust or other form of association, the parent organization will have a board of directors, to which each member plant or firm may send a representative. The board is to deal with coordination of and conflicts between the smaller units. Eventually, ". . . the new legal form can create a framework for transforming the present dependencies [i.e., the smaller entities] into independently taxed economic units, whose former center acts as an agent, rather than as the boss of the member plants."[17]

This initiative may prove to be a major step in the direction of market socialism, but it may also result in little change. Enterprise directors must still be approved by party and state superiors and may continue to view such approval as the key to a successful career. The number of blue-collar workers on the supervisory councils appears to be low, and the councils need not meet more often than once per year. Moreover, prices of most producer goods are still rigid, preserving excess demand and keeping firms dependent on their planning superiors. Besides the Ministry of Industry, these now include the National Prices and Materials Board, the State Economic Commission, and other state organs. Because the division of responsibility between these agencies was not well defined at the outset (in 1980), a struggle to establish and expand areas of control and influence has been underway.

(e) Because of widespread resistance, successful reform also requires efforts to expand the sector of firms that are already subject to the market. It is here that the Hungarian system now threatens to make a decisive break from its command-economy roots. Thus, there are many reports of private owners and cooperatives taking over state stores, restaurants, and workshops since 1982—generally leasing the facilities in competitive bidding—and turning chronic loss-makers into profitable enterprises. This is just one facet of new regulations that make it easier to start small private or cooperative ventures. Individuals can now more easily invest their money in such enterprises, and there are fewer bureaucratic roadblocks, less red tape and paperwork, and less harassment than before 1982. Limits on permissible numbers of employees are higher, and small ventures can more easily import tools, machinery, and materials, provided they have the necessary convertible currency or demonstrate export potential. The importance of private companies and small cooperatives in construction, services, and industry is greater than at any time since 1960. In contrast to large state firms, there is full freedom for these enterprises to take losses and go bankrupt, and there is still some political risk of another about-face in the party's attitude toward them.

However, the potentially revolutionary changes are embodied in the new Corporation Law, passed in October 1988, that took effect in 1989. It overturns the 1949 Nationalization Law—which was part of the legal foundation of the Soviet-type economy—by allowing private firms with up to five hundred workers, when they are Hungarian-owned, and of unlimited size when they are foreign-owned. It also provides the legal basis for limited liability and a stock exchange—including the rights for individual Hungarians to buy, sell, and own shares—and makes it easier for foreign investors to buy into Hungarian firms. Some state enterprises will probably convert to the joint-stock form and issue shares, although no widespread denationalization is expected. Nevertheless, the provision for limited liability, which is new in Hungary, should attract capital to private enterprise—unless the soft budget constraint undermines this by continuing to lock up savings in loss-making state firms. Laws to make it easier for private and cooperative enterprises to get established have now appeared in several other socialist countries including China, Yugoslavia, Poland, and the Soviet Union. But Hungary is allowing larger private firms than most and is also going a step further (and beyond what has been considered a boundary of socialism) by allowing a full-fledged secondary stock exchange, with share prices to be set by supply and demand.

From one perspective, the new possibilities for private and cooperative firms since 1982 are part of a broader reform that has expanded the variety of legal contracts which firms and individuals may use in taking business initiatives and in cooperation on a cost or profit sharing basis. These include cooperation agreements involving only state firms and/or collective farms, as well as joint public-private ventures and other forms of collaboration between the public and private sectors. They also include the right of an enterprise to found a subsidiary company, which may turn out a different line of products from the parent. As noted earlier, the parent is allowed a claim on the profits or losses of its offspring. The central authorities hold *de facto* veto power over such a founding, however, because of their control over the allocation of producer goods.

(f) By November 1987, bankruptcy proceedings were underway against fifty-five firms (most of which were small), and there had been more than thirty bankruptcies among state and cooperative enterprises within the state planning network. These have led to some layoffs, and there has also been an increase in strike activity, which may now be legalized when it seeks purely economic aims.

In 1985, 15,000 workers were made redundant by factory closures or reorganizations, although most found new jobs quickly in Hungary's tight labor market. In September 1986, a new bankruptcy law took effect, which also provides "job search support" for workers made redundant by closure or restructuring of an enterprise. When ten or more employees of a firm lose their jobs, they become eligible for benefits equal to full former earnings for up to six months, then to 75 percent of former pay for another three months, and, finally, to 60 percent of former pay for three more months, provided no suitable work is found. (Work is "suitable" when it pays at least 90 percent of former earnings, requires no more than an hour's travel from home, and has skill requirements that match an individual's training.) In addition, most enterprises must now make public information relating to their sales, assets, profits, bond issues and other loans, etc. However, there is still no guarantee that loss-making firms (of which there were more than two hundred in 1987) will be forced into bankruptcy. As of early 1988, just two enterprises had been declared bankrupt under the new law, and there have been few claims for job search support, although these will increase as (or if) the enterprise budget constraint begins to harden. In 1987, the State Wages and Labor Office also began a small public-works program for hard-to-employ workers.

   (g) A crucial part of the drive to promote efficiency is an effort to transfer investment funds to those enterprises or uses where yields are highest. Thus, Hungary has been trying to build genuine financial markets in recent years, through which the bulk of outside funding for investment projects would flow. As noted under (e), firms could already pool their savings for major investments more easily than before 1982. Individuals can more easily invest in their own businesses or borrow from supplier or user enterprises. Joint public-private ventures in several forms are also possible.

   In 1982, Hungary also witnessed the rebirth of a bond market, which firms and public bodies are using as an avenue to borrow from other enterprises and the general public. Over 1983–87, there were more than three hundred separate issues valued at over 27 billion forints, and during 1987, bonds financed about 5 percent of investment by state and cooperative enterprises. Thus far, bond issues are strictly regulated and fall into two categories—one which may be sold only to households and the other which may be sold only to enterprises and other organizations. Some bonds pay a return which depends on company performance, while others pay a fixed rate of interest, and the state guarantees payment of principal and interest to household buyers. Although prices of some bonds are variable, the gain from buying them is mainly their interest return. In at least one case, bond issuers have also taken advantage of the excess demand for their product. Telephone bonds purchased by households have come with a promise of phone line installation within three years, instead of the usual ten- to fifteen-year waiting period.

   In section 6-1, we also described the 1987 banking reform, which converted Hungary's "monobank" or Soviet-type banking system into one organized more along Western lines. At least four of the specialized investment banks created by the reform are supposed to promote innovation—and, in particular, to help develop marketable products from promising research results—and another is intended to promote expansion of exports to convertible currency markets. The National Bank controls interest rates, reserve requirements, and other conventional instruments of monetary policy and owns a majority of shares in each of the new commercial banks. As in China, however, this reform is threatened by persistence of the soft budget constraint, which would force the central bank to restrain credit expansion with direct controls over lending, in order to keep down open and repressed inflation, as well as investment completion times.

(h) Financial markets would work more efficiently if the enterprise budget constraint would harden, which implies more uniform tax-subsidy treatment of different firms. Thus, Hungary instituted a tax reform in 1988 to bring its system more in line with those in Western Europe. At the same time, it is trying to reduce enterprise subsidies and to restructure some firms to enable them to produce in a cost-effective manner. The basis of taxation has shifted toward enterprise value added and personal incomes. The new personal income tax is progressive, with marginal rates ranging from 10 percent to 60 percent, and the average income initially lying in the 25 percent or 30 percent bracket. It will treat most sources of income uniformly. Thus, it will tap incomes, such as bond interest payments, that have so far been tax free for households. In addition, a new value added tax will be levied on enterprises to replace the former turnover tax on consumption. The VAT rates are supposed to be the same, regardless of whether a firm is large or small or owned by the state or by private individuals. At the outset, there will be three basic rates—0 percent, 15 percent, and 25 percent, with most firms paying the last. This partly replaces a system which has treated nearly every enterprise differently, and in time, even these differences are supposed to disappear. As in Western Europe, VAT will be levied on imports, but forgiven on exports, to encourage the latter. Enterprise profits taxes are to decline, but will still take 50 percent of the profits of most firms (which is high by West European standards), with more uniform treatment of different enterprises, regardless of industry or ownership. Wages have risen, since the tax burden on earnings has shifted from firms to households, and consumer price inflation was on the order of 15 percent in 1988. To partly compensate for the latter, welfare payments are also rising.

VAT payments were expected to provide 26 percent and individual income taxes 10 percent of central government revenues in 1988, with social insurance contributions providing 29 percent. The latter have risen to over 40 percent of wages and salaries. If the number of different VAT rates remains small, it will be harder for the government to take away most increases in profit, except by changing prices. Thus, a major retreat from administrative pricing and controlled markets for producer goods is likely to become a key to further reform progress.

(i) Finally, the best guarantee of economic reform could be the political reform proposed in 1988, which has allowed new political parties to form and to compete with HSWP for legislative seats. A similar statement holds for the Soviet Union—

where electoral competition and the beginnings of a political opposition have begun to emerge under Glasnost—and for other socialist countries. If allowed to go far enough, such competition is incompatible with a Soviet-type economy, by the argument in section 2-3.

C. Prospects

> Marxism is not the theory of egalitarianism, but [rather] of the necessity for equal opportunity.
>
> —Karoly Grosz
> (former General Secretary of HSWP)
>
> Q: What is socialism?
> A: The longest distance from capitalism to capitalism.
>
> —a recent Hungarian political joke

The changes associated with the New Direction of 1979 are necessary if Hungary is to achieve a socialist market economy, but not sufficient. Most can still be neutralized or reversed through a cumulation of efforts by planning authorities to solve specific problems, in combination with a hostile party attitude. The latter will also be crucial to political reform and in determining how the all-important Corporation Law of 1988 is interpreted and applied in practice. The possibility that it could be applied so aggressively as to erode the socialist nature of the Hungarian economy also exists and has spawned some cynical political humor. Yet, from the standpoint of creating a viable market economy, the key ingredients of price flexibility and competition are still missing, for the most part, and state management of interenterprise exchange continues. Hungary is now halfway between command and market and is reaping some of the worst results of both worlds. Growth is stagnant; resources are still misallocated and underutilized; inflation and the convertible currency debt are rising; terms of trade with the rest of the world are deteriorating, and it risks losing its favorable credit rating in the West.

Like previous reforms, the New Direction represents a quest for efficiency, but it also redistributes or threatens to redistribute income, authority, job and career prospects, etc., and, in the process, to create winners and losers. Many of the latter are government officials and enterprise managers with power in the Hungarian Socialist Workers' party, as well as blue-collar workers in inefficient heavy industrial firms, while the former are often outside the party and vulnerable to attack on ideological grounds. As a counterweight, it is necessary to promote the growth of a body of managers and officials within the party who can prosper in a market environment with Japanese or Western-style planning and who therefore have a vested interest in decentralization. Among young professionals in Hungary, the proportion who want to become managers and entrepreneurs has been growing. In addition, a change of political leadership in 1988 has increased HSWP's willingness to push ahead with reform, at least in the party's upper echelons. It replaced Janos Kadar as General Secretary of HSWP.

Kadar had come to power following the 1956 uprising.

Part of the problem is the reduced potential for extensive growth, but the external environment for the smaller East European countries has also grown harsher since the first energy crisis than it was in the two decades prior to 1973. The need to expand export market shares or halt economic growth for want of imports—the very dilemma which the strategy of import substitution over 1950–73 was designed to avoid—is now more compelling than ever. These economies are more dependent on imports than they were in the early 1950s, and quality demands on exports to both Eastern and Western markets are greater. The days when it was possible to combine high rates of growth with widespread job and income security, low inflation, low business risk, and moderate income differentiation are probably gone forever. This is why the long-run prospects for marketization in Hungary, Poland, and perhaps elsewhere in Eastern Europe are good, but there are still three basic constraints which must be overcome. These are the job and egalitarian constraints and the political constraint on reorienting foreign trade and payments too much toward the West or in straying too far from traditional command-economy practices. In addition, there is a small-economy constraint that prevents these countries from achieving self-sufficiency at acceptable cost, and we have seen that Hungary is the most trade-dependent nation among them.

The political constraint has eroded, but still tends to mandate import substitution and strict controls over imports, as well as protection of domestic industry and efforts to be overly self-sufficient. For Hungary, it also limits specialization according to comparative advantage (which lies in agriculture and light industry) and restricts integration into the international division of labor. It has produced a wide range and variety of industrial products, in many of which it enjoys no comparative advantage, and is unable to realize scale economies, which would require larger export markets. The organizational structure of its large enterprises is partly the consequence of industrial concentration in combination with efforts to build self-sufficiency, which tend to raise the variety of products turned out by each firm.

The job and egalitarian constraints are the main reasons for preserving much of the remaining excess demand, as well as state control over the allocation of scarce inputs at low prices. These protect the jobs of workers and managers, especially in large enterprises with good political ties. But they also remove much of the incentive for firms to produce in a cost-effective manner, to take risks, to respond to shifts in demand, and to seek export markets. The egalitarian constraint makes it hard to use profit or profit-based bonuses as a motivating force. To do so would require more income differentiation on this basis than has been socially or politically acceptable.[18] The government and HSWP have also had to guard against creating too much political opposition to reform. This has limited job loss and demotion of managers unable to shed their dependence on the planning hierarchy.[19] Passage out of the state-managed sector into the one oriented toward the market can be traumatic, not only because of the paternalistic, protective nature of state control, but also because the success indicators change dramatically. A model firm can quickly become a failure, as is illustrated by the following account:

> The agricultural cooperative Aranykalasz of Rackeve . . . each year in 1977–80 received the Grand Prix of the Ministry of Agriculture and Food, before going bankrupt in mid-1982, and the construction company, TANEP of Heves County, whose bankruptcy is also illustrated by the prosecution of its corrupt managers, received awards of the regional offices and of the ministry of Construction and City Development on ten occasions, the last in the year of its bankruptcy.[20]

The state has tried not only to avoid open unemployment, but also to provide a measure of traditional socialist protection against loss of specific jobs in specific factories. This is made more necessary by Hungary's lack of infrastructure—in the form of job placement and worker retraining facilities—for recycling displaced employees, and by the absence of comprehensive unemployment insurance. In Western Europe, a large part of the motivation for these institutions has been exposure of the domestic economy to shifts in demand and supply on world markets. Domestic political pressures have forced Western governments to cushion the impact of these shifts on domestic labor, and the government budget has borne the burden of this. In Hungary, as in other socialist economies, the budget bears this burden indirectly, since any factors that reduce enterprise profits or increase losses tend to reduce budget revenues and to increase state subsidies.

Over the near future, Hungary will continue to be a kind of dual economy, in which larger state enterprises are mainly responsive to directives from above, while much of the rest of the system becomes more privatized and more oriented toward the market. The main hope for further reform and renewed economic growth lies in relative expansion of the market-oriented sector, which is also less subject to regulation and redistribution, and here the 1988 Corporation Law provides a major potential stimulus. As it expands and as the high incomes earned by some of its participants receive growing publicity, political pressures to control it more closely and to tax it more severely are bound to intensify. Nevertheless, the job and egalitarian constraints—which many consider to be the essence of socialism—will ultimately have to loosen, as part of the price for renewed growth in a harsher economic climate, and this process has already begun. Employment guarantees are becoming more general, and the state is starting to shoulder the burden of resulting unemployment and increased need for vocational training. The 1986 Bankruptcy Law institutionalizes unemployment compensation, in the form of Job Search Support, although some firms have avoided paying benefits by laying workers off in groups of nine.

The 1988 political changes replaced no fewer than seven of the eleven HSWP Politburo members, generally bringing more reform-minded officials to power. In 1989, the party signaled its acceptance of full political democracy (in place of its former insistence on "dictatorship of the proletariat") by dropping "Workers" from its name. Yet, there is still lack of agreement on the nature of the system to which reform should ultimately lead, and because of Hungary's vanguard role, there are no good socialist models for it to follow. Several small capitalist economies, such as the Scandinavian or Benelux nations, are prosperous and highly developed, but also closely integrated into the world economy. Comparative advantage plus the social insurance requirements associated with being open to and deeply involved in world trade play a major role in determining what menu of goods and services these nations produce and how. They exercise far less direct control over imports than does any COMECON country, in addition to which their currencies are all convertible. Japan has sometimes looked like a model for Eastern Europe, partly because of its tighter constraints on imports, but the internal Japanese market is also fifteen to twenty times as large as Hungary's. This allows efficient enterprise size to go hand-in-hand with competition between domestic producers in supplying the home market. Moreover, Japanese firms routinely use this as a proving ground on which to gain the scale and experience economies and the proficiency they will need to compete abroad.

Traditional Marxist-Leninists viewed socialist planning as an instrument for loosening constraints on economic development, allowing mankind to take control of its destiny within an egalitarian environment. Being forced to specialize according to comparative advantage appears to be at odds with this aspiration (even though nations do shape and profit from their evolving comparative advantages to varying degrees). The energy crises shattered the traditional vision—although not entirely its egalitarian values—and clarified the costs of defying comparative advantage. The search for a replacement continues.

9-3. The Chinese Economy after Mao

> We are trying a number of experiments. Those that work, we will call socialism. Those that don't we will call capitalism.
>
> —An official of Yunnan Province

> Ten young people were given the honorary title, "entrepreneur," at a recent national meeting in Beijing to congratulate 100 young business directors and managers. The business leaders, all between the ages of 28 and 37, were elected from nine provinces and cities.
>
> —*Beijing Review*, March 4, 1985

> Recently, a departmental head of the manufacturing subsidiary, VW Shanghai, was wanted for a meeting. He was nowhere to be found. After a desperate search, he was discovered on the factory floor—sweeping it. A West German technician asked, with astonishment, what the man was doing. The reply was that the party leadership required him to do manual labor regularly, so as not to lose touch with the working class.
>
> —*Hannoversche Allgemeine*, April 10, 1985

With the death of Mao Zedong in September 1976, the power of leading Chinese radicals (the Gang of Four) collapsed almost overnight, and most of their followers were subsequently purged from important posts. This set the stage for a more conventional conflict between centralizers and decentralizers. The men who succeeded Mao agreed that material incentives were legitimate means to promote economic development. They were also more willing to import foreign technology, and in this context, have instituted the open door policy. But they disagreed about the priority of heavy industry, and, more generally, over the need to orient economic growth to demand. Thus, they have been at odds over the role that markets should play vs. administrative allocation of goods and resources.

At first, the centralizers under Party Chairman Hua Guofeng sought to reaffirm the Soviet-type economy—a move made easier by recentralization over most of 1970–76—together with rapid growth and priority development of heavy industry. As a result, China quickly ran up large external and internal deficits, in addition to which its rate of saving climbed to over 30 percent of GNP. Since the large capital construction projects being undertaken could not hope to come on stream for several years, this placed a heavy burden on a poverty-stricken people. These projects were of doubtful value, since heavy industry was already producing below capacity, due to shortages of raw materials and electric power. Bottlenecks in the transport system almost immediately grew worse. Yet, in the midst of shortages and breakdowns, many goods of unsaleable quality were piling up in warehouses.[21] China also began switching away from coal toward oil as an energy source, although it did not have the means to achieve further rapid increases in crude-oil production.

Meanwhile, in Sichuan Province, the local party Secretary, Zhao Ziyang, began to decentralize and to loosen administrative controls. After the Cultural Revolution and the turmoil of 1974–76, Sichuan was in desperate straits. Although normally a grain-surplus region, it was forced to import grain from other parts of China, and some families sold their children for grain ration coupons. Under Zhao, the province achieved solid economic gains; between 1977 and 1979, industrial output rose by 81 percent and grain production by 25 percent. Unemployment among young people was greatly reduced, partly by expanding urban cooperatives. The contrast between performance in Sichuan and in other parts of China helped propel Zhao to the leadership. Once the centralizers had lost power, his reforms and others undertaken in Anhui province became a model for the whole country.[22]

Besides decentralization, there was a readjustment of priorities, mainly over 1978–81, in which outputs of light industry, agriculture, services, energy, and transportation were raised relative to those of heavy industry. Thus, ''the output of TV sets increased 10.4-fold; radios and cameras, 3.5-fold; bicycles, sewing machines, wristwatches, and wines more than doubled. Cotton yarn, cloth, woolen fabrics, sugar, leather shoes, and cigarettes each grew between 27 percent and 42 percent. In 1981, 5,000 new light industrial products were trial-produced and more than 70,000 new varieties and patterns were added. . . .''[23] The product assortment of heavy industry also changed to better serve the input needs of light industry and agriculture, and growth rates of heavy and light industry have been about the same since 1981. The investment share of GNP has fallen from its 1978 peak, leaving room for more private consumption.

In agriculture, Zhao's reforms have strengthened private property rights under the rural responsibility system and raised state purchase prices for farm produce. In industry and services, reformers have expanded the market sector of mainly small firms, while trying to increase enterprise autonomy and market links within the state planning network. Since 1978, cooperative and private enterprises have been the main avenues of employment expansion in the cities, and they will continue to play a major role, since state enterprises are over-staffed. About 20 million people were working in 12.3 million small private businesses (with fewer than eight employees) in urban areas as of 1987, and by the end of 1988, there may have been as many as one million "large" private companies (with eight employees or more) employing about 30 million workers, although estimates vary widely. As noted earlier, 20 percent of the labor force was working in rural enterprises in early 1989, most of which were privately or cooperatively owned. Moreover, the state's share of retail sales fell from 90 percent in 1978 to 40 percent in 1986, while the cooperative share rose from 7.4 percent to 36 percent and the private share from 2.5 percent to 24 percent.[24] The cooperative and private share of industrial output expanded from 10 percent in 1970 to 33 percent in 1987. Most of these firms are subject to the market, and even state enterprises are supposed to be governed by market prices after fulfilling their mandatory plans (although in practice, many of them lack this much freedom from state control). By 1989, decentralization had gone furthest in the countryside and made the least progress in state industry. Here, we shall focus mainly on changes outside agriculture and foreign trade or investment. The latter were discussed in chapter 8.

A principal goal of China's reforms is to raise enterprise independence, while reestablishing or strengthening customer-supplier relations between firms. The central government has therefore relinquished some of its authority to determine what to produce and in what quantity and variety, along with part of its control over the distribution of materials, investment funds, and labor. In 1984, the State Council announced a 50 percent cut (from 120 to 60) in the number of industrial products subject to mandatory output targets and a 65 percent decrease (from 29 to 10) in the number of farm and peasant sideline products purchased by the state. In each case, basic means of production or consumption are still included. Centrally-managed distribution now covers just 20 kinds of producer goods vs. 256 over most of the period of Communist rule. Workers have modestly increased powers to choose decision makers within their firms, and efforts have been underway to separate economic management from political administration. The idea is that political criteria should become less important in economic decisions and that contractual relations should more frequently extend across political boundaries.

The name, "contract responsibility system," given to the industrial reforms also implies that the transfer of use and income rights over capital to state firms carries corresponding responsibilities—to be entrepreneurial, to produce in a cost-effective manner, to pay taxes to the state, and to meet contractual obligations. In this context, the management of a state enterprise now negotiates a contract, not only with a customer or supplier, but also with the central, provincial, or local government body which owns the firm. The latter contracts generally cover three to five years and detail the enterprise's responsibility to meet minimum output and profit targets, as well as other mandatory plan commitments. Subject to this obligation, management is supposed to enjoy greater freedom to take decisions that are normally the province of enterprise management in a market economy. At least in form (although to a lesser degree in substance), reforms in rural and urban areas are therefore similar, and workers are also supposed to be hired on contracts with expiration dates, in place of the former lifetime employment ("iron rice bowl") in the state sector.

A national plan will continue to be the centerpiece around which economic activity revolves—in part, to protect party and central government priorities. During the early 1980s, the official view was "that the planned economy plays the leading role and regulation by the market the supplementary role. . . . Only by applying mandatory planning to key products and enterprises can our economy truly be a planned economy." For many products and firms not included in mandatory planning, output targets are to become guidelines which indicate priorities, and the state will try to induce firms to meet them by manipulating prices, credit, taxes, and subsidies, rather than by tying penalties and rewards directly to fulfillment. In addition, "Both mandatory and guidance planning must conform to objective reality [and] constantly study changes in market supply and demand," meaning that plan targets should conform to demand.[25] To encourage cost consciousness, the planners have also sought to replace gross output with net output value as the main index of enterprise plan performance.

Recalling the three categories of producer goods, mandatory planning is now supposed to apply mainly to category I, considered most important, while "guidance" planning applies mainly to categories II and III. The role of the market is supposed to be greatest in III, although in practice, this will depend on the willingness of local governments to relax control. At end-1987, official sources claimed that mandatory planning covered half of total output and would cover only 30 percent by 1991.[26] In terms of day-to-day operations, however, enterprises are likely to be governed more by state plans (and interference by party and government officials) and less by market prices than this implies. In many instances, guidance planning will prove to be more like mandatory planning than the reformers intend.

The fact that mandatory output targets are "negotiated" with enterprises does not necessarily make them different than before. However, they are also supposed to be low enough to allow efficient firms a margin to produce above the plan. Above-plan production must be sold on the market, with no guaranteed state outlet, but potentially at higher prices, and above-quota inputs are also supposed to be purchased at higher, market prices. Thus, production decisions are to be governed by market prices at the margin, although in many firms this is still more aspiration than reality—in part, because a system of rational, market-clearing prices has not yet evolved. If planners set targets that producers can overfulfill and refrain from adjusting these upward as performance improves, and if firms are able to retain part of the profit earned on above-plan production, they will have an incentive to produce on their production-possibility frontiers. One reason for multiyear contracts is to inhibit planning from the achieved level, and in fact the share of output covered by obligatory targets is supposed to fall over time as part of efforts to increase the role of the market. Enterprises are now officially able to keep after-tax profits and to exercise greater control over the use of their depreciation funds. Rates of depreciation have been raised to more realistic levels.

Following experiments, the government introduced a new system of enterprise taxation in 1985, which includes a basic 55 percent tax on targeted profits for most large- and medium-sized state firms. Above-quota profits are taxed more lightly (or not at all), but there are other taxes as well, and each firm's tax obligation is in effect negotiated separately as part of management's contract with the state. Formerly, firms had to pay nearly all profit to the state, which also absorbed most losses. The average share of profits retained by state enterprises rose from 3.7 percent in 1978 to about 25 percent in 1986, although it appears to have fallen again over 1987–88, and tax evasion is widespread. After-tax profits are divided between several funds—including a bonus fund, an investment fund, and an employee welfare fund. Worker delegates are to have a voice in formation and use of the latter.

A major goal of tax reform was to give the state a secure source of revenue consistent with tying rewards to performance at the enterprise level. The government thus hopes to harden budget constraints, or as official sources put it, to end the practice of firms "eating from the big pot of the state [budget]." In this context, firms are now required to borrow most of their outside investment finance with obligation to repay principal and interest. Supply expansion and price reform are supposed to reduce the excess demand for most industrial goods, and as this occurs, the importance of credit control as a lever for implementing state priorities is to grow. The access of light industry to investment funds, energy, and other inputs has been raised, and several thousand inefficient state enterprises have been closed, forced to merge with more viable firms, or required to change their product lines. Laid-off workers continue to receive their wages, which are financed by a "labor insurance" fee, equal to 5–8 percent of each firm's payroll. As direct ties between enterprises become easier to establish, the supply system will hopefully improve, allowing each firm to specialize more completely in its main lines of production.

However, the forces impeding reform in Eastern Europe for over twenty years are also at work in China. A major problem has been an inability of reformers to establish an acceptable market allocation of goods and resources, which allows state management to persist or to regain control. Reforms face strong opposition from enterprise managements, especially of large and politically powerful firms who feel threatened by the wider demands of marketization, and from bureaucrats who are threatened with loss of status and authority. We recall that party secretaries exercise more power in China than in most socialist countries. They have often resisted changes that would make managerial competence more important within the firm or raise the risk and range of responsibilities placed on the enterprise. In addition, a number of successful firms have found control over their retained earnings to be illusory. Party organs have pressured them to buy government bonds (as "their share" of financing the budget deficit) or to "donate" their profits to the state for projects normally financed from taxes. In other cases, higher authorities have dictated how enterprise investment funds would be spent. Within the firm, it has proved difficult to tie bonuses to performance, after years of egalitarian distribution. Efforts to do this have encountered resistance from planning superiors and created friction within the work force.[27] Real wage increases have tended to exceed productivity gains, and often, the main determinants of individual pay and promotion are still seniority and political factors rather than job performance.

In section 5-1, we listed five barriers that reform efforts to raise enterprise autonomy in Soviet-type economies must overcome. These are the unwillingness of state authorities to yield control; the aversion of enterprise managements to greater independence and responsibility; the reluctance to soften full employment or job security guarantees or to harden enterprise budget constraints; the problems associated with price distortions and price increases when controls are loosened; and the tendency to continue setting some plan targets from the achieved level. All five are potential roadblocks to reform in China. In particular, some enterprise managements have been reluctant to take on wider responsibilities or to accept business risk, from which they are largely shielded under command planning by excess demand, absence of competition, cost-plus pricing, and the soft budget constraint. Price restraints have been too weak to stop growing inflation, but they have preserved excess demand, and many Chinese enterprises have complained that inputs they need are unavailable.

In addition, prices are often irrational. For example, Chinese profit-to-cost ratios in the latter 1970s averaged 73 percent in petroleum, 29 percent in industrial machinery, and 0.7 percent in coal mining. These variations did not reflect differences in efficiency, but rather administrative decisions which, in particular, set most raw materials, minerals, and energy prices far too low. Even in 1988 the state price for coal made a ton of it cheaper than a ton of sand and required large state subsidies for coal mines. The opportunity for mines to sell part of their production at higher, market prices is therefore important as an incentive to expand coal output, which now supplies nearly 80 percent of China's energy consumption and again has highest priority in its energy development program.

Thus, while pricing has become a principal focus of the Chinese reforms, China still lacks a system of rational or flexible prices capable of coordinating production and resource allocation.[28] Without flexible prices, the effort to raise enterprise autonomy is doomed (because markets will be unable to allocate goods), and the absence of this key ingredient is the major immediate cause of reform failure in Eastern Europe. But price reform also implies that some prices will increase dramatically. Given the excess demand, price flexibility will generally mean rising prices until approximate supply-demand equilibrium is reached. The result will be dislocations and at least short-term financial hardships for many households and firms. China has had nearly the world's lowest retail food prices, for example, and food price inflation since the reforms began has caused hardship for some families.[29] Generally speaking, open inflation has risen whenever price controls have been relaxed.

Firms and planning jurisdictions, especially in heavy industry, which enjoyed high access to scarce inputs under centralized allocation, but which subsequently have to pay more for these goods and are not fully compensated via price increases for their own products, are strong potential opponents of price reform. These same enterprises are often large and inefficient, but also politically powerful, as indicated by their priority access. Because of this and of reduced living standards for some state employees caused by inflation, the transition to a more decentralized system may never be completed. In China, the reforms have encountered resistance from the planning bureaucracy and from many large firms. Complaints of unauthorized or unjustified price increases have appeared regularly in the press. A number of enterprises have used their greater autonomy plus shortages of goods they produce plus the régime's emphasis on performance-linked bonuses to raise prices and distribute much of the resulting profit to their employees. In some cases, these bonuses have been charged as costs and often end up being paid at least partly by the state, in the form of reduced profits taxes. Thus, over 1978–88, government expenditure fell from 34 percent to around 20 percent of GNP, with the biggest decline occurring in budget grants for investment. But revenue fell even further, from 34 percent to under 19 percent of GNP, with taxes collected on state enterprise profits showing the largest decrease.

We have also seen that reform has led to higher market prices for above-plan production of many goods, which coexist with lower, controlled prices for the same products, when the latter are obtained or delivered within plan quotas and targets. Market prices can be up to eight times as high as controlled prices for the same goods. Firms obtaining supplies at low prices are supposed to use these as productive inputs, but some enterprises have simply resold these goods instead at their higher, market prices. Together with government agencies, enterprise managements have even set up new companies existing only on paper, which were endowed with input quotas. This allowed them to buy low and sell high in such a fashion. Similar arbitrage between the official and second economies went on before the reform, but such acts were less well publicized than they have been recently.

There have been numerous reports of other kinds of corruption related directly or indirectly to continuing shortages of goods, in combination with increased opportunities for trading and the system of dual prices. Decentralization has also increased investment spending, along with the ratio of unfinished to total investment. The country went on a runaway investment boom after a renewed commitment to reform in 1984. This resulted from failure to harden the budget constraint for enterprises or for local bank branches after the new loanable funds market partly replaced the system of investment finance by budget grants. Bank branches expected to be subsidized from the "big pot" of the state, if their loans were not repaid, and there was some expectation that future lending quotas would depend on current loan volumes. Thus, they lent too freely, and demand was high because borrowers also perceived that they would be bailed out in the event of financial difficulties. Since then local bank branches have been under pressure from local officials to finance major investment projects and have often ignored appeals from Beijing to curtail lending. Similarly, decentralization of import decisions caused buyers to plunder China's foreign-exchange reserves, which are underpriced (since the yuan is overvalued).

As a result, several components of the reform are going through cycles of reversal and renewal, and this is especially true of freedom from price controls. China has also established Western-style facilities to train managers to operate in a market environment, and thousands of young Chinese have gone to Western countries to obtain advanced degrees. According to the head of the State Economic Commission, "By the end of 1984, about 80 percent of all state-owned enterprises and commercial units [had come] under the leadership of younger and more competent directors. This greatly improved management."[30] However, many large firms were among the hold-outs.

As indicated above, China is following a dual approach to pricing, reminiscent of Hungary. A few prices are free of direct controls, and the present goal is to expand this sphere until it includes nearly all prices (hopefully by the mid-1990s). Those of basic necessities and key industrial goods (category I) are set centrally and will be the last to be freed. Other prices are set by regional authorities or are flexible within limits that are set by the center in some cases (including industrial goods in category II) and by provinces or local governments in others. Usually, the upper limit then becomes a binding ceiling. Thus, in effect, there are two kinds of prices—"free" or "market" and controlled—and controlled prices may either be fixed by the state or subject to state-set ceilings. In 1987, fixed prices covered just over 40 percent of the total value of industrial plus agricultural output.[31] Even here, however, free prices are supposed to guide above-plan production and resource allocation. As noted, the existence of two prices for many goods is a source of "corruption." Although dual pricing is supposed to be a temporary phenomenon, it is also a means by which the state tries to get the incentive effects of rational, market prices, while partly shielding urban households and state firms from the redistribution effects of price increases. Thus, it may endure for a long time.

Moreover, even "free" prices are subject to downward pressure, in the form of moral suasion and threat of punishment, should producers be found guilty of price gouging. Instead of allowing prices to adjust quickly to equilibrium levels,

China is trying to raise many prices in stages, while expanding supplies of scarce products and using subsidies to maintain the living standards of state employees and pensioners. Such an approach is designed to ease the pain and dislocation of adjustment. Ideally, the sphere of mandatory planning would retreat as prices approached their equilibrium levels, until, finally, prices would guide nearly all production and ration nearly all goods among users. With the role of the market expanded, the government would rely more on the instruments of a mixed economy—taxes, subsidies, public spending, leverage over credit allocation—to achieve its goals, and Japan provides a model for such an approach to planning.

But such a phased approach may never reach its goal or require so much time that it is overtaken by a backlash against reform. If marketization is to succeed, the upward movement of prices must go hand-in-hand with a reduction of inflationary pressure (or excess demand). This requires hardening of the enterprise budget constraint and assumption of business risk by the management of each firm, plus a reduction of excess household and enterprise liquidity. But hardening of budget constraints is proving to be slow and painful, and liquidity was rising, at least through 1987. The subsidies used to cushion the impact of price hikes, to maintain low prices for basic means of consumption and production, and to prop up loss-making enterprises are the major reason for budget deficits, which have been largely financed by money supply increases. The example of Yugoslavia shows that such subsidies can persist over many years and cause severe inflation. In addition, the state has been setting lower tax rates on enterprises producing less profitable goods. This may be equitable, but it reduces the role of profitability and, thus, of prices in determining what goods each firm will produce, thereby increasing the management role of state agencies. Use of taxes and subsidies to insulate firms from profit-and-loss variations has a similar effect. In 1986, about 20 percent of state-run enterprises made losses, subsidized from the budget, and in 1988, such subsidies still came to nearly 3 percent of GNP, suggesting that budget constraints remain on the soft side. Earlier, a top planning official noted that reform was making good progress in only 15 percent of China's key industrial enterprises. About 65 percent were going along as before, and 20 percent were having financial difficulties. In particular, efforts to reduce the role of the party in enterprise management have met strong resistance.

A smoothly functioning market system requires competition, free response of prices to supply and demand, and restraints on money-supply increases to hold down inflation. It also requires producers to respond to changes in prices, so that elastic supply responses will limit price increases or decreases resulting from shifts in demand. Prices (or availabilities of goods) are less volatile when supply curves are more elastic, which makes advance planning by firms and households easier and less error prone. However, basic elements of command planning—notably, targeting from the achieved level and the range of measures that insulate firms and their employees from the financial results of their decisions and work—act to reduce supply elasticities. The adjustment of enterprises to these "rules of the game," and the evolution of managements able to thrive, or at least survive, under them complicates the task of reform and increases the pressure on reformers to use price controls as a substitute for creating the conditions under which prices will be stable naturally. This treats the symptoms, while prolonging the disease.

As of mid-1989, reform progress is mixed, and ultimate success is not guaranteed. Often, practices appear to vary widely from region to region. Tight party and state controls in some areas coexist with much private initiative and loose government restrictions on economic activity elsewhere. Many firms are now more subject to the market and less constrained by central controls than before 1980. In this context, China's efforts to decentralize have several potential advantages over those in Eastern Europe. For one, China has carefully studied East European experience, and is in a position to learn from mistakes made there, but not in a position to be restrained by the Soviet Union, should that country's present reform-minded leadership be replaced. For another, many of China's top leaders have been firmly committed to reform, although this may no longer be true after the events of May and June 1989, which caused many reformers (including Zhao) to be purged, and which are likely to prove a setback to reform as well as to the open door policy. The reformers understand the need for flexible pricing, enterprise autonomy, and improved management. They are prepared to stop protecting backward enterprises and even to allow them to go bankrupt when they are persistently unable to cover their costs. However, "bankruptcy" has increasingly meant replacing existing management and/or merging the loss-making firm with a viable partner, rather than closing an enterprise and liquidating its assets. The latter has been quite rare in the state sector since the early 1980s.[32]

Moreover, as long as irrational prices, supply deficiencies, excessive labor costs, and other command-economy hold-overs continue to influence enterprise profitability, it will be hard to isolate the effect of management on the bottom line. Thus, it will be hard to punish and reward managers on the basis of enterprise profits and losses, and many excuses for poor performance will be available. One such hold-over, even among reform-minded officials, is an intervention mentality common to countries ruled by communist parties and with deep roots in Communist ideology. Thus, a cotton mill in Zhengzhou recently built a fifteen-story hotel with its retained earnings, instead of using them to upgrade its technology and product quality, which were considered poor. The mill's managers were held up to the nation as an example of "unhealthy tendencies" due to the reform.[33] Yet, construction of the hotel may have represented an efficient use of investment funds. Success of the reform requires that firms be free to take up new, profitable lines of production, regardless of whether this conforms to central plans or intentions.

A third potential advantage is the rapid economic growth that has so far accompanied the reforms and for which the reforms themselves are partly responsible, especially in agriculture. China fulfilled its Sixth Five-Year Plan (1981–85) more than a year ahead of schedule. This contrasts with the growth slowdown in the USSR and Eastern Europe, and in some cases the resulting supply increases have reduced demand pressure on prices. Unfortunately, rapidly rising excess liquidity is an offsetting danger signal, as are bottlenecks in transportation, energy, and some raw materials. Eventually, the overriding goal of quadrupling 1980 material output by 2000 could lead to ambitious mandatory targets that worsen shortages and intensify pressures for recentralization, along lines familiar from Eastern Europe. (Up to 1989, however, growth has been faster than necessary to reach this goal.) The size of China's economy is a fourth advantage. Regional diversity makes it harder to roll back reform progress throughout the country. Some regions will remain relatively advanced in terms of the reform, and if they become more prosperous in consequence, they can always serve later on as a model for the rest of the country to emulate.

Moreover, even regional markets are potentially large enough to accommodate several firms of efficient size in each industry and, thus, to permit effective competition. In this context, the reforms have included horizontal and vertical mergers of enterprises designed to improve the supply system, increase product specialization, and realize scale economies. One result may also be to increase monopoly power, but it seems more likely that the effect will be to strengthen competition by creating more viable firms and leapfrogging political boundaries, which have been segregating markets and sustaining uneconomic duplication of production facilities. Effective competition requires firms to invade each other's markets whenever it is profitable to do so—a major part of the elastic supply response referred to earlier—but bureaucratic control at all levels poses a formidable barrier to this kind of expansion. Like their counterparts in other socialist countries, Chinese bureaucrats have shown ingenuity in hanging onto their leverage over enterprise output profiles, and redistribution through the tax-subsidy system has given them some reinforcement.

To get around bureaucratic approval procedures, a 1980 article in the *People's Daily*, the party newspaper, suggested that firms sell shares of equity and invest the proceeds in new production facilities. It continued:

> In general, we can completely adopt the capitalist countries' method of issuing stock. This would help break through the bureaucracy's suffocation of economic advance and help to change the unreasonable distribution of industry in some cities. It would also help to develop new technology and products, help to achieve full utilization of each person's talents and each material's potential, and help to concentrate now dispersed funds for use in areas of most pressing need. It would [also] help to solve youth unemployment problems.

The author acknowledged that the "issuance of stock in a socialist country could encounter many problems."

While the article was a trial balloon, stock markets of a sort did begin to appear in 1986. Buyers of shares receive claims on the profits of the firms in which they invest, but most share prices remain fixed, and shares may not be resold to third parties. (Most of the buyers appear to be employees of the enterprises whose shares they purchase.) Where large firms are concerned, moreover, the state and/or the enterprise itself (in the name of its employees) will retain the vast majority of shares. Without secondary markets, people cannot make money speculating in share prices—or so official thinking goes—which, according to Marxian theory, would constitute unearned income, deducted from labor's rightful reward. Primary stock markets are a means of channelling investment resources to firms less subject to control through the planning bureaucracy and more responsive to demand and cost pressures than are most Chinese enterprises. Such means are crucial to success of the reforms. However, firms issuing shares may prefer to have secondary markets, since these would probably lead to higher demand for shares and, thus, to higher share prices. (Rumors suggest, moreover, that such markets have already become part of the second economy.)

Many small firms, especially in supply and services, are being sold to private individuals or small groups, while other small- and mid-sized factories, repair shops, and workshops are being leased by the state, under the constraint that lessees may not reduce the value of the company's assets. In each case, buyers or lessees must operate the enterprise themselves. A major goal is to get managers and workers to take responsibility for company performance, as if they were the owners. For radicals, bureaucratization and individualism were the twin paramount evils. China's reformers can get just as incensed about bureaucratic suppression of initiative, although they seek more room for individual, as opposed to collective initiative.

And yet, long-term survival of bureaucratic control over industry and even agriculture cannot be ruled out. Should the reform faction lose power (as may already have happened), the new régime would have its power base in the state bureaucracy, the PLA, and surviving radical elements. Almost half the present party members joined during the Cultural Revolution, and most of these are probably not enthusiastic reform supporters. Many are career ideologues. Such a government would retain as few reform measures as it could get away with. Since radical-style decentralization has proved unworkable, its only viable option would be a strengthening of command planning. As this would not be an adequate vehicle for realizing the four modernizations, however, it would only be a question of time before agitation for reform begins again.

Ultimately, the political prerequisite for successful decentralization is a basic change in the nature of the Communist party. In the future, it will have to co-opt the best managers, engineers, skilled workers, and peasants, and these people must come to constitute its most powerful internal group. Instead of awarding managerial posts as prizes for being good party members, it will have to give party memberships, promotions, and recognition as rewards for successful management. Managerial labor, within a market environment and taking responsibility for profits and losses, will have to rise in esteem and political status, relative to administrative labor, allocating goods and resources in an environment of excess demand. Such a transformation may well be possible, while preserving some of the "redness" that has been historically prized, as well as the order and discipline valued by conservative party elements. But neither should we underestimate the magnitude of the change required in an organization whose roots are antibourgeois, anti-intellectual, fervently revolutionary, deeply ideological, and most of whose members have historically come from the poorest segments of society.

Notes

1. Zdenek Srein, "Principal Goals of the Present Economic Reform in Czechoslovakia," paper delivered at Carleton University, Institute of Soviet and East European Studies, Ottawa, Canada, February 15, 1968, pp. 7–9.

2. Tamas Bauer, "The Contradictory Position of the Enterprise Under the New Hungarian Economic Mechanism," *Eastern European Economics*, Fall 1976, p. 5.

3. Annamaria Inzelt, "Disappearing Companies, Lost Functions (in Hungarian)," *Valosag*, No. 9, 1985, abstracted in *New Hungarian Quarterly*, Autumn 1986, pp. 176–77.

4. J. Timar, "Employment Policy and Labour Economy in Hungary," *Acta Oeconomica* 17, 2, 1976, p. 134n.

5. On "storming" in Hungary, see M. Laki, "End-Year Rush Work In Hungarian Industry and Foreign Trade," *Acta Oeconomica* 25, 1–2, 1980.

6. T. Laky, "The Hidden Mechanisms of Recentralization in Hungary," *Acta Oeconomica* 24, 1–2, 1980, p. 106.

7. Prices were divided into four categories—those that were "free," those subject to ceilings, those subject to floors and ceilings (although only the latter mattered), and those that were fixed. Where retail trade was concerned, most necessities had fixed prices—to protect lower-income families from price increases—whereas luxuries were more likely to have free prices. In practice, there was little difference between the last three categories, and even free prices tended to be rigid. Today, most prices are free, as indicated below. See Tamas Morva, "Planning in Hungary," in Morris Bornstein, ed., *Economic Planning: East and West* (Cambridge, Mass.: Ballinger, 1975), pp. 281–94 and David Granick, *Enterprise Guidance in Eastern Europe* (Princeton: Princeton University Press, 1975), pp. 257–70, as well as Marton Tardos, "The Role of Money: Economic Relations between the State and the Enterprises in Hungary," *Acta Oeconomica* 25, 1–2, 1980.

8. Within a normal socialist pricing structure, turnover taxes are highest on luxuries and lowest on necessities. The most basic necessities are subsidized. Generally, producer goods prices are lower, relative to average costs, than are consumer goods prices, and a special effort is made to keep down prices of basic raw materials and industrial goods. Regarding the Hungarian price reform, see Bela Csikos-Nagy, "The Hungarian Price Reform," *New Hungarian Quarterly*, Winter 1979. Regarding the recalculated consumer price index mentioned below, see Thad Alton et al., "Official and Alternative Consumer Price Indexes in Eastern Europe, Selected Years, 1960–80," Research Project on National Income in East-Central Europe, occasional paper no. OP-68, New York, June 1981.

9. In chapter 5, we saw that the number of firms in state industry reached a low of 699 in 1980 and rose to 1,043 at end-1987. The number of industrial cooperatives increased from 661 to 1,392 during the same interval. (The latter figure excludes "new-type economic units" set up after a January 1982 change of regulations made it easier to start small private firms and cooperatives, which still produce a tiny fraction of industrial output.) See Laszlo Csaba, "New Features of the Hungarian Economic Mechanism of the Mid-Eighties," *The New Hungarian Quarterly*, Summer 1983, pp. 58–60, along with G. Varga, "Enterprise Size Pattern in the Hungarian Industry," *Acta Oeconomica* 29, 3, 1978, and E. Szalai, "The New Stage of the Reform Process in Hungary and the Large Enterprises," *Acta Oeconomica* 29,

1–2, 1982. Finally, see Z. Roman, "The Conditions of Market Competition in the Hungarian Industry," *Acta Oeconomica* 34, 1–2, 1985.

10. J. C. Kramer and J. T. Danylyk, "Economic Reform in Eastern Europe: Hungary at the Forefront," in U.S. Congress, Joint Economic Committee, *East European Economic Assessment*, Part I (Washington, D.C.: U.S. Government Printing Office, 1981), p. 560.

11. In 1975, COMECON changed from pricing goods at world-market prices of a previous year, with revisions every five years, to pricing them at averages of world-market prices over the previous five years, with revisions every year. For 10–15 percent of her imported oil, Hungary had to pay world market prices during the 1970s and early 1980s, when COMECON prices were lower.

12. See Thad Alton et al. "Economic Growth in Eastern Europe, 1970 and 1975–86," Research Project on National Income in East Central Europe, Occasional Paper No. 95, Table 15, p. 23, July 1987.

13. To date, most of Hungary's cooperation agreements have been short-term, and over one third have been with West German firms. Thus, most have expired, and Hungary wants to increase the number of long-term, large-scale agreements.

14. After noting that Soviet oil exports to Eastern Europe would probably decline, Robert Campbell pointed out a decade ago that "the USSR's position as a supplier of gas; nuclear plant, fuel, and reprocessing; and electric power may be in the process of becoming an adequate substitute for control of oil supply" in maintaining economic control over the region. See Robert Campbell, "Implications for the Soviet Economy of Soviet Energy Prospects," *ACES Bulletin*, Spring 1978, quote, p. 48.

15. Szalai, "The New Stage of the Reform Process," p. 41.

16. Csaba, "New Features of the Hungarian Economic Mechanism," pp. 51–52.

17. Ibid., p. 52.

18. However, this may really be part of the political constraint mentioned above. That is, the root of such an objection may be fear of the bureaucratic élite—whose status depends on differentiation of incomes and access to goods according to hierarchical rank—of being displaced by a new "bourgeois" élite.

19. In 1978, a Hungarian official wrote that no manager had been dismissed "merely for profitability problems, if he has fulfilled other tasks well." Partly, this is because enterprise profitability depends on central as well as managerial decisions. See K. A. Soos, "Some General Problems of the Hungarian Investment System," *Eastern European Economics*, Fall 1980.

20. Csaba, "New Features of the Hungarian Economic Mechanism," p. 51.

21. Zhou Zhiying, "The Economy: Successes in 1980, Targets for 1981," *China Reconstructs*, December 1980, p. 12. Zhou implies that the official growth rates of industrial output of 14.3 percent and 13.5 percent, respectively, for 1977 and 1978 were inflated. Regarding the discussion below, see, as well, Bian Fa, "Reform—China's Second Revolution," *China Reconstructs*, October 1987.

22. However, it was by no means the only one, especially since China had already experimented with decentralization during the Great Leap Forward (1958–61) and subsequent Liu Shaoqi era (1961–66).

23. Zhang Zhongji, "Economic Re-adjustment: Results Since 1979," *Beijing Review*, August 30, 1982.

24. See "Rural Enterprises in China: Too Many, Too Soon?" *China News Analysis*, no. 1380, March 1, 1989. "The Privately-Run Enterprises," *China News Analysis*, no. 1382, April 1, 1989. Gao Shangquan, "Progress in Economic Reform (1979–86)," *Beijing Review*, July 6, 1987.

25. "Renmin Ribao" Commentator, "Institute an Economic Planning System Better Suited to China's Conditions," *Beijing Review*, October 11, 1982, pp. 21, 23, 26. This article was probably by a top political leader or economic expert.

26. See *Beijing Review*, November 15, 1987, pp. 10–11. Regarding the paragraph to follow, see Zhou Yongkang, "Developing a Responsibility System in Industry," *China Reconstructs*, September 1982.

27. Firms have also tried to award bonuses that authorities considered to be too high. This has led to limits on enterprise bonus funds, which reduce pay differentials between firms based on comparative profitability. Regarding this and enterprise disposal of profits, see Jan S. Prybyla, "Some Questions Concerning Price Reform in the People's Republic of China," Pennsylvania State University, Department of Economics, Working Paper no. 9–87–16, September 1987, and "Reassessing the Tax Reform," *China News Analysis*, no. 1352, January 15, 1988.

28. See Tian Jiyun, "Price System Due for Reform," *Beijing Review*, January 29, 1985, and Dong Shaohua, "On Re-Structuring the National Economy—II," *China Reconstructs*, May 1985. When these articles were written, Tian and Dong were, respectively, Vice-Premier of the State Council and Director of the Investigation and Research Office of the State Economic Commission. Finally, see Qian Jiaju, "Why China Needs Price Reforms," *China Reconstructs*, October 1988.

29. See Guo Zhongyi, "Combatting Price Rises," *China Reconstructs*, May 1988. Between July 1987 and July 1988, official consumer price inflation in urban areas was 24 percent, more than double the average pay increase for state employees. Official statistics probably understate both increases, and food prices may even have doubled during this period. Sample surveys have indicated that some urban households are finding it nearly impossible to make ends meet. However, over 87 percent of respondents to a survey in early 1988 said that their living standards were unaffected by recent price rises. If recorded prices are moving toward market equilibrium levels, the discussion in part E-1 of section 1-1 indicates that living standards of many urban dwellers may even be improving, since demand prices would be rising more slowly than recorded prices. See Economist Intelligence Unit, *Country Reports: China*, No. 3, 1988 (London: Economist Intelligence Unit, July 1988), p. 8.

30. Lu Dong, "Reforms Invigorate 1984 Economy," *Beijing Review*, March 11, 1985.

31. See Liu Guoguang, "Price Reform Essential to Growth," *Beijing Review*, August 18, 1986, and Guo Zhongyi, "Price Reform and Peoples' Lives," *China Reconstructs*, January 1988.

32. See Yan Kalin, "How to Deal with Losing Enterprises," *Beijing Review*, March 11, 1985, and Gao Yangliu, "Signs of Capitalism in China? The Shenyang Experiment," *China Reconstructs*, March 1987.

33. Wu Naito, "Delegates Assail Unhealthy Tendencies," *Beijing Review*, April 15, 1985, p. 23.

Questions for Review, Discussion, Examination

*1. In the idealized version of reform, the incomes of enterprises become fully dependent on their financial success. What feature of a Soviet-type economy would this most directly negate? If financial success is to be a reasonably good measure of efficiency, what does this presuppose about pricing and competition?

Given Hungary's small domestic market, does this suggest that a choice might have to be made between limiting reform in some sectors and drastically changing national priorities, as well as the organization and conduct of foreign trade? Which sectors are most likely to require continuing protection in some form? Discuss.

2. Discuss the reform implications for labor market policy in Hungary and other socialist countries, in the event that a genuine socialist market economy emerges.

3. How did reform alter the allocation of producer goods in Hungary after 1968? Have producer goods prices become flexible?

4. Is Hungary's industrial structure competitive or concentrated? Why do you suppose this is? In particular, how easy is it for firms to take up new lines of production where excess profits can be earned? (Does this depend on the type of enterprise?)

Is there room to increase competition in Hungary without thwarting the realization of scale economies?

5. Why did the energy crisis hit Hungary especially hard, causing a 20 percent deterioration in her terms of trade with other nations and a large increase in her foreign debt? Why did it initially help to recentralize investment decision making?

6. What was responsible for the "New Direction" of 1979? Briefly, what measures are included in the New Direction?

Do you believe it really constitutes a new beginning or is a major reversal of reform again likely (as over 1972–78)? On what crucial factors does reform success hinge, in your view?

7. Why does persistence of the soft budget constraint threaten the banking reforms in both Hungary and China?

*8. Suppose you are an economic advisor to the Hungarian government. Assume that you will have the backing of the USSR for whatever proposals you make and that you also enjoy the luxury of being able to ignore ideological constraints. Bearing in mind that Hungary is a small country without a diversity of natural resources and with a comparative advantage in agriculture and light industry, what type of economic system would you recommend? Would you select a market economy, a Soviet-type economy, or a mixture of the two? In the latter event, what kind of mix would you select? Also say something about labor market policy, nature of and control over enterprise management, and the handling and finance of investment.

9. Basically, why did efforts to reaffirm the Soviet-type economy over 1976–78 lead to a shift of power toward the reformers in China?

10. Why is the Chinese reform referred to as a "responsibility" system?

How do reform goals reflect Zhao's view that socialism has just three requirements: public ownership of most of the material means of production; payment according to labor input, and some form of central planning?

11. Why is there considerable opposition to reform in China within many large firms, as well as in the planning bureaucracy?

*12. Why are supply elasticities in a Soviet-type economy apt to be low? What difficulties does this pose for efforts to reform (or to introduce genuine markets into) such a system?

*13. A problem with reforms in China, as in other Soviet-type economies, has been the rigidity of prices.

(a) Explain why planners are reluctant to free up prices when a reform begins. Why does successful decentralization tend to require that prices be flexible?

(b) Explain how past experience with command (or administrative) planning acts to increase the perceived cost of price flexibility to the planners.

(c) Over the long run, how must the nature of the Communist party change to accommodate successful decentralization of the command economy, to the point where most firms are subject to a competitive market environment?

*14. Between July 1987 and July 1988, consumer prices rose more rapidly than incomes of state employees in China. Using the argument in section 1-1, part E-1, show why this would not automatically cause the living standard of a "typical" state employee to fall, despite the apparent fall in his or her real earnings. (*Hint*: Suppose consumer prices generally moved closer to their market equilibrium levels. Did demand prices of urban consumers rise as rapidly as recorded prices? Of what significance is this?)

15. What advantages do China's efforts to reform have over those in Hungary and other East European nations?

16. Why has China launched stock (equity) markets of a sort? What is the socialism-preserving feature of this reform? Do you expect this feature to survive or to disappear over the long run? Why?

* = more difficult.

10

THE YUGOSLAV ECONOMY
AND WORKERS'
SELF-MANAGEMENT

This does not mean that we place the role of the Communist party of the Soviet Union and the social system of the USSR in the background. On the contrary, we study the Soviet system and take it as an example, but we are developing socialism in our country in somewhat different forms.

—J. B. Tito, April 1948
(replying to Cominform expulsion of Yugoslavia)

10-1. Introduction: The Nationalities Question and Regional Income Distribution

In 1946, Yugoslavia became the second country after the Soviet Union to establish a command economy. By this time, the League of Communists under Marshall Tito was firmly in power, after leading a legendary wartime resistance against the Nazis, and the Yugoslav system was closely patterned after the Soviet model. But while Tito was anxious to adopt Communist ideals and to imitate Stalin's economic and political organization, he insisted on Yugoslavia's independence as a nation. This infuriated Stalin, who expelled Yugoslavia from the East European bloc of nations, or Cominform, in 1948. Subsequently, Tito decided to pursue a separate road to socialism, and he dismantled much of Yugoslavia's command economy during the early 1950s. Greater autonomy passed to firms, which began to be managed, at least in principle, by elected representatives of their employees. Producers and users of goods were also allowed to establish direct ties through the market.

Thus, Yugoslavia became the first socialist market economy—and, to date, the only one—with the added dimension of workers' self-management. Over 1953–64,

Yugoslavia had a mixed or market-planned economy, in which the federal govern-ment played a dominant role in allocating investment resources. However, regional and ethnic diversity within the country bolstered forces working toward further decentralization. This drive culminated in the 1965 reforms, which strengthened the role of the market, but weakened those of the federal government and the League of Communists. By 1972, it was clear that these reforms had helped to break the system into regional blocs without adequate coordination or integration for the country as a whole. They also raised unemployment and inequality, helped to spark ethnic tensions, and led to a mass emigration of Yugoslavs, who became "guest workers" in Western countries. Yet, growth over 1965–71 was slightly lower than in the period before 1965. Thus, from 1972, efforts were made to rebuild economy-wide planning and to restrengthen the party's role. A new constitution was adopted in 1974, and the 1976 Law on Social Planning asserts that the market is just a transitional means of coordinating economic activity.

It now appears that the transition will be a long one. The reforms of the 1970s generally reduced efficiency, and the energy crises dealt Yugoslavia a double blow. First, they exposed a strategy of economic development that defied comparative advantage—as in several other East European economies—and that required large imports of energy, raw materials, and sophisticated machinery and machine tools. Yet, the industries being promoted lacked the export potential to pay for their import requirements, even before the first explosion of oil prices in 1973–74. Second, Yugoslavia has covered an almost continuous trade deficit since World War II from aid and, after 1965, from remittances (portions of their paychecks) which Yugoslav workers in Western Europe send home, as well as from tourism and other invisible receipts. By the latter 1970s, aid was down in real terms from earlier levels, and Yugoslav employment in Western Europe was falling, as the energy crisis had slowed economic expansion there. Yugoslavia's foreign debt soared during this period, in part because the federal government was unable to adequately restrain borrowing by regional (or republic-level) governments. Finally, the federation was forced to curtail imports, and this nearly brought economic growth to a halt after 1979.

The 1980s have witnessed a return to the spirit of the 1965 reforms, although with a growing willingness to transfer powers from regional governments to the federal level. These reforms had sought to stress efficiency and cost effectiveness within a decentralized environment. From one perspective, the rest of the socialist world has come around to Yugoslavia's way of thinking. In the early 1950s, the label, "Titoist," usually meant death or imprisonment in most of Eastern Europe, but recent reforms or reform proposals in Hungary, Poland, China, and even the USSR would strengthen the role of market relations and give employees more power over enterprise management, in line with the basic self-management model. However, a closer look at Yugoslavia's economy reveals that it also needs an overhaul to remain viable and growing—not least because it has yet to develop sufficient financial discipline at the enterprise level.

As a rule, while the League of Communists is able to impose its industrial priorities on the economy, it has been unable to bring about an efficient specialization and cooperation between different regions, a problem that has bedeviled Yugoslavia from the first day of its existence. Regional diversity is also ethnic, cultural, and linguistic diversity, and there are large gaps in living standards between regions. Aside from this Yugoslav-specific dilemma, the country suffers from Western-type problems of inflation and lack of jobs, as well as Eastern-type problems of chronic subsidies to inefficient firms (the soft or elastic budget constraint), plus difficulties in generating intensive growth and Western markets for exports. The two kinds of problems are related, since subsidies are often financed by money creation, which leads to inflation. Among the root causes of these troubles are a politicization of economic decisions, especially investment choices, as well as a "socialist" reluctance to tie earnings too closely to financial performance and an unwillingness to accept business risk, which is partly built into Yugoslav-style self-management.

In practice, the power of worker representatives in Yugoslav firms is greatest in areas of traditional blue-collar concern—namely, in matters related to working conditions, job security, wages and benefits, and hiring. Most power over investment and other "business" decisions is shared between the League of Communists, local and regional governments, and professional managers and technocrats. Since the early 1970s, party and government bodies have generally had the upper hand, although the growth slowdown, declining real incomes, and balance-of-payments pressures of the 1980s are restrengthening the position of professionals. Yugoslavia's industrial priorities have been the same as those of other socialist nations, with whom it shares a common ideological heritage. Like them, it has subsidized the growth of heavy industries, without being particular about their efficiency. Like them, it has weakened the link between performance and reward in state-owned enterprises. The most heavily subsidized industries have also been the most capital intensive—which have relatively low capacities to absorb labor, for any given investment—and subsidies have gone mainly to reduce the cost of capital, which makes recipient firms more capital intensive still. Because enterprises in the socialist sector have been unwilling to hire all job seekers, Yugoslavia now has significant unemployment plus around 650,000 guest workers (as of 1988) in Western countries. Because subsidies to support wage-employment guarantees plus enterprise solvency and liquidity have been rising since the mid-1970s, inflation has shot up as well. Between April 1988 and April 1989, the official cost of living index rose by more than 340 percent. On average, consumer prices were already over 55 times as high in April 1988 as in mid-1980. Unofficially, inflation has been even greater.

Geographically, Yugoslavia lies in the Balkan region of southeastern Europe, astride the historical boundary between the "crescent and the cross," or between the Turkish Ottoman Empire and predominantly Christian Europe. Thus, the inhabitants of Yugoslavia descend from peoples who have witnessed and battled countless invaders and been subjected to many foreign rulers, including Turks, Austrians, Huns, French, Italians, and Venetians. Prior to December 1918, Yugoslavia did not exist as a nation, and when formed, it was a patchwork quilt of eight major and numerous smaller ethnic groups or "nationalities" inhabiting six constituent republics. Journeying from north to south, we first encounter the Slovenes, who are the most prosperous of the southern Slav peoples. In terms of income per capita (Table 10.1), they are followed by the Croatians to the southeast, along with Vojvodina, an autonomous region within the republic of Serbia. Magyars or Hungarians are the ethnic group native to this region, but they now comprise just 19 percent of its population, 55 percent of which are Serbs. Just south of Vojvodina, Serbia proper has generally enjoyed a level of per capita income and output about the same as that of Yugoslavia as a whole.[1] Immediately west of Serbia (and southeast of Croatia), Bosnia-Herzegovina is the most ethnically mixed Yugoslav republic, as well as one with a significantly lower per capita income than the national average. Bosnian Moslems are the ethnic group most unique to this republic, constituting 40 percent of its population, which is also 32 percent Serb and 18 percent Croat.

To the south of Bosnia-Herzegovina, Montenegro is the smallest republic in area and population—and also the poorest, although it has achieved the most rapid per capita growth since World War II. Just east of Montenegro (and south of Serbia proper) lies Kosovo-Metohija, a province or autonomous region within the republic of Serbia. Kosmet is the poorest and most densely populated area in the country and also the one with the highest population growth rate. It borders on Albania, and Albanians are by far the dominant ethnic group. Finally, to the south of Kosmet lies Macedonia, the land of Alexander the Great, and another developing republic, where the influence of the Turkish Ottoman Empire made its deepest cultural penetration.

Each nationality above has its own national history. In partial recognition of its cultural diversity, the new nation formed in 1918 was originally called the Kingdom of Serbs, Croats, and Slovenes, the name being changed to Yugoslavia (Land of the South Slavs) in 1929. Ethnic diversity is also divergence in terms of economic development, as Table 10.1 bears out, and regional income inequality in Yugoslavia is greater than in the USSR, Canada, or virtually any other country. It has also increased over the past 30 years, and the poorer regions have been gaining population, relative to the country as a whole. Regional inequality makes the overall distribution of income in Yugoslavia less equal than in most socialist and probably than in most capitalist nations as well.

Regional income differences predate 1918 and reflect a division of Yugloslavia's territory along a north-south axis for most of the five centuries prior to World War I. The northern republics of Slovenia and Croatia, along with Vojvodina, were long part of the Austro-Hungarian Empire and, thus, subject to European culture and influence. They were relatively free of warfare, and by mid-nineteenth century, economic development was fairly brisk. Both Slovenia

Table 10.1

Index Numbers of Regional Income Per Head for Yugoslavia, Compared with Canada
(in percentages and thousands)

A. *Yugoslavia (social product per head) (countrywide average = 100)*

Republic or Autonomous Region	1947	1953	1979	1986	Population (mid-1986)
Kosmet	58	53	31	30	1,804
Bosnia-Herzegovina	72	79	70	72	4,356
Macedonia	71	69	68	66	2,041
Montenegro	43	58	64	78	619
Serbia Proper	100	91	96	94	5,803
Vojvodina	125	96	120	121	2,049
Croatia	105	111	125	123	4,665
Slovenia	157	182	200	211	1,934
All Yugoslavia	100	100	100	100	23,271
Highest ÷					
Lowest	3.65	3.43	6.45	7.03	

B. *Canada (personal income per head) (countrywide average = 100)*

Province	1947	1963	1980	1986	Population (mid-1986)
Newfoundland	—	59	64	67	568
Prince Edward Island	56	62	71	71	127
New Brunswick	72	66	72	75	710
Nova Scotia	80	74	79	81	873
Saskatchewan	96	109	91	92	1,010
Quebec	83	87	95	94	6,540
Manitoba	103	96	90	93	1,071
Alberta	109	101	112	105	2,375
British Columbia	115	113	111	99	2,889
Ontario	115	116	107	111	9,114
All Canada (except far North)	100	100	100	100	25,278
Highest ÷					
Lowest	2.05	1.97	1.75	1.66	

Sources: Yugoslav data from *Indeks* (monthly bulletin of statistics), Canadian data from *Canada Yearbook*, and Statistics Canada: Information Bulletins of the Division of National Income and Expenditure.

and Croatia had achieved autonomy within Austria-Hungary, and many Croats longed for a status even closer to national independence. The southern parts of Yugoslavia—Serbia, Bosnia-Herzegovina, Kosmet, Montenegro, and Macedonia— were ruled as part of the Turkish Ottoman Empire, except for tiny Montenegro, which expended its energies in successfully fighting off the Turks. Macedonia and Kosmet were under Turkish rule for over 500 years prior to 1912. Serbia had effectively gained independence from Turkey by 1829 (for the first time since 1389, when the armies of the Serbian Empire were routed at the Battle of Kosovo) and achieved formal independence as a nation in 1878. Bosnia-Herzegovina was under Turkish rule until 1878 and was then occupied by Austria-Hungary, which formally annexed it in 1908.[2] Under Turkish control, economic stagnation was the rule. Not only did local inhabitants have to help fight Turkish wars against outsiders, they often fought each other within the Empire. Over 1876–1918, the eastern and south-eastern regions of what is now Yugoslavia were involved in six wars, including World War I.

No wonder that, when the new nation was born, the southern regions were much less developed than the north. Neither the royalist government between World Wars I and II nor the socialist government since World War II has been successful in reducing regional income inequalities. The overriding difference is that all regions have grown more rapidly since the advent of "self-management socialism" in 1953. Over 1950-86, real GNP per person grew to 3.94 times its original level—averaging just under 3.9 percent per year—one of the best performances of any country in the world. Per capita gross material product (GMP)—the Marxian version of national income and output (also called "social" product)—grew even faster, at nearly 5 percent per year. Investment and growth priorities are indicated by the relative expansion of industry and agriculture, whose outputs grew, respectively, to 14.8 times and to 3.3 times their 1950 levels by 1986, according to official statistics. This turned an agrarian nation into a modest industrial power. By 1987, there were about 120 cars, 140 telephones, and 220 TV sets per 1,000 residents. Before 1950, the economy had been comparatively stagnant, under both the interwar royalist régimes and command planning, over 1946–50.

However, during the 1980s, growth has fallen sharply in Yugoslavia, as in many other nations, because of the need to restrict imports of energy, raw materials, and other products on which its industries have come to depend. Despite being the most decentralized socialist economy, Yugoslavia's growth has also been largely extensive—the result of rapid accumulation of capital and transfer of labor from agriculture to industry, rather than of technological progress. This has sharpened the impact of the energy crisis, which turned the Yugoslav economic miracle into an economic crisis, although it may simply have pushed forward the inevitable. Real personal incomes from employment have risen more slowly than real GNP, and have fallen in recent years, according to official statistics, as cost-of-living increases have outpaced the expansion of money incomes. This mirrors a fall in labor productivity (both of GNP and GMP per worker) during the 1980s. In 1985, average real personal income from work was down about 35 percent from its 1979 peak (although still 23 percent above the 1963 level) and has since fallen further. Both it and average labor productivity were less than a fourth of corresponding averages in the West European Common Market.

The above income data exclude social insurance receipts and remittances from abroad, as well as most income earned in the private sector, where recent trends have reportedly been more favorable, but the official cost-of-living index also understates consumer price inflation, by leaving out most second-economy transactions. When such adjustments are taken into account, the average Yugoslav living standard peaked in 1980, according to a Western estimate, and then fell by just over 6 percent during 1980–87.[3] In 1987, it was 24 percent above 1970, the smallest net increase in eastern Europe. The current decline is punctuated by an austerity program, which features wage regulation, along with formal rationing of gasoline, electricity, and some foodstuffs, plus a tax on Yugoslavs each time they leave the country.

As a rule, the poorer regions have been less able than developed areas to generate the savings and investment required for sustained growth, and this has tended to widen the regional income gap. Attitudes inherited from Turkish rule are also inimical to development, and an "attitude gap" between the northern and southern parts of the country remains.[4] Self-management socialism—one of whose guiding principles has been the taking of decisions at the lowest level of government at which an issue can reasonably be resolved—has often worked against interregional coordination and integration. The wealthier regions have consistently favored limiting the powers of the federal government, in order to reduce its ability to redistribute income to poorer areas. Slovenia, Vojvodina, and Croatia have been the largest net contributors to redistribution, with Slovenia transferring more than a third of its GMP. Montenegro has been the main beneficiary, receiving amounts greater than 90 percent of her GMP. For every less-developed region (Kosmet, Macedonia, Montenegro, Bosnia-Herzegovina), supplementary funds from the federal budget are the most important source of republic-level government finance. There is also a Fund to Aid the Less-Developed Regions (FAD), which transfers just over 1 percent of GNP from more- to less-developed areas, and during the 1980s, more than two-thirds of World Bank loans to Yugoslavia have gone to the less-developed regions. The above measures partly compensate for the differences in per capita output shown in Table 10.1.

Nevertheless, several factors have limited the helping hand which better-off regions are willing to extend through the federal government to their poorer neighbors—and which, in the case of Kosmet, the main current beneficiary of redistribution, is partly offset by loss of income due to price controls on basic products. The first is that investment in the south bears a much lower average yield than investment in the northern regions.[5] Industrial workers in the south have nearly as much capital to work with, on average, as those in more developed areas, but still produce much less output. The southern regions have shortages of workers with industrial skills and acute shortages of qualified managers and engineers. As well, machinery has been misallocated, misused, and combined inefficiently with other inputs.

Moreover, investment resources transferred from north to south have often been used to promote regional or even local self-sufficiency, rather than specialization according to regional comparative advantage. Partly, this is because farming, mining, electric-power generation, building materials, nonferrous metals, and other industries in which the less developed regions have a comparative advantage have either had a low priority or else low, controlled prices that have discouraged investment. The traditional low priority granted to agriculture in socialist countries has been further reduced by the private ownership of most farms, particularly in less-developed areas. Relatively slow growth of agriculture, mining, and infrastructure has helped to increase regional income disparities and has led to a basic defect in the country's production structure. Yugoslavia has excess capacity in processing industries, but not enough in sectors supplying these industries with raw materials, energy, and fuel, or which transport their products or supplies. Yugoslavia imports timber, sugar, bauxite, and other raw materials to feed processing industries that were built to use domestic raw materials (and many of these still operate at low capacity).

Self-sufficiency is common, as well, in the developed republics. One consequence is that Yugoslav republics have a lower propensity to trade with each other than do nations of the European Economic Community. A second result is an uneconomic duplication of facilities, which increases overcapacity, especially in periods of tight import controls. For example, Yugoslavia has twenty-three sugar mills, most of which also operate at less than 50 percent capacity, owing to low domestic production of sugar beets. Each republic has insisted on meat-processing facilities and slaughter houses, which operate at less than half capacity, as well as steel mills and electric-power generating plants, even though electricity is much costlier to produce in most less-developed areas than in Slovenia, Croatia, or Bosnia. Power grids have been badly coordinated between and sometimes even within republics, and there have been frequent power shortages. In addition, Yugoslavia's lignite reserves, most of which lie in Kosmet, have been underexploited, which raises the cost of generating electricity in that province. Potentially, coal and lignite production could be expanded to over three times current levels, thereby reducing dependence on imported oil, which accounts for nearly 75 percent of domestic consumption of petroleum. Today, steps are being taken to remedy this dilemma. Coal has become the focus of Yugoslavia's energy policy, and the physical volume of output grew by about 85 percent over 1976–86, following a long period of neglect. Plans call for production to double over 1986–2000.

Unemployment in the south could also be reduced by further migration northward, but this is limited by ethnic diversity. "Ljubljana [the capital of Slovenia] has more in common with Graz or Salzburg [in Austria] than it has with Pristina [in Kosmet], and the Moslem peasant from Kosovo would feel more at home in Damascus than in Ljubljana."[6] When asked their nationality, 95 percent of Yugoslav citizens gave their ethnic origins in the 1981 census, rather than state that they were "Yugoslavs." While barriers to migration are eroding—in 1980, over

10 percent of Slovenia's labor force, holding the least attractive jobs, came from other republics—they remain a part of the north-south schism that threatens Yugoslavia's survival as a nation.

Unemployment and social welfare benefits also vary from region to region, and the level of benefits is often low by Western standards. Average old-age, survivors', and disability pensions, for example, came to just 57 percent of average personal income in the socialist sector in 1984, and many elderly were not covered, while others received far less than the average. The real value of these incomes declined over 1980–87. In 1987 pensions were indexed to wages in the socialist sector, which may lead to further decreases in their purchasing power. Unemployment compensation has been paid for three to twelve months, depending on length of previous employment, generally at 60 percent or better of previous earnings. But less than 3 percent of those registered as unemployed have qualified for such benefits in recent years, which require the recipient to have worked for twelve straight months or for eighteen months in the previous twenty-four. Over 60 percent of the unemployed in 1986 were under twenty-five and without previous work experience, except (in some cases) in private sector jobs which did not qualify them for coverage. (Once hired, employees of socialist firms usually enjoy a strong guarantee against job loss.)

Regional unemployment variations are also high and closely correlated with variations in per capita income. If we define the rate of unemployment in Yugoslavia as the ratio of registered unemployment to domestic labor force, this was just 0.7 percent in 1952. It rose slowly to 3.1 percent in 1965 and 4.2 percent in 1973. Then came the energy crisis. By 1979, it was over 8 percent and by 1988, it was about 10.6 percent, with more than ten registered unemployed for every job vacancy. The energy crises slowed growth both at home and in Western Europe, reducing job openings in both places for Yugoslav nationals. Around 650,000 Yugoslavs were working abroad in 1988, down from over 1.3 million before the first energy crisis in 1973–74. Many of those still working in foreign countries have effectively emigrated. As elsewhere, the average age of Yugoslav unemployed has been falling (over 60 percent were under twenty-five in 1985), and the average duration of unemployment has been rising. However, Yugoslavia's unemployment statistics are difficult to compare with Western data, because its domestic labor force is hard to estimate (it is close to, but not identical with the number of economically active people in the country), and because many registered as unemployed have at least part-time jobs or are really students. Registered unemployment is to some extent a measure of the number of people working in the private sector (mainly agriculture), who are queuing for better-paying jobs in the socialist sector. Studies suggest that between 20 percent and 30 percent of registered unemployed in recent years really have a job, but want to change. This would make the "true" rate of registered unemployment between 7.4 percent and 8.5 percent in 1986.

However, from Table 10.2 we can see that there is no serious unemployment problem in Slovenia. (In addition, the number of Slovenian workers abroad is more than made up for by guest workers from other parts of Yugoslavia.) Slovenia has a serious shortage of skilled workers. By contrast, we find heavy unemployment and comparatively few job vacancies in the less-developed regions, and the situation in Serbia proper, Vojvodina, and Croatia has not been very encouraging in recent years. Yet, some vacancies (especially in construction and mining, where wages are low) have been hard to fill in all areas. Well over half the job seekers were women in 1986, although they constituted only about 40 percent of the domestic labor force.

The less-developed regions especially need investment in their areas of comparative advantage—which include labor-intensive light industry and mining—plus improved training and educational opportunities (including exchanges of management and technical personnel with the developed regions). Because of their rugged terrain, power, transport, and communications networks that will give them cheap access to markets for their products and supplies for their industries are also essential. Without such access and without substantial investment in other infrastructure and education, investment yields are likely to remain below those in Slovenia, Croatia, and Vojvodina.

The nation as a whole has come a long way with social overhead and infrastructural investment. For example, average life expectancy has risen from 46 in 1939 to 68 in 1984 (66 for men and 73 for women), and infant mortality is less than a third of the 1950 level, although it is still higher than in most European nations. Almost the entire population is now covered by some form of health insurance, although coverage and benefits are generally better for those working in public enterprises than for those in the private sector. The number of inhabitants per doctor is now about 625, or less than 17 percent of the 1950 level. Illiteracy has fallen from 45 percent of the population before World War II to under 9 percent today, while the number of students in advanced vocational schools and universities was, by 1980, about 25 times the low level of 1938–39 (vs. an overall population increase of 40 percent). However, these figures conceal vast regional differences in favor of the developed areas, and over 80 percent of Yugoslavia's illiterate citizens live in the countryside. The energy crisis also had a devastating impact on social investment. Over 1979–84, real investment in education decreased by two thirds, in health care by 62 percent, in housing by 55 percent, and in public utilities by 40 percent.

In 1981, the transport network was carrying around 10 times the 1939 traffic volume and more than 5.5 times the volume carried in 1955, largely in line with the overall growth of industry. However, "transport costs are two to three times higher than in other European countries with similar transport and geographical conditions."[7] Moreover, prior to the early 1960s, transport costs were largely neglected in deciding where to build factories. In combination with other administrative errors, this led to irrational location patterns in all republics, the cost of which was probably higher in less-developed regions. Overall development and coordination of transportation—between different modes and between different

Table 10.2

Regional Indicators of Unemployment in Yugoslavia

Region	Registered unemployment (A)		Number of vacancies (B)		(A) + (B)		Number of unemployed per 100 "economically active" people, 1984
	Monthly average 1984	January–June average 1987	Monthly average, 1984	January–June average 1987	Monthly average 1984	January–June average, 1987	
Kosmet	101.2	128.5	1.6	1.6	64.6	80.3	22.9
Bosnia Herzegovina	220.3	242.0	7.4	9.5	29.8	25.5	12.5
Macedonia	128.3	141.2	5.8	7.2	22.1	19.6	14.9
Montenegro	34.9	39.3	1.6	2.4	21.8	16.4	15.8
Serbia Proper	268.1	300.3	23.1	30.6	11.6	9.8	9.0
Vojvodina	92.7	90.2	13.0	13.0	7.1	6.9	10.9
Croatia	114.0	125.2	16.2	21.0	7.0	6.0	5.2
Slovenia	15.3	14.3	8.9	10.2	1.7	1.4	1.5
All Yugoslavia	974.8	1,080.9	77.6	95.5	12.6	11.3	9.5

Sources: Indeks, September 1987, p. 10; Milenko Pavlovich, "Employment in the Socialized Sector, 1979–1984," *Yugoslav Survey*, August 1985, p. 12; *Statisticki Godisnjak Jugoslavije, 1986* (Statistical Yearbook of Yugoslavia), pp. 466–67.

*Numbers are in thousands, rounded to one decimal place.

regions—has left much to be desired. In particular, management of the railway network is entrusted to 365 quasi-independent units (BOALs) and is fragmented along regional boundaries.

Railway investment has also been neglected, although in many less-developed areas, railroads are potentially the most efficient way to haul goods. There has been no net addition of length to the 10,000 kilometers of track inherited from before World War II. In 1985, total length was less than 9,300 km. Instead, "there has been an expansion of road carriage, whose per unit costs greatly exceed rail costs. River transport, too, is not up to the level of navigable rivers and canals. Coastwise maritime transport is almost extinct." Most of the rail system is neither electrified nor double-tracked, although the electrified share (about 38 percent of the total in 1985) has been rising. An expansion of the transport network in less-developed regions would increase market size, as well as access to supplies and technical know-how, for many producers there. This would help to reduce fragmentation of the national market. Because scale economies are considerable, it is probably efficient to operate all transport systems at a loss in such areas. (Marginal-cost pricing would probably require this.) The need to develop a more integrated and cohesive society reinforces this conclusion. On balance, Yugoslavia has not invested enough in its transportation infrastructure, especially in the less-developed regions.[8]

Finally, less than 2 percent of Yugoslavia's agricultural land is irrigated, although irrigation is capable of raising crop yields in parts of Kosmet, Macedonia, and Vojvodina by up to five times. Partly because private farming (which has a low priority) would be the main beneficiary, only in the mid-1970s did Yugoslavia start to invest in irrigation in a big way. The schemes undertaken since then are likely to be beneficial, but also capital intensive, and they rely partly on foreign loans.[9]

Like many countries, Yugoslavia has tried to follow a path of economic development that is too capital and energy intensive, given its resource endowments. The net result is a dual economy, featuring many large-scale, capital-intensive firms, especially in heavy, processing industries, alongside a multitude of small, labor intensive enterprises with low access to investment credits. The latter include the entire private sector. The distorted pricing structure has encouraged overemphasis of processing industries, and especially since the 1965 reforms, excessive capital intensity has been promoted by artificially low interest rates in all regions. Low borrowing costs help to ensure a local excess demand for locally generated savings, as well as survival of some enterprises without too much aid in the form of direct subsidies. They also allow credit rationing, which guarantees that priority industries will have the best access to investment loans. The local shortage of savings helps to limit pressures for their transfer across ethnic frontiers, although the Fund to Aid the Less-Developed Regions (FAD) partly compensates for this. (However, FAD itself consists of compulsory loans at extremely low interest rates.)

Many firms with high access to loans have gorged themselves on capital. Often these enterprises are among the least efficient in the country. If capital were better utilized, industrial output could be quickly raised, since Yugoslav industry has been operating at about 60–65 percent of capacity or less over 1986–88. The developing regions suffer most from excessive capital intensity, not least in their ability to generate jobs. By contrast, the small-scale sector has been restricted, even though it can generate more jobs with smaller investment outlays. Still other firms, both public and private, have not been founded because credit was unavailable. Private farms have had poorest access of all, because the League of Communists and governments at all levels have been mainly interested in promoting industry and have given preference within agriculture to the relatively small socialist sector. The low-access enterprises use too much labor and too little capital, just the reverse of firms with high access to credits and subsidies. Private agriculture still has a reservoir of underemployed labor, and incomes there are low, especially in less-developed areas.

Given Yugoslavia's heterogeneity, ethnic conflicts are inevitable. Historically, these have been heightened by tension and rivalry between the two largest nationalities, the Serbs and Croats, comprising 39 percent and 20 percent of the population, respectively, in the 1981 census. This rivalry has a long history and is made more intense by the fact that Croatia is the major contributor to redistribution—not only through FAD and the federal budget, but also because of price controls, notably on crude oil, and redistribution of foreign currencies earned in Croatia to other parts of the country. (Croatia has higher foreign exchange earnings than any other republic, and foreign currencies are undervalued in terms of the Yugoslav dinar.) Croatian terrorists living abroad have made worldwide headlines, and Tito himself initiated a purge of nationalistic Croatian Communist leaders in 1971. Tensions in that year came to a head over the foreign exchange issue. More recently, conflict with Bulgaria over Macedonia and rioting in Kosovo, which has claimed many lives and made worldwide headlines, have highlighted the two other ethnic flash points.

10-2. The Yugoslav Economy and Workers' Self-Management

A. *The Organization of Self-Managed Firms*

Self-management and marketization of the Yugoslav economy essentially date from 1953. Although workers' councils first came into existence in 1950, it was over two years later when they received the right to decide how to use the firm's capital. This signalled the formal demise of command planning. The industrial ministries were also dismantled, along with formal rationing of key inputs via materials balances. The state continued to be the legal owner of enterprise capital, but management by elected representatives of a firm's workers replaced, in principle, the former management by higher level bureaucrats. Firms did not do away with professional managers any more than they tried to get along without other kinds of skilled labor, but the enterprise director became responsible to its workers' council, much as the management of a privately owned firm is responsible to its owners via the board of directors. This system is sometimes referred to as "social ownership."

Workers' councils emerged as legislative bodies, consisting of fifteen to one hundred-twenty members (depending on firm size), elected for two-year terms by all employees, including top management personnel. The formal duties of workers' councils are "to examine and approve the annual economic plans of their enterprises, to contract investment loans, to approve balance sheets, and to [decide how to] dispose of profits."[10] In firms with fewer than thirty employees, the entire personnel, except (in principle) the top management, constitutes the workers' council. Otherwise, any employee not part of top management may be elected to the council, and the top executives of a firm usually form a business committee. In practice, the director often belongs to the council as well, although this is illegal. In order to broaden participation, a rotation rule prohibits anyone from serving two successive terms on the same council. This probably strengthens the director's authority, since he is not subject to such a rule.

Each large enterprise is divided into BOALs (basic organs of associated labor), on the principle that each division producing a saleable good or service constitutes a BOAL, and also into "work communities," which perform auxiliary functions, such as administration, bookkeeping and accounting, secretarial work, maintenance, and various technical services. Independent enterprises are called OALs (working organs of associated labor), regardless of whether they are divided into BOALs, but we shall mainly refer to these entities as "enterprises" or "firms." At end-1985, there were about 14,280 undivided enterprises in the socialist sector, along with 4,062 large OALs, which were divided into 18,927 BOALs and 4,835 work communities. Less than 2 percent of these BOALs belonged to OALs whose headquarters were located in a different republic or autonomous region, partly because regional governments have discouraged expansion of enterprises across ethnic boundaries.

The workers in each BOAL and each work community elect their own council, along with delegates to the OAL council, which must have at least one representative from each of these divisions. Otherwise, the OAL council follows the rule of proportional representation. Delegates to it must present the views of their respective work-unit councils on issues that directly affect these units. Each council is also supposed to reflect the social composition of the employees it represents, in terms of jobs performed, age, sex, and nationality (or ethnic group). In practice, unskilled and semiskilled workers have been underrepresented on the councils and, thus, the most likely group to resort to informal grievance methods, such as strikes.

Historically, the enterprise (OAL) level has tended to dominate its BOALs, and a 1971 law sought to redress this situation by giving each BOAL the right to secede from its parent firm. In principle, the latter is now only a voluntary contractual arrangement among BOALs, who agree to delegate certain powers to central management organs. Thus, each division or BOAL must ratify enterprise decisions about investment, pricing, finance, income distribution, and so forth. When possible, the BOALs take decisions themselves, especially concerning wages and working conditions. Each BOAL has a share of enterprise income. This is based either on negotiated transfer prices at which it sells to and buys from other BOALs in the same OAL, as well as its transactions with the outside world, or else on a negotiated return to the labor and capital supplied by the BOAL to its OAL. With rapid inflation, the second type of agreement has become predominant. By directly linking each worker's wages to the earnings of his division, rather than to the income of the entire firm, the reform sought to establish a closer bond between individual productivity and reward.

In practice, however, most OALs appear to be more centralized than the reform would suggest. By law, a BOAL may not separate from its parent OAL, if this would "substantially disrupt work in other basic organizations" of the enterprise. If it does secede, it must pay damages to other BOALs, and actual secession is rare. Efficiency requires the major production and investment decisions to be made centrally, since more than one BOAL is bound to be affected. Those firms which have become highly decentralized—and are generally scenes of internal struggles over distribution—have suffered in consequence. In section 2-1, we pointed out that the product and profit created by a firm will usually result partly from cooperation between its constituent divisions—here, BOALs and work communities. There will usually be no unique way of dividing the OAL's total profit between these entities and, hence, no unique outcome to any struggle between BOALs over profit shares. Such wrangling could consume so many resources as to cancel all benefits from cooperation. Thus, we would expect governments to be vigilant in keeping these tendencies under control, although any formula for sharing profits between BOALs might still have to be renegotiated when new BOALs are added to the firm. (One consequence of this is that the willingness to make investments that might result in new BOALs has declined.)

An average-sized workers' council has 20–25 members. Since 1965, candidates for the councils in each BOAL or individual OAL are nominated at a general meeting of all employees, any four of whom may place a given name in nomination. However, it is virtually impossible to be elected to a council without endorsement by the enterprise labor-union committee, which is an avenue for League of Communist influence. As a rule, fewer than three candidates are nominated for every two vacant council positions, and half or more of all elections to the various councils go uncontested. At the enterprise level, the workers' council meets relatively infrequently and confines itself mainly to basic policy decisions. In some firms, its day-to-day responsibilities are delegated to a smaller management board, of five to eleven members, elected by the council for one-year terms. At least 75 percent of the members of each management board must be blue-collar workers. Because of the rotation principle, no member may serve more than two successive terms on the board. However, it is possible to serve a term on the workers' council, to then be elected to the management board for two consecutive terms, to follow this with a term on the labor-union committee, and, finally, to start around again. In larger firms, delegates can also alternate between BOAL and OAL councils.

The director of a BOAL or OAL is an ex-officio member of its management board, which is supposed to assist him and also to supervise him to ensure that he obeys the council's wishes. The management board "draws up basic plans, approves monthly operating plans, decides on internal organization, personnel problems, and grievances, establishes working hours, and is generally responsible for the proper functioning of the enterprise and the fulfilment of its plans."[11] Until 1969, management boards were mandatory in all firms. However, a December 1968 constitutional amendment gave each working collective more freedom to determine its own internal organization. Most firms have since abolished their management boards, replacing these with advisory committees chosen by the director. This may signal an erosion of worker influence, although most workers' councils still choose their own executive committees, with responsibility for making proposals to the council and for ensuring that council decisions are implemented.

At least in the short run, the rotation rule also reduces the influence of the workers' council vis-à-vis the director and his staff. However, because of it, the majority of skilled and white-collar workers have by now served at least one council term. The Yugoslavs claim that this widens the perspective of workers and educates them as to their rights and responsibilities under workers' management. In the long run, employees would plausibly become more insistent on those rights. Nevertheless, a 1986 sample survey of 6,000 young people from all over Yugoslavia found that just 28 percent reacted favorably toward self-management, while 17 percent were negative and 55 percent were indifferent. Regionally, favorable ratings ranged from 41 percent in Bosnia-Herzegovina to 18 percent in Slovenia, the most developed republic.

Figure 10.1 shows the flow of funds in a social sector firm. By way of explanation, we note that membership fees go mainly to organizations called general associations and economic chambers, described below, to which all socialist enterprises must belong. The collective consumption fund pays for vacations, education, recreation, communal feeding, and other employee benefits in kind, while the housing fund helps to finance workers' housing, which is provided to limited numbers of employees far below cost. Payments into these funds have come to around 15–20 percent of net personal income, on average, but plans now call for housing funds to decline and wage increases to make up the difference, as Yugoslavia seeks to privatize home ownership and finance. The reserve fund is to ensure that the firm can pay its debts, along with minimum wages. (In practice, real wages may not fall by over 30 percent per year as of May 1988, unless the enterprise goes bankrupt.) To strengthen the latter guarantee, part of the reserves of each enterprise go to an interfirm solidarity fund, which makes up the difference between minimum wages and what an unprofitable firm can afford.

The above scheme appears to treat labor mainly as a residual claimant to the

Figure 10.1. **The Flow of Funds in a Yugoslav Social Sector Firm.**

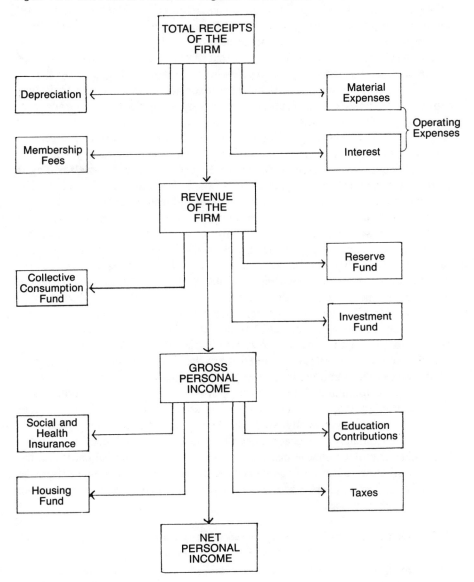

firm's income—and thus as its principal owner in the property-rights sense—rather than as a cost that must be met before profit is calculated and divided up. In practice, however, labor is largely a cost, beyond minimum wages, for reasons that we shall explore. It has a *de facto* prior claim on the firm's revenues, with the state holding the residual claim. (The government therefore becomes the owner in terms of property rights, as well as the legal owner.) Moreover, enterprise taxes and obligatory health and social insurance contributions have been based largely on its wages and salaries bill (gross personal income), as in other socialist countries. These raise the cost of labor relative to that of capital, which tends to increase capital intensity and to reduce employment in the socialist sector. Recently, the tax system has become more neutral between labor and capital, but the basic bias remains. Enterprise taxes also vary significantly from republic to republic and even from one locality (or "commune") to another.

Finally, nearly all aspects of Yugoslav society conform to the self-management principle. In particular, this is true of government bodies (officially known as sociopolitical communities) and of quasi-government bodies called "self-managed communities of interest." The latter control social insurance, public utilities, and provision of a variety of public goods, including education, science, culture, and health. Self-managed communities receive revenues in the form of obligatory contributions, mainly from social sector firms, which amount to almost half the public sector's income. The top management of any community is, in principle, a two-house assembly—one chamber consisting of elected representatives of producers and the other of elected representatives of users of its products. Where education, science, culture, health, and social welfare are concerned, the assembly of the relevant self-managed community becomes part of the communal or republic-level legislature, whenever legislation in its sphere of interest is considered. Without its participation, no such laws may be passed.

Self-managed communities of interest are therefore joint producer-consumer cooperatives. The same could be said of any democratic government, but the existence of communities for each of several types of public goods and services gives users more freedom of choice, at least in principle, than would be normal in a political democracy. Usually, voters in Western countries cannot express their preferences separately on education, health, medical care, social security, and other such issues, but must choose instead between alternative political parties on the basis of an expected provision by each of all these services. As an offset, the Yugoslav system requires a series of costly, cumbersome, and time-consuming decision-making processes.

B. The Distribution of Power in a Social-Sector Firm[12]

The comparative authority of worker representatives vis-à-vis the League of Communists and its political allies or vis-à-vis professional managers has varied across space and through time. A general rule is that worker representatives mainly occupy themselves with questions of wage determination, fringe benefits, conditions of work, labor discipline, hiring and firing, and the distribution of enterprise revenues between wages, funds for investment in the enterprise, and funds for housing and collective consumption. These areas of traditional blue-collar interest are also where the power of worker representatives is greatest, except for constraints on hiring and firing the director, and with the proviso that legal and political constraints on firing ordinary workers are substantial. Workers' councils also have the formal right to hire and fire the director's immediate subordinates and to determine the organization of the enterprise. In principle, the director may advise, but the council must consent. In practice, the director is likely to win the day, provided he has the support of local Communist and union officials.

More generally, decisions covering the business policy of the enterprise—investments, pricing, product research and development, changes in product line, marketing, finance, and so forth—are largely controlled by professional managers, the League of Communists, and local or regional governments. When this type of issue comes up at workers' council meetings, attendance falls off, which is not surprising, given that members serve without pay and that meetings take place after hours. Worker representatives have had an inadequate incentive to learn to understand complex engineering and financial reports, particularly in light of the rotation principle.

A similar division of effort has appeared between professional management and labor representatives in West Germany's system of quasi-workers' management, called codetermination, and has served in both Yugoslavia and West Germany as the basis for claims that workers' management is not genuine. Yet, for any given working conditions, workers' councils are likely to be profit oriented, and they can motivate professional managers in the same direction by tying their salaries to enterprise profitability. Labor relations, the humaneness of the workplace, and other work-related issues involve more intangible benefits, and these are among the areas where the influence of worker representatives is greatest.

This having been said, there are still grounds for suspecting that the practice of workers' management falls short of principle, even in more developed regions.[13] For one thing, control over major investment decisions rests more with politicians than with experts, and the track record of the former has been poor. For another, workers' councils have limited powers over income distribution. Taxes plus floors on the amounts of revenue that must be allocated to investment and reserves closely constrain net personal income from above, while effective wage guarantees constrain it from below. Moreover, within a typical BOAL or OAL, over two-thirds of all proposals passed by the workers' council originate with professional management, which has usually cleared them with local party or labor-union officials. These submissions are rarely rejected (although they are sometimes withdrawn after an informal sounding). Within the councils, "deliberations are dominated by high-level managers and technical experts, most of whom are League of Communist members and have better-than-average educations—with the result that rank-and-file members participate less actively than theory might suggest." Workers lack independent access to information, which is controlled by technocrats and often presented too late to allow genuine consideration of alternatives or in technical terms that most workers do not understand.

Thus, membership in a workers' council appears to lower alienation for those whose desire to participate in decision making is low to moderate. But membership does little to raise satisfaction for those with a high desire to participate. Nonetheless, most workers' councils are more than rubber stamps—especially when it comes to questions of wage and bonus distribution, working conditions, and personnel policy—but also, on occasion, where production, pricing, marketing, or investment policy is concerned.[14]

In fact, directors often claim that their responsibilities exceed their authority. Their freedom of action is constrained, in business-related matters by government bodies and the League of Communists and in personnel-related matters by their workers' councils.[15] Government and the League also put pressure on firms to hire the unemployed, and many enterprises are overmanned, even though their basic choices of production technology are too capital intensive, as noted earlier. Directors find it hard to dismiss workers, even for gross incompetence, negligence, or insubordination. In industry, absenteeism averages 10 percent—high by West European standards—and, on average, employees appear to work no more than five to six hours per day.[16] A major reason for this is that over a third of them have second jobs in the private sector, most often in agriculture.

As in other socialist countries, Yugoslav workers often have a specific right to a specific type of job in a specific place, as opposed to a general right of employment. Compared to the USSR, however, Yugoslav directors have a slightly freer hand in dismissals and can be more confident that appeals by dismissed workers will be disallowed. On the other hand, strikes are not forbidden in Yugoslavia, as they are in the USSR. About 3,000 work stoppages occurred over 1950–80, and no fewer than 1,570 were officially recorded in 1987, which involved 365,000 workers. Most strikes arise spontaneously as a result of disputes over wages or working conditions, last less than five days, and achieve their immediate demands.

Workers' councils have also limited the director's salary, as well as the dispersion of wages and salaries in the enterprise. The spread of wages in a Zagreb textile factory, circa 1961, when wage inequality was relatively high, appears in Table 10.3. Workers' councils approve the assignment of a number of work points to each job, based on such factors as those given in the table. Thus, the director's job is worth 730 work points (the last column in the table) while that of a charwoman is worth just 130. The 730 work points assigned the director's post can be broken down into 100 points due to relatively high educational requirements, 170 for skill and experience requirements, down to only 10 for working conditions, since the director's surroundings are presumably as pleasant as any.

A similar breakdown occurs for each occupation. There are also work-point bonuses and penalties for individual performance and a substantial payment in kind to many employees, including of subsidized housing and education. Each worker's income depends on number of work points received plus the firm's net personal income. The latter is divided by total number of work points awarded to all

Table 10-3

An Example of Work-point Assignments in a Zagreb Factory, 1961

	Level of education	Skill and experience	Authority	Responsibility	Physical effort	Mental effort	Working conditions	Total
Managing director	100	170	150	190	10	100	10	730
Technical director	100	140	140	160	10	90	10	650
Works manager	100	130	100	120	10	90	30	580
Foreman	80	60	40	50	10	40	40	320
Skilled weaver	50	40	0	40	35	30	40	235
Skilled spinner	30	20	0	20	30	10	40	150
Sales manager	100	130	100	140	10	90	10	580
Accountant	100	100	50	90	10	80	10	440
Truck driver	80	60	0	70	30	40	40	320
Charwoman	20	10	0	10	40	10	40	130

Source: Rudolf Bicanich, "La Politique des Revenus Ouvriers en Yougoslavie," *Économie Appliquée*, October-December 1963, p. 587.

employees combined to get a money value for each point. As profits are never exactly known in advance, a Yugoslav worker is never sure of his pay until he opens his envelope.

Table 10.3 reveals a low spread between the director's salary and those of ordinary workers. The former was only about 5.6 times that of a charwoman. Historically, directors have generally received even less relative to other employees. A director will usually enjoy, as well, the use of a chauffeured limousine and a comfortable home. However, many workers have obtained dwellings through enterprise housing funds at a tiny fraction of cost, while others are poorly housed and/or pay up to half their incomes for rent, since there is a pronounced shortage of socially-financed homes. One management expert (Granick) found the relative earnings of Slovenian managers to be lower than was customary in other East European countries (where the use of state-owned housing and autos is also part of managerial remuneration), and noted that "Yugoslavia is the only country, socialist or nonsocialist, where I have heard complaints as to the difficulty of recruiting top managers from among the most competent personnel of industry."[17] Similarly, shortages of skilled workers persist amid high and rising unemployment, and it is frequently hard to get people to take responsibilities or risks or to perform heavy, dirty, or dangerous work—in part, because earnings differences are often not allowed to become great enough to fully reward differences in education, training, or job responsibility.

Finally, we might expect that in a labor-relations system which seeks to unite labor and management, labor unions would wither away for want of anything to do. Instead, Yugoslavia has a thriving union movement, which more closely resembles unions in the USSR and in Eastern Europe than those in the West. They actively defend some worker interests, but they are also an arm of the League of Communists and a medium through which the League exercises influence. Strikes are led, not by unions, but by informally-chosen workers. When a strike occurs, the head of the enterprise labor union is likely to bargain on behalf of management, since he wants to maintain production. All employees have the right to join their firm's labor-union branch, but the union committee, which heads the branch, is likely to consist almost entirely of leaders of the local League of Communists cell.

Within the firm, the union is responsible for holding elections, and, in particular, for drawing up and approving lists of candidates. It also conducts vocational training programs. The union movement founded and still operates the "workers' universities," or adult education programs for employees who have not finished high school. Over 1.5 million take these courses every year, and unions have played a major role in stamping out urban illiteracy. In addition, they help employees with work-related personal problems, and they delve into the financial and technical aspects of managing an enterprise, in an effort to better prepare future workers' council members. Beyond this, they play no formal role in management, although both in law and in practice, they have a substantial advisory role. Legally, the workers' council and professional management must consult with the union local, which will have views on wage distribution, pricing policy, the division of profit between wages and investment, and other important issues. Actual union influence varies from firm to firm and is held in some check by the ability of workers' councils to raise or lower budgets for union activities. Neither the unions, the League of Communists, nor government officials have had much luck in persuading enterprises to limit wage increases or to tie them to productivity gains.

In Soviet-type economies, the role of the Communist party is to enforce the spirit of economic plans, and the role of the Yugoslav League of Communists is consistent with this basic philosophy. The League does not generally involve itself in the details of running an enterprise, although enterprise management will always consult with it (and the League may take a position through the labor union committee). Instead it tries to align the firm's activities with general government policy, and it seeks to influence the values of workers, as well as their long-range outlooks. It will try to induce them to take a broader perspective, which goes beyond their individual work places. An important source of Communist influence in any firm is the customary requirement for its professional management, the executive committees of its workers' councils, its labor-union committee, and other important officials to be League members in good standing.

C. The Role of the Private Sector

Yugoslavia also has a large private sector, accounting for a third of domestic employment, but no more than 20–25 percent of legally generated GNP. Most of this sector consists of over 2.1 million tiny private farms, which produce about 70 percent of total farm output. As well, in 1987, about 620,000 people officially worked in the nonfarm private sector, in 457,000 enterprises. They comprised nearly 9 percent of employment outside agriculture and produced a somewhat smaller share of non-farm output. During the 1980s, employment here has expanded at a much higher rate than employment in the social sector. Moreover, because of underreporting, official statistics understate the size of the private sector. Income from private activity is subject to steeply progressive taxation when it exceeds the social-sector average for a given region and occupation, and there are legal constraints on the size and nature of private firms. Even so, small private companies build two-thirds of all homes, operate nearly half of all hotels and restaurants, drive most of the taxis, and supply over a third of all transport by truck. These companies have been legal throughout the era of self-management, provided they did not hire more than five employees, who were not close relatives of the owners. In 1987 (and earlier in Slovenia), this legal limit was raised to ten, and private tourist enterprises may hire up to twenty employees during the high season.

In principle, according to Article 31 of the Constitution, managers and workers in the private sector are treated like those in the social sector. In practice, the authorities can discourage private firms by raising taxes, refusing licenses, cutting off supplies and credit, or even resorting to direct intimidation. The private sector has also been starved for investment funds and foreign exchange, while much of the social sector has enjoyed high access on favorable terms. When socially owned firms have complained about private competitors, the latter have often been restricted or suppressed.[18] Nevertheless, labor productivity has grown more rapidly in the private sector, largely because the out-migration from private agriculture has reduced underemployment there. The strength of the private sector also depends on the political climate, which varies over time and from one republic to another. Slovenia is the most and Serbia the least receptive to private enterprise, although enough excess demand exists in Serbia's service sector to absorb nearly all that republic's unemployed. During the 1980s, the political climate for private enterprise has grown more favorable in most regions, and the nonfarm private sector is expected to continue to increase its shares of income, output, and labor force during the 1990s.

Lower access to capital has reduced average incomes in the private sector, especially in agriculture, below those paid in the social sector. But politicization of investment decision making, along with price controls and a tendency to weaken the link between performance and reward in socially owned firms, has also created opportunities for private entrepreneurs to supply goods and services in excess demand. Some have become wealthy, e.g., in tourism, and are denounced for their wealth during periods of ideological retrenchment. However, like the second economy in other socialist countries, their success lies mainly in their ability to provide useful products that the social sector cannot or will not supply in adequate amounts.

We have also seen that jobs in the social sector are rationed. Social-sector OALs or BOALs will not hire additional workers, it is argued, if this would lower incomes for those already employed.[19] To see how this might happen, define a firm's *net* revenue to be its total receipts minus all *non*labor expenses, including taxes, depreciation, interest, cost of materials, allocations to reserve fund, etc. Define its average net revenue product of labor ($ANRP_L$) to be its net revenue divided by number of workers employed (or its average net revenue per worker). In Figure 10.2, L indexes employment, and the $ANRP_L$ curve shows how net revenue per worker may vary with L. Suppose, initially, that every worker receives the same earnings (= wages plus all benefits), which we index by w. Then, we must have w = $ANRP_L$, since $ANRP_L$ measures what is left from the firm's receipts to be paid to each worker.

In these conditions, the shape of the $ANRP_L$ curve is important. We have drawn it rising as L increases from zero to $\overline{L}$. Initially, in other words, the firm has increasing returns to labor. In the short run, this would result from declining fixed costs per worker, as the number of workers rises, plus gains from increases in capacity utilization. In the long run, it would result from increasing returns to scale at low rates of output (and employment). Beyond $\overline{L}$, falling $ANRP_L$ would result from downward sloping product demand and/or diminishing returns to labor in the short run and/or decreasing returns to scale in the long run. In Figure 10.2, the firm's

Figure 10.2. **Job-rationing in a Worker-managed Firm.**

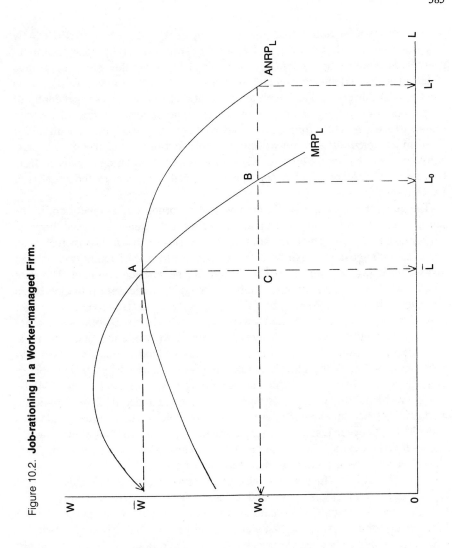

working collective would like to set employment at $\overline{L}$, where $ANRP_L = \overline{w}$ is maximized. It will resist efforts by party, government, and professional management to expand employment beyond $\overline{L}$, since this forces the firm's net revenue "pie" to be divided into smaller and smaller slices. Yet, more than $\overline{L}$ workers may want jobs in this enterprise, which tends to set its employment independently of supply conditions in the labor market. Suppose the opportunity cost of labor in Figure 10.2 is w_0 (which might be the earnings available in private agriculture). If the firm accepted all who are willing and able to work for it, it would expand employment to L_1. However a social-sector OAL contemplating expansion from $\overline{L}$ to L_1 must also consider the corresponding need to cut wages and benefits of existing staff from $\overline{w}$ to w_0.

The government could tackle this problem by promoting competition, in the sense of expanding output and employment through creation of new firms in industries and regions where social investment yields are highest. But investment decisions in Yugoslavia have been less responsive to rate-of-return criteria than this would imply, and its antimonopoly law has never been enforced. The state could also try to expand employment by encouraging wage discrimination based on seniority within social-sector firms. Suppose an OAL pays relatively high wages to workers with high seniority and lower wages to newly hired workers. Specifically, let each additional worker beyond $\overline{L}$ receive w_0 while the first $\overline{L}$ workers continue to get more than w_0. Let MRP_L measure labor's marginal (net) revenue product—that is, the addition to total net revenue caused by each new worker, as employment expands. Then, increasing employment from $\overline{L}$ to L_0, where $MRP_L = w_0$, will benefit the OAL's customers, suppliers, and also its L high-seniority workers. For such an expansion creates additional net revenue equal to the area under MRP_L between $\overline{L}$ and L_0. After paying $w_0 \times (L_0 - \overline{L})$ to low-seniority workers, a sum equal to the area of triangle ABC remains to be shared among high-seniority workers, which will raise their earnings *above* $\overline{w}$.

A "capitalist" firm facing the same cost and revenue conditions would also hire L_0 workers, since MRP_L is its demand for labor. However, while expansion from $\overline{L}$ to L_0 is consistent with Western notions of economic efficiency, it is also classic Marxian exploitation, since high-seniority employees are taking part of the surplus value created by newly hired workers. Such wage discrimination also runs contrary to egalitarian principles and would leave high-seniority workers vulnerable to wage cuts, should they be unable to maintain control of wage setting. These considerations tend to reduce wage discrimination based on seniority and cause social-sector OALs to ration jobs (in the manner suggested by the solution at A in Figure 10.2). As a result, the private sector must serve as an employment sponge, absorbing workers who would otherwise have no job. This, plus provision of goods and services in chronic short supply, plus preservation of the principle of small-scale private ownership of land and other means of production, are its main socioeconomic roles in Yugoslavia.

From time to time, the private sector's ability to supply some goods and services more efficiently, as well as to achieve a greater employment expansion for a given investment, creates pressure for a loosening of constraints and a more liberal attitude toward it. The rise in unemployment, since the energy crisis closed off West European demand for Yugoslav guest workers, has intensified these pressures. Legally, it has become easier to start small private firms. More spheres of activity are now open with fewer restrictions than before, and many returning guest workers have founded small businesses with money they had saved. In principle, returnees are eligible for tax relief and improved access to credit, and a 1976 law allows them to import capital equipment duty free, in order to get started. However, the spirit of these laws is not always honored by regional or local officials in practice. About 30 percent of returnees with jobs are working in the private sector—most of these in agriculture.

In 1987, there was just one private factory in Yugoslavia that was larger than a workshop and not worker managed. This is the Lestro Power-Saw and Machine-Tool firm in Slovenia, founded in 1986 as a cooperative of eight owner-managers, each of whom brought his legal limit of ten employees into the enterprise. Whether it will be a precedent for future mid-sized private firms is unclear. However, Articles 64–68 of the 1974 Constitution also provide for self-managed private enterprises, whose size could be unrestricted. The owners of such a firm—those who put up the capital to found it—must also constitute its professional management. These self-managed private firms are called Contractual Organs of Associated Labor (COALs), because the owner makes a contract with his employees to govern the division of net income between wages and profits, as well as other basic ground rules of the firm's operation. Legally, the owner-managers of COALs have a final veto over workers' council decisions not enjoyed by the directors of OALs or BOALs, although the practical difference may not be very great. The 1976 Law on Associated Labor strengthened the legal sanction for COALs, of which there were 249 at end-1985, the majority in industry and construction. Most were fairly small, but some employ more than 100 workers.

Eventually, COALs are supposed to shed their private status and pass into the socialist sector. This would happen when the original owner-managers retired, and it could happen sooner if the firm generated enough profit to pay back their original investment. In one such company, the owner withdraws a fifth of his original investment every year (this sum is not taxed) plus a fifth of the remaining profit plus a salary three times that of the average worker (a figure in line with the social sector). Thus, if the firm is profitable enough, and if the owner does not renew his investment, the company passes into the social sector after five years, although the original owner could continue to manage if he was doing a good job. As a rule, COALs may not operate in banking or finance, insurance, wholesale trade, mining, or some branches of manufacturing. The idea is to stimulate production of goods in short supply, as well as goods that were previously imported, and to generate employment. Ironically, a constraint on their formation has continued to be a hostile political climate in some areas.

Finally, to mobilize the savings of guest workers abroad, as well as to increase the number of social sector jobs for returnees, the Law on Associated Labor allows them to invest their savings in BOALs at home. These savings are earmarked for creation of new workplaces, to be ready for guest workers when they return. In this way, workers abroad are able to buy social-sector jobs as an alternative to starting their own businesses, and about 70 percent of returnees with jobs have done this. Potentially, the scheme is a form of wage discrimination based on seniority if a newly hired returnee does not receive a return on his investment, in addition to the usual wage paid by the BOAL for his type of work.

10-3. Financial and Industrial Structure of the Economy

A. *The Banking System*

Yugoslavia's financial institutions are mainly banks, and its banking system has evolved away from structures common to Eastern Europe. Under command planning, the National Bank of Yugoslavia was virtually the sole bank, with branches throughout the country, many of which had been independent commercial banks in previous years. Its main role was to enforce the physical plan by monitoring flows of funds between enterprise accounts, the state budget, and itself to ensure that these flows conformed to the plan. (This was "control by the dinar.") Nearly all investment was financed by state budget grants to investing firms.

With marketization and workers' management came a 1954 Bank Law allowing communal (or local) governments to set up their own banks (called "communal banks") which were still subject to National Bank control. These were not yet commercial banks, although many of today's commercial (or "business") banks trace their origins to them. The state continued (and continues today) to monitor flows of funds involving social sector firms. Socialist enterprises must use bank credit in their dealings with other firms (including private companies). Thus, a form of control by the dinar remained, although the state decentralized short-run decisions to a greater degree than it did investment decisions. It also established the Yugoslav Investment Bank and the Yugoslav Agricultural Bank to implement its investment priorities, along with a special bank to finance foreign trade, which remained under central control. Communal banks were not allowed to accept time deposits or to make long-term loans on their own initiative until after 1963. However, they did manage social investment funds under the control of local governments, much as the Yugoslav Investment Bank managed the General Investment Fund under federal control, and the six republic-level banks managed the investment funds controlled by the governments of the republics.

The 1965 Law on Banking and Credit established a system that in many important respects still prevails. The nine specialized banks at the federal and republican levels became investment banks, specializing in long-term lending and deposits, while the 220 communal banks went through a merger movement and came out, in 1970, as 55 "mixed" banks, permitted to carry out both long and short term operations under a stipulation that these be kept separate. A 1971 law then transformed all 64 commercial banks into "universal" banks, with rights to perform both long and short term operations. Today, all business or commercial banks (of which there were 191 at end-1985) are universal in this sense. They also became more autonomous in managing their investment resources after 1965.

A second 1971 law established eight republic-level "national" banks by expanding the autonomy of the former republic-level branches of the National Bank. The nine-man Board of Governors of the National Bank now consists of the eight governors of the republic-level banks, together with the Governor of the National Bank, who acts as chairman. Major decisions require a consensus of republic-level governors, which often makes it hard to stop the regional banks from operating semi-independently. In particular, each republic-level bank has covered public deficits and protected firms in its region from financial difficulties or the need to make major wage cuts by extending low-cost loans or outright grants, ultimately financed by expanding the money supply. The inflationary pressures generated by any single republic-level bank's creation of money are far less than the pressures generated by all together. Especially in a region running a balance of payments deficit with the rest of the country, the inflationary costs of one bank's bail-out operations are partly shifted to other regions. In this way, fragmentation of central bank authority has magnified basic inflationary forces (described below) at work in the economy.

Formally, firms in the socialist sector do not keep their current accounts with the banking system. Instead, each firm holds several accounts—which are segregated according to type of payment (wages, collective consumption, raw materials, reserves, etc.)—with a supervisory agency called the Social Accounting Service (SAS). SAS is responsible for implementing government policy and is controlled by federal and republic-level governments, for whom it maintains a comprehensive financial picture of the economy. It also retains extensive auditing and inspection powers and monitors flows of funds between as well as within socialist enterprises, thereby exercising a weakened version of control by the dinar. However, SAS is a supervisory rather than a financial institution. It lends no money; instead, accounts with it serve as financial backing for bank loans and are otherwise treated as bank deposits. Like the business banks, SAS has a strictly limited degree of internal self-management. Whereas the former are essentially credit unions owned by their largest business borrowers, SAS is primarily an arm of the federal government.

Finally, the present financial system includes a Post Office Savings Bank and a number of other savings banks, as well as savings and loan cooperatives, insurance companies, and credit funds. Except for the Post Office Bank, the savings banks also grant loans to individuals. In addition, firms and government bodies have increasingly borrowed by selling bonds to the public, although the securities market remains underdeveloped.

B. Credit Rationing

Just 30–40 percent of all gross fixed investment in Yugoslavia's socialist sector has been financed from own funds, a share that many officials and economists believe is too low, and one which has been rising in recent years. The main effect of the 1965 reforms—which were supposed to raise the proportion of self-financing—was to substitute the banks for government investment funds as the main source of investment finance. This change was partly superficial since government bodies transferred their funds to the banks, but continued to control placement of loans from them with ultimate borrowers. However, the relative importance of these funds has since declined, and today banks probably have formal control over most of the investment credits that they lend. Nevertheless, communal and republic-level governments still exercise leverage over bank loans by directly and indirectly influencing decisions made within banks and firms.

There is room to exercise such leverage in the first place because of the high percentage of investment that has been loan-financed, and because interest rates have been kept low enough to ensure a large excess demand for loanable funds.[20] In recent years, inflation has exploded, while interest rates on loans have risen too slowly to keep pace. Nominal interest rates have been less than the rate of inflation, and real interest rates—nominal rates minus inflation—have been negative. They are raised by bank requirements for borrowers to keep portions of their loans on deposit with the lender and to finance part of any investment from own funds. But even after this adjustment, real rates have been below levels that would ration loanable funds among would-be borrowers. Banks must therefore use administrative criteria to ration loans, which provide an avenue for government influence over their allocation.

The high percentage of external financing stems from the low cost of borrowed funds, as well as from the fact that the state is legal owner of firms in the social sector. Because of this, no worker has a share in a firm to sell when he leaves. Thus, suppose a workers' council agrees to lower current wages in order to invest more of the firm's income. The reward to employees will come as higher future profits and wages when the investment pays off. But some of these higher profits will probably be realized after part of the present work force has left the enterprise. Moreover, in contrast to private savings accounts, workers can never withdraw the principal of their investment, which remains in the firm. This increases employee preferences for profits sooner rather than later, which shortens enterprise decision-making horizons. It also makes worker-managed firms prefer to pay out their profits as wages—which employees can always deposit in private savings accounts—while borrowing the funds they need for investment.[21]

The second reason for the low percentage of self-financed investment is the tendency to avoid business risk and responsibility, sometimes described as a national pastime. By nature, Yugoslavs are not necessarily more risk averse than anyone else. However, the reluctance of workers' councils to grant high salaries, even to successful directors, plus the high probability of survival and career advancement for managers who avoid making mistakes, has acted as a disincentive for management to take entrepreneurial risks. Additional risk-bearing has, at best, a weak positive effect on managers' expected lifetime earnings—in part, because they are judged on political, social, and ideological factors, at least as much as on business success, and, in part, because many Yugoslav firms operate in sellers' markets, which reduces their need to innovate, to upgrade quality, or to reduce costs in order to keep their customers.

On top of this, a worker-managed firm is by nature an enforced risk-sharing agreement among its employees, whose pay depends on its profits or losses. Each worker automatically absorbs part of the risk of its business operations, no matter how risk averse he or she may be. It is not possible, as under private ownership, for some individuals (the owners) to specialize in risk bearing by agreeing to be residual claimants to enterprise income, while employees work for wages that are largely independent of profitability. Neither is it possible for employees to diversify away part of this risk, since their claims to profits and losses are not transferable. Finally, to properly supervise investment and other business decisions by managers, employee delegates must at least make large investments of their own in time and effort. Profit sharing reduces the (extrinsic) return on this investment, and the rotation principle acts as a further disincentive. As a result, employees are reluctant to accept responsibility for business decisions.

Consequently, worker-managed enterprises would like to avoid risky investments—and most investment bears some risk—unless part of the risk and responsibility is borne by outside parties, specifically banks and subfederal governments, in most cases. Risk avoidance is well documented and lies at the root of a contradictory view of the Yugoslav firm. According to Tyson, the "pure cooperative" view holds that "enterprise members should share equally in the fruits of profitable operations and the penalties of unprofitable operations, the ultimate penalty being loss of job and enterprise bankruptcy." By contrast, the "worker-manager" view distinguishes between the roles of worker and professional manager. It "sees all members of an enterprise, except the director and his managerial staff, as workers with an inalienable right to a steady income and a steady job. According to this view, individual workers should not be made to bear the cost of enterprise actions, provided they perform their own specific production tasks. This view leads to the conclusion that only the managers, whose specific task is . . . supervision . . . should be penalized by poor financial results."[22]

Most Yugoslav workers take a "worker-manager" view, even though it seems at odds with the essence of workers' management. To accommodate it, a system has arisen which allows workers to share in enterprise profits, but which shields them from losses, default, and bankruptcy. In a typical year, at least 10–15 percent of all socialist firms, employing perhaps 20 percent of the social sector work force, operates at a loss—ultimately made good by government subsidy. Bankruptcy has been rare, and when it has occurred, the employees of the bankrupt firm have not usually been stuck with most of its losses.[23] Instead, they have shared losses with creditors, the local and/or regional government, and, possibly, with one or more banks. This phenomenon, which also operates when there are serious losses short of bankruptcy, dulls the profit-and-loss incentive to operate efficiently. Indeed, relatively efficient firms pay higher-than-average rates of tax on their revenues and are also likely to be hurt more by price ceilings and other restraints. The upshot is a Yugoslav version of the soft budget constraint encountered in all socialist economies. The state protects inefficient enterprises from failure or the need to pay low wages relative to other firms and redistributes income from profitable to unprofitable enterprises. This tends to divorce reward from performance at the level of the firm. In Yugoslavia, subsidies are often financed by creation of new money, which fuels inflation.

In short, enforced risk sharing within an enterprise leads to external risk sharing, in which the rest of society absorbs part of a firm's business risk. The specific device used to shield enterprises against losses is a guarantee from a bank to a firm's creditors that it will repay them, should the enterprise default (that is, not meet its obligations on time). The bank then gets a similar guarantee from the communal government, which may be passed up to the republic-level government and even to the federal government, if the enterprise is important enough. One consequence is that firms grow careless about repaying their debts on time, preferring to use their proceeds to pay wages first, debts second, and to undertake new investments third. Much of the risk associated with investment is also covered by a system of guarantees, extending in most instances back to the founding of a firm. As a rule,

> the founder must set up the new enterprise with assets borrowed from a bank, [and] the bank has gotten a guarantee from the local government, [which] expects that, when serious difficulties are encountered, the republic government will bail out the new enterprise through special tax rebates, loans, pressure on business associates, etc.[24]

However, local and republic-level governments do not provide this service free of charge. In return for accepting ownership responsibilities, they are able to claim some management rights—specifically, to increase their influence over enterprise investment, production, and marketing—and to play a major role, together with the League of Communists, in the selection of the director of each firm. One consequence is that enterprise directors have had dual loyalties—to party and government officials, as well as to their employees—throughout the era of self-management. This has reinforced the reluctance of workers' councils to grant large salaries to directors (although egalitarian considerations have also played a role in this). It has also reinforced the worker-manager view and tended to raise the share of enterprise income that councils want to pay out as wages and other current benefits, at the expense of the investment share. Thus, it runs headlong into party and government preferences favoring rapid growth, and the state uses its leverage to enforce its own growth and industrial priorities.

Unfortunately, this does not ensure that investment decisions will be wise or that capital will be efficiently used. As we have indicated, political rather than economic criteria often determine which companies will have best access to government guarantees, and these are more likely than not to be inefficient enterprises in priority industries. Given this plus the low cost to firms of default, the volume of unpaid business debt is usually high, and it is common for receivers of goods not to pay for them on time. Historically, the cost of delay to sellers has been reduced by their ability to borrow against accounts receivable, a process that results in creation of new money and is therefore part of the inflationary process associated with the soft budget constraint. Wages, salaries, and taxes have also been calculated with most accounts receivable included in enterprise revenues.

Through the system of guarantees, workers' management indirectly makes the Yugoslav economy more subject to government influence, but also helps to cellularize it into overly self-sufficient regional blocs. Banks are discouraged from lending to enterprises in different republics—and, sometimes, even in different communes—because when default occurs, the bank can only turn to a government agency to recoup its losses. Moreover, when one firm sells to another, it must reckon on a significant probability that it will not be paid on time, for in the climate just described, those who do pay promptly are penalized most by shortages of liquid funds. Uncollected business debts have become an important means of extending credit from enterprises with high access to bank loans to enterprises (in the social sector) with lower access. When bank credit is restrictive, inter-enterprise credit expands to take up the slack and insulates firms from the tightening of monetary policy. Once again, guarantees are important, with the result that enterprises are more reluctant to sell to firms in other republics.

C. The Role of the Commune in Selecting Enterprise Directors

Especially at the local level, public authorities can also influence enterprises by influencing the career prospects of professional directors. As a rule, a web of mutual support is woven between commune officials, directors of local firms and banks, the local League of Communists cell, and officials at the republic level. An important element in this web is the role of the commune in hiring and firing enterprise directors. One might believe that workers' management would require the director to be hired and fired by the workers' council and fully accountable to it, just as he was accountable to his superior ministry under command planning (and just as the management of a private corporation is, in principle, responsible to its shareholders). But this is not quite how it works.

As communal governments gained power and independence during the early 1950s, they also got the authority to appoint enterprise directors:

> In 1953, public competition for the director's office was introduced, and in the selection committee, the communal representatives retained a two-thirds majority, [the other members being chosen by the workers' council]. Only in 1958, did the councils achieve parity with communal authorities on the joint committees authorized to appoint and dismiss enterprise directors.[25]

While the 1950–53 reforms reduced the influence of the League of Communists at the local level, this remained strong, and the idea of a director not acceptable to local party and government officials was unthinkable, then as now.

Thus, directors have had dual loyalties. Prior to the 1965 reforms, local political connections were probably more important than the support of the working collective, and party loyalty and standing were more important than expertise in management. The Yugoslav view was that "the development of workers' councils must be considered a gradual process . . . of long duration. For the dangers are numerous: formalism in management, reduction of democracy to a mere formula [and] failure to see existing rights and to use them fully."[26] As a general rule, the power of the councils vis-à-vis the director and the rest of professional management grew irregularly over 1952–67, and the director became increasingly dependent on acceptance by the working collective. Yet, the local labor union branch has always played a major role in voicing this acceptance or rejection, which has provided an avenue for League of Communist influence.

Nevertheless, the influence of the League declined after 1953, and in 1965, the party formally lost the right to "request" acceptance of its recommendations for vacant directorships. Finally, in December 1968, workers' councils obtained sole legal rights to hire and fire directors.[27] Yet, by 1973, the influence of the League and of the commune in determining who the director would be was again rising. More than two-thirds of all "competitions" for the post have only one candidate. While the council can theoretically dismiss a director at any time for incompetence, and this sometimes happens, directors can generally expect to be reelected at least once, if they wish, provided they make no major economic or political errors. Moreover, not only the workers' council, but also the local union and the communal assembly can start dismissal proceedings at any time.

Because they must have dual loyalties, which conflict to a degree—and because their qualifications are political, as well as economic—directors often feel insecure and suffer from identity crises. Both the relatively low salaries and the tensions and frustrations associated with the job reduce the supply of candidates and raise the probability that a given director will view his job as a stepping stone to something better. Such an individual is more prone to influence by government and party officials, who can help him with his career.

D. Industrial Structure

Jaroslav Vanek, a staunch crusader for workers' management, once argued that "a labor-managed industrial conglomerate is as likely as the apocalyptic beast with seven heads and 10 horns."[28] However, not only does Yugoslavia have worker-managed conglomerates, the 200 largest social sector firms account for over 60 percent of all social sector sales and 40 percent of social sector employment. About half the employees in the social sector work in firms with payrolls of over 2,000. The largest 130 industrial firms account for 70 percent of all social sector sales and two-thirds of all capital assets. The largest enterprises do not invariably reduce competition, however, because they are often threats to established market posi-tions—as well as sources themselves of monopoly power—owing to their ability to mobilize resources in order to expand their product lines or to establish them-selves in new locations.

Nevertheless, Yugoslavia's industrial structure is highly concentrated, and concentration has been rising since the late 1960s. There are many complaints of sheltered regional markets within which monopoly power is exercised—often with the active promotion of local or republic-level governments. In part, monopoly elements stem from the close ties between banks, firms, and local or regional government bodies. This exercise of market power has helped to produce un-derinvestment in some industries, together with overinvestment and excess capac-ity in others, as well as subsidies for loss-making firms. Only exceptionally, moreover, do prices respond flexibly to supply and demand. As in other socialist countries, the norm tends to be administrative, cost-plus pricing, with frequent use of price controls, many on a continuing on-again, off-again basis. Over 1980–85, much price-setting authority devolved onto regional "communities for prices," quasi-government bodies like the self-managed communities of interest discussed earlier, which tried to set prices high enough to cover costs in the least efficient firms within their jurisdictions. In 1985, the federal government increased its control over pricing, which reduced some of these abuses. Still, price controls at all levels have been ineffective in stopping inflation, but together with restrictions on entry of new competitors, they have preserved excess demand and sellers' markets for many goods.[29]

In this context, market sharing and other forms of collusion are both widespread and accepted in Yugoslavia.[30] These arrangements are protected by local and regional governments and also by lobbying on the part of two types of associations of enterprises. The *general associations*, such as the Association of Shipbuilders and the Association of Iron and Steel Works, are organized according to industry, being the legal replacements for the industrial ministries that were dissolved in 1952 with the end of command planning. Every social sector firm must belong to at least one of these, and they also play a role in promoting productivity, research, and development. The *economic chambers*, much like chambers of commerce in Western countries, are quasi-government, regional organs. They have the task of harmonizing and coordinating the plans of different enterprises, under Yugoslavia's system of contractual planning (described in chapter 11), into a consistent regional plan.[31] The chamber's evaluation of a firm's investment pro-posal can determine its access to borrowed funds. However, like the general associations, the economic chambers tend to frown on overt competition or enforcement of Yugoslavia's antimonopoly law.

The closest form of collaboration between firms probably takes place through the combine (kombinat), also called a Joint Organ of Associated Labor (JOAL), of which there were just over four hundred as of end-1985. In principle, a JOAL is a contractual linking together of firms (OALs), which can withdraw from it or collectively dissolve it at any time. However, according to one source,

> Yugoslav industrial enterprises, although legally independent, are in the great majority of cases not operating autonomously, but are grouped with others in kombinats. The individual enterprises cede, through contractual arrangements, certain functions to the "group," which frequently operates under its own name . . . and assumes all contractual arrangements with third parties. Frequently, the integration is so close . . . that legal autonomy is a fiction. . . .[32]

Sometimes the JOALs consist only of vertically integrated companies, forming a supplier-user chain from raw materials to final use. Often, however, they comprise firms producing the same or substitute goods and therefore constitute regional or even nationwide monopolies. In some cases, they are conglomerates, such as those formed around foreign-trade companies. Here, the motive to unite is often that of obtaining access to scarce foreign exchange or bank loans. In other cases, the combines enable scale economies in research and development, marketing, and even production to be realized. (They often make subcontracting easier, for example.) Frequently, they raise the competitiveness of Yugoslav industry on the world market, or so it is claimed. But they have the opposite effect on the domestic market. And while they are supposed to be self-managed, they often take authority away from member firms.

In determining how competitive an industry will be, the most important factor is often the ease with which firms can take up new lines of production or expand into new markets, when this is profitable. Under competitive conditions, this is part of the supply expansion which keeps down prices. Just the threat of entry by new competitors into a market can prevent established firms from putting up their prices to monopoly levels. However, the founding of new enterprises or the expansion of existing ones into new product lines is usually a risky form of investment. If most venture capital to found new enterprises is put up by individuals or by other firms, the need to share resulting profits, but not losses, with employees of the new entity will act as a deterrent to such investments. Thus, most Yugoslav firms are started by government bodies, who are also heavily involved in financing or in guaranteeing the financing of major expansions. Aside from private companies and small cooperatives, there have been virtually no citizen-founded firms since 1967, although enterprise foundings have been of some importance since the 1950s.[33]

When one or several firms found another, the founders usually retain some claim to the profits of their offspring. This is necessary as an incentive to call forth venture capital, although strictly speaking, it constitutes a departure from workers' management. However, when an investment will result in a new OAL or in an entity that could reconstitute itself as a BOAL, there is a risk to the investor that the new OAL or BOAL will be able to sever its obligations to its founder. This deters the founding of firms by other enterprises and also involves government more closely in such investment decisions—both because its risk-absorbing role is made more important and because it will be in a position to put pressure on the newly founded entity.

When government is the founder—generally at the communal or republic level since 1964—profitability is just one consideration, along with the expected social contribution of the new enterprise (e.g., its ability to create attractive jobs, its ability to serve as a catalyst for further growth, and its prestige or compliance with industry-by-industry priorities of the League of Communists). As price controls have preserved a somewhat irrational structure of prices, profitability has often been a rather poor guide to comparative worth of investment projects in different industries, and many government-founded enterprises have been poor profit prospects. Unfortunately, many have also been badly located, away from markets or sources of supply, and/or have produced doubtful product mixes, from the standpoint of need or cost advantage. Nor have they created as many jobs as one could hope for, given the amount of capital invested in them, and good jobs have been rationed as noted earlier. Political criteria, notably regional lobbying pressures, have motivated their founding, and a number have received large subsidies year after year.[34]

Differences between average wages and salaries paid for comparable skills in different industries have also been widening over time. These interindustry differentials cannot be explained by the regional problem, because interregional wage differences for the same kinds of work have been falling.[35] Instead, firms have not entered markets where excess profits are being earned, or at least have not brought about supply expansions great enough to eliminate these profits. Yet, some enterprises have been chronic loss-makers in recent years. Profitability differences between industries have been growing—another sign that the pattern of expansion has been inefficient—and these have translated into growing wage differences. In addition, some firms in high-priority industries pay higher than average wages, even though this requires them to receive regular subsidies.

Finally, since 1967, foreign investment in Yugoslavia has been legal, in the form of joint ventures or firms jointly founded by a Yugoslav and a foreign firm in cooperation. Until December 1984, the foreign partner could own no more than a 49 percent share of such a venture, except in cases where the Federal Assembly had given specific approval to raise this limit. Now, foreign equity participation is, in principle, unrestricted, although as of mid-1989, a new hotel in Belgrade is the only joint venture with more than 50 percent foreign ownership. Joint ventures are possible in all industries, except banking, insurance, commerce and social welfare. Theoretically, each joint venture is worker managed, at least as far as the Yugoslav participation is concerned. In fact, however, a joint operations board takes most management decisions. The foreign partner has a 50 percent representation on the board, regardless of the extent of its participation in the joint venture (which has ranged as low as 2 percent). The workers' council has less power than usual, even over the distribution of profit.

As of early 1984, there were only 170 joint ventures, involving a total foreign investment of under $125 million, or just over 25 percent of the total investment in these firms. There were no new joint ventures over 1978–84. An important purpose, from Yugoslavia's standpoint, is to gain access to Western technology, for which a large foreign participation is not necessarily required. However, other goals have been to create jobs and to expand exports to the West, where Yugoslavia's foreign-trade deficit is concentrated, and here, progress has been disappointing. Often, the Western partner wants to take advantage of relatively low Yugoslav wages and to tap the Yugoslav or East European markets. The latter has been a source of friction between the two sides, although a 1978 law explicitly allows for joint ventures designed to fill gaps in domestic supply or to improve the performance of Yugoslav firms.

Potential Western investors have complained about poor management and low labor productivity, which, they say, often eliminates the cost advantage. They have also been put off by import and foreign exchange retention quotas, which have been applied to joint ventures in the same way as to other firms in a given region. These and other measures have limited the transfer of earnings back to the foreign partner. However, the November 1984 amendments freed the latter from obligations to contribute part of his earnings to housing, education, national defense, and other collective consumption and made it easier for him to repatriate his profit share. The government also plans to create free trade zones, similar to those in Hungary, where firms established with the aid of foreign investment can benefit from tariff and tax advantages. Although several joint ventures have come to Yugoslavia since 1984, no great rush of foreign investment has occurred or is expected.

Notes

1. By "Serbia proper" here we mean the republic of Serbia, excluding the autonomous regions of Vojvodina and Kosovo-Metohija. This roughly coincides with the independent kingdom of Serbia prior to the Balkan Wars of 1912–13. With regard to the discussion below, Macedonia has not been an independent country since the time of Alexander the Great, over 2,000 years ago.

2. Bosnia-Herzegovina was part of the Austro-Hungarian Empire when World War I began, and the immediate cause of the war may be traced to this. A young Bosnian nationalist, Gavrilo Princip, assassinated Franz Ferdinand, the Austrian Archduke and heir to the throne, along with his wife, in Sarajevo on June 28, 1914, the anniversary of the Serbian defeat at the Battle of Kosovo. (Ferdinand's visit to Sarajevo on this day would be roughly akin to Prince Charles visiting the Catholic section of Belfast on St. Patrick's Day.) Princip was a member of "Young Bosnia," a secret organization dedicated to the violent expulsion of Austro-Hungarian rule from Bosnia-Herzegovina and to Bosnia's union with Serbia. The chief of the Serbian secret police helped to plot the assassination, which gave Austria-Hungary an excuse to attack Serbia. This conflict quickly expanded into world war.

3. See Thad Alton et al., "Money Income of the Population and Standard of Living in Eastern Europe," Research Project on National Income in East-Central Europe, Occasional Paper OP-103, New York, July 1988, Table 5, p. 14. Calculations for Yugoslavia are by J. T. Bombelles.

4. As an example of this gap, Dirlam and Plummer write, "One of the authors visited a newly-constructed hotel in an underdeveloped area in the summer of 1966. The local community and various development funds had invested heavily in the project and hoped for an influx of tourists. By the summer of 1971, the hotel had so deteriorated that there were no overnight guests, and half of some 24 expensive tourist cabins were unfit for human

habitation. The hotel had had five different managers, the latest one was nowhere in evidence, and by 4 o'clock in the afternoon, a group of waiters and friends had taken over the lobby for coffee and *slivovica.*" Joel B. Dirlam and James L. Plummer, *An Introduction to the Yugoslav Economy* (Columbus, Ohio: Merrill, 1973), p. 153.

5. See, for example, The World Bank, *Yugoslavia: Development with Decentralization* (Baltimore: Johns Hopkins, 1975), ch. 8, and Tripo Mulina and Milos Macura, "Employment," *Yugoslav Survey,* August 1980, p. 43. Regarding regional redistribution in Yugoslavia, see J. T. Bombelles, "Transfer of Resources from More to Less Developed Republics and Autonomous Provinces of Yugoslavia, 1971–1980," Research Project on National Income in East-Central Europe, Occasional Paper OP-69, New York, July 1981, and Toussaint Hocevar, "Inter-Regional Economic Integration: the Yugoslav Case," paper presented at Third World Congress for Soviet and East European Studies, October 30–November 4, 1985, Washington, D.C.

6. F. B. Singleton, "Problems of Regional Development: The Case of Yugoslavia," *Yearbook of East European Economics,* vol. 2 (1971), Part II, p. 376. See, as well, F. B. Singleton and Bernard Carter, *The Economy of Yugoslavia* (London: Croom Helm, 1982), ch. 17. This book gives an excellent general discussion of the Yugoslav economy.

7. This quote and the one in the next paragraph came from Lazar Drakul, "Economic Development, 1971–82," *Yugoslav Survey,* May 1984, p. 77.

8. In this context, Yugoslavia's roads are among the most dangerous in Europe, partly because of a 52-fold explosion in the number of registered vehicles, from 55,000 in 1954 to 2,874,000 in 1985.

9. One major project, costing around $125 million U.S. and supported by a $56 million loan from the World Bank (a regular source of Yugoslav borrowing) is now irrigating about 21,000 hectares (over 50,000 acres) in Kosmet and providing most urban areas there with drinking water. This irrigation network should eventually make it possible to raise fruit and vegetable output by over 6 times and to double livestock production, by comparison with 1980. A second irrigation project is connected with construction of the three huge Iron Gates hydroelectric dams on the Danube River, a joint undertaking with Romania. The irrigation works alone are to cost about $100 million and to be financed entirely by Yugoslavia, with the benefits being concentrated in Vojvodina. Eventually, the Iron Gates power stations will generate 20 billion kilowatt hours per year, or more than Yugoslavia's entire output in 1968.

10. J. T. Bombelles, *Economic Development of Communist Yugoslavia* (Stanford: Stanford University Press, 1968), p. 48.

11. Ibid., pp. 48–49.

12. The most accessible discussions of decision making in Yugoslav firms are Dirlam and Plummer, *An Introduction to the Yugoslav Economy,* chs. 2, 3; Jiri Kolaja, *Workers' Councils: The Yugoslav Experience* (London: Tavistock, 1965); Ellen Commisso, *Workers' Control Under Plan and Market* (New Haven: Yale University Press, 1979); Idzhak Adizes, *Industrial Democracy: Yugoslav Style* (New York: The Free Press, 1971); Paul Blumberg, *Industrial Democracy* (London: Constable, 1968), ch. 9; Howard Wachtel, *Workers' Management and Workers' Wages in Yugoslavia* (Ithaca: Cornell University Press, 1973), ch. 4; David Granick, *Enterprise Guidance in Eastern Europe* (Princeton, N.J.: Princeton University Press, 1975), chs. 11, 12; and H. Lydall, *Yugoslav Socialism: Theory and Practice* (Oxford: Clarendon Press, 1984). The last gives an excellent general discussion of Yugoslav self-management in theory and practice.

13. See, for example, Lydall, *Yugoslav Socialism,* along with Granick, *Enterprise Guidance,* ch. 12, and the references cited by him, notably (on p. 380) to J. Obradovich, J. R. P. French, Jr., and W. L. Rodgers, "Workers' Councils in Yugoslavia," *Human Relations,* October 1970. The quote below is from J. Obradovich, "Workers' Participation: Who Participates?" *Industrial Relations,* February 1975.

14. Granick, *Enterprise Guidance,* ch. 12, cites the case of one Slovenian enterprise

(p. 372) where the director was fired because of a policy disagreement with the workers' council. However, this sort of dismissal appears to be rare.

15. See J. Zupanov, "Is Enterprise Management Becoming Professionalized?" *International Studies in Management and Organization*, September 1973.

16. As a proportion of working time, absenteeism in 1978 came to 2 percent in Japan, 3.5 percent in Canada and the U.S., 7.7 percent in West Germany, 8.3 percent in France, 10.6 percent in Italy, 12 percent in the Netherlands, and 13.8 percent in Sweden. Regarding the discussion in the text below, see Granick, *Enterprise Guidance*, pp. 382–89, and references cited, particularly M. McAuley, *Labour Disputes in Soviet Russia, 1957–65* (Oxford: Clarendon Press, 1969), chs. 6, 7; and D. Gorupich and I. Paj, *Workers' Self-Management in Yugoslav Undertakings* (Ekonomiski Institut: Zagreb, 1970).

17. Granick, *Enterprise Guidance*, p. 355.

18. See, for example, the Zagreb daily, *Vjesnik*, March 20, 1976, and the Belgrade weekly, *Nedeljne informativne novine*, June 20, 1976. Some of the arguments used by social sector firms to explain their problems with private competition have also been used by public enterprises in Western countries. For instance, social sector bakeries have complained that they must serve distant towns and villages, while private competitors are free to concentrate on the most profitable kinds of bread and cake and serve only the most profitable market areas. Nevertheless, it is also conceded that private bakers are forced to use nineteenth-century production methods, while social sector bakeries have up-to-date equipment.

19. See Saul Estrin, "The Effects of Self-Management on Yugoslav Industrial Growth," *Soviet Studies*, January 1982, along with the references he cites on p. 69, especially Ben Ward, "The Firm in Illyria: Market Syndicalism," *American Economic Review*, September 1958. Ward first indicated the job-rationing thesis, along with several other hypotheses relating to labor-managed firms. However, see, as well, Janez Prasnikar, "The Yugoslav Self-Managed Firm and its Behaviour," *Economic Analysis and Workers' Management*, no. 1, 1980. Finally, see M. Pauly and M. Redisch, "The Not-For-Profit Hospital as a Physicians' Cooperative," *American Economic Review*, March 1973.

20. See, for example, Jaroslav Vanek and Milena Jovicic, "The Capital Market and Income Distribution in Yugoslavia: A Theoretical and Empirical Analysis," *Quarterly Journal of Economics*, August 1975. A May 1988 reform seeks to achieve positive real interest rates by indexing all savings deposits of three months or more and all loans of one year or more to the retail price index. The principal of each loan and deposit will rise at the same percentage rate as retail prices (according to the official index).

21. Employees can privatize the firm's profits in other ways, e.g., by allocating more funds to housing or collective consumption. The basic point in the text has been made in numerous articles by S. Pejovich and E. Furubotn. See their "Property Rights and the Behavior of the Firm in a Socialist State: The Example of Yugoslavia," *Zeitschrift für Nationalokonomie*, nos. 3–4, 1970.

22. L. D'Andrea-Tyson, "Liquidity Crises in the Yugoslav Economy: An Alternative to Bankruptcy?" *Soviet Studies*, April 1977, pp. 288–89. The risk avoidance of Yugoslav workers is documented, e.g., by J. Zupanov, "The Producer and Risk," *Eastern European Economics*, Spring 1969. See also Adizes, *Industrial Democracy*, for discussions of responsibility avoidance.

23. Tyson, "Liquidity Crises," p. 288, who also notes (p. 290) that "the Yugoslavs have tried to develop a variety of penalties for financial irresponsibility . . . consistent with [the worker-manager view], such as forcing illiquid enterprises to change management, placing such enterprises under state directorship, requiring insolvent enterprises to present local governments with plans for 'rehabilitation', and allowing the creditors of an insolvent enterprise to choose its management and future business policy. . . ."

24. Stephen Sacks, *Entry of New Competitors into Yugoslav Market Socialism* (Berkeley: University of California, Institute of International Studies, 1973), p. 75.

25. Branko Horvat, "Labor-Managed Enterprises," paper presented to the Workshop on Economic Organization and Development, Carleton University, Ottawa, Canada, April 1972.

26. Albert Waterston, *Planning in Yugoslavia* (Washington, D.C.: Economic Development Institute, 1962), p. 54.

27. However, in many cases, it appears that the joint selection committees, composed of enterprise and local government representatives, were never disbanded. No one can hold the post of director until he or she has been approved by such a committee in places where it still exists. While the firm nominates two-thirds of committee members, half the enterprise representation is chosen by its union local.

28. J. Vanek, *The General Theory of Labor-Managed Market Economies* (Ithaca: Cornell University Press, 1970), p. 288.

29. Cost increases, low average employee earnings, and financial difficulties have been reasons for granting firms higher output prices in the past. Increases in the prices of imported goods are passed through the economy. Moreover, firms can sometimes push up controlled prices, simply by holding supplies off the market until shortages become acute.

30. See (e.g.) Sacks, *Entry of New Competitors*; Werner Sichel, "The Threat to Market Socialism: The Case of Yugoslavia," *Antitrust Bulletin*, Summer 1971, and World Bank Staff, *Yugoslavia*, pp. 48, 119–20.

31. They also perform other useful functions, such as dissemination of technological information, research and development, and product standardization. However, many of the general associations fix prices and set production quotas for member firms, just as a cartel would. In principle, both economic chambers and general associations obey the self-management principle. That is, they are managed by councils consisting of employee representatives of member firms.

32. World Bank Staff, *Yugoslavia*, pp. 119–20.

33. Citizen founders must raise their own capital or borrow from nonbanks. They are not allowed to pass along their risk to the government. Together with the profit-sharing requirement and tax disadvantages noted earlier, this has been a powerful deterrent.

34. Sacks, *Entry of New Competitors*, pp. 65–78.

35. H. Wachtel, "Workers' Management and Inter-Industry Wage Differentials in Yugoslavia," *Journal of Political Economy*, May–June 1972. See, as well, Peter Miovich, *Determinants of Income Differentials in Yugoslav Self-Managed Enterprises*, unpublished Ph.D. dissertation, University of Pennsylvania, 1975, and Laura D'Andrea-Tyson and Gabriel Eichler, "Continuity and Change in the Yugoslav Economy in the 1970s and 1980s," in U.S. Congress, Joint Economic Committee, *East European Economic Assessment, Part I* (Washington, D.C.: U.S. Government Printing Office, 1981).

Questions for Review, Discussion, Examination

*1. After roughly a quarter century of rapid economic growth, 1953–79, Yugoslavia now faces serious economic problems, which we may divide into three categories: (a) "Western-type" problems, (b) "Eastern-type" problems, (c) "Yugoslav-specific" problems. Briefly give examples of each and explain how (b) may contribute to (a) in Yugoslavia's economic system (which is more decentralized than in most socialist economies).

2. What specifically caused the sharp decline of economic growth during the 1980s in Yugoslavia, as in some other East European nations?

3. Why is regional income inequality so high in Yugoslavia? Why has inter-regional coordination and specialization been hard to achieve?

What do you suppose has made the regional problem tolerable, at least until the 1980s?

4. Why did the replacement of state management of much of the economy by workers' self-management push Yugoslavia toward a market economy? Basically, what does workers' self-management imply about enterprise management?

5. What is the difference between an OAL and a BOAL? Why have OALs tended to dominate their BOALs in practice?

*6. In theory, workers should "own" labor-managed firms, at least in the property-rights sense of sharing in profits and losses. This would require them to be residual claimants to enterprise income. Is this true *de facto* in Yugoslavia?

In what way do state tax-subsidy policies toward firms in Yugoslavia resemble those in other socialist countries?

7. In what areas of enterprise decision making do worker representatives exercise greatest influence? In what areas do they exercise least influence? Where does power lie in the latter areas?

8. Yugoslavia has had an inadequate supply of competent people who are willing to assume top management posts. Why is this? (See also question 16 below.)

9. Despite being a socialist market economy, Yugoslavia has a large private sector, which plays much the same role as the second economy in other socialist countries, and also supplies many badly-needed jobs.

(a) Why is there such a large private sector?

(b) Why are *average* incomes in the private sector below those in the social sector?

(c) Why are there nevertheless opportunities for some private entrepreneurs to become wealthy?

*10. Why is there a tendency for jobs in the social sector to be rationed, despite government pressure on socialist firms to hire more employees? What kind of role does this suggest for the private sector?

*11. Recalling the insider-outsider dichotomy in section 3–5, suppose that Yugoslav workers with secure rights to good social-sector jobs are "insiders," while most other workers are "outsiders." What is likely to be the result of expansionary policy designed to increase employment? Could inflation and unemployment coexist? Explain.

12. Yugoslav guest workers in western countries are able to use their savings to invest in the creation of new workplaces in social-sector firms, which they may occupy when they return to Yugoslavia. In effect, the worker buys himself or herself a social-sector job.

Why may this be a form of wage discrimination, if the returnee does not receive a sufficient return on this investment, over and above the usual wage for his type of work?

*13. Why has quasi-independent operation of republic-level banks magnified inflationary pressures in Yugoslavia? (*Hint:* What has this to do with the notion of "externality?")

14. What has been the main source of investment finance in Yugoslavia? Why has the percentage of self-financed investment been low?

*15. In connection with question 14, what is the difference between the "pure cooperative" and "worker-manager" views of a Yugoslav firm? Which view do most Yugoslav workers take?

How does the view taken by most workers relate to enterprise willingness to finance investment from retained earnings? How does this help to increase the influence of local and regional governments over business decisions? How does it help to cellularize the economy into overly self-sufficient regional blocs?

16. Why do directors of social-sector firms often feel insecure and suffer from identity crises (according to psychological studies)?

17. Are markets in Yugoslavia generally competitive? How are prices of many goods usually set?

18. What are JOALs in theory and in practice?

19. Who is most often the founder of social-sector firms? What criteria are used in deciding what kinds of enterprises to start, and what problems has this caused?

*20. Has development in Yugoslavia been demand-oriented? Explain.

* = more difficult.

11

THE YUGOSLAV ECONOMY: PLANNING, AGRICULTURE, AND FOREIGN TRADE

We are back to the basic contradiction between unworkable, centralized systems and a consumer society. If managers use their initiative and are enterprising, some are bound to get richer or they wouldn't bother.

—Milovan Djilas
(author of *The New Class*)

11-1. Approach to Planning and Policy

A. Formal Planning

The demise of the command economy by 1954 did not mean the end of formal planning in Yugoslavia, although the drawing up of one- and five-year social plans is less important than the informal interaction between government bodies, banks and firms. Planning became more bottom-up and, to a degree, more participatory. The Federal Planning Commission in Belgrade was renamed the Federal Institute of Economic Planning (FIEP), and its staff was cut. Many of the discharged personnel went to the enterprises or to republic-level or communal governments, which gained authority, as well as control over their own budgets, a guarantee that federalism was real. A fairly complex planning network replaced the previous chain of command. Participatory planning meant, in theory, that social plans—covering investment and production forecasts, as well as projections of national and personal income, consumption, housing, labor productivity, and imports and exports—were to be worked out cooperatively. Ultimately, plans must also be approved by the federal legislature, and Table 11.1 lists a few main targets and realizations for each of the five-year plans completed since World War II.

Table 11.1

Medium-Term Growth Targets and Realizations in Yugoslavia, 1947–85 (percent per annum)

Sector	1947–52		1957–61		1961–65		1966–70		1971–75		1976–80		1981–85	
	Plan	Actual	Plan	Actual	Plan	Actual	Plan	Actual	Plan	Actual	Plan	Actual	Plan	Actual
Social product	12.5	2.3	9.5	10.6	11.4	6.0	8.0	6.2	8.0	6.3	7.3	5.7	4–4.5	0.7
Agriculture	8.7	−0.4	7.4	7.7	7.2	0.5	5.0	3.7	3.0	4.1	4.0	1.9	4.5	0.7
Industry	37.6	6.2	11.0	12.2	13.0	10.6	9.5	6.7	9.5	8.1	8.5	6.9	4–4.5	2.7
Construction	n.a.	1.1	10.9	15.9	13.3	9.3	7.0	8.0	8.5	3.7	8.0	8.0	n.a.	−6.3
Trade, tourism, catering	n.a.	8.0	7.1	12.3	12.2	8.7	9.0	7.9	9.5	6.3	7.5	4.5	n.a.	−0.9

Sources: J. T. Bombelles, *Economic Development of Communist Yugoslavia* (Stanford: Stanford University Press, 1968), p. 48; OECD, *Annual Economic Survey of Yugoslavia, 1970* (Paris: OECD, 1970), Table 15, p. 43; Economist Intelligence Unit, *Quarterly Economic Review of Yugoslavia,* Annual Supplement, 1975 (London: Economist Intelligence Unit, 1975), p. 4; Spasoje Medenica, "Basic Targets of the Social Plan of Yugoslavia for 1981-85," *Yugoslav Survey,* February 1981; *Statisticki Godisnjak Jugoslavije* (Statistical Yearbook of Yugoslavia), various years.

n.a. = not available

Plan targets were not binding on firms over 1954–75—this is the essence of indicative planning—although they were supposed to be obligatory for government bodies. In practice, when the League of Communists and different levels of government have been able to agree on priorities, the state has had powerful means of implementation. These include such conventional levers as taxes, subsidies, and influence over the allocation of credit, plus the system of guarantees and the control over career prospects of officials and managers described above. Over 1953–64, the federal government had greater control over the allocation of investment credit—exercised largely through the General Investment Fund (GIF)—and over imports, access to foreign exchange, and taxation than it has today. With the demise of GIF in 1964, the central government lost some of its leverage over economic activity, as did the League of Communists. However, as early as 1972, the League was beginning to reassert its leading role, and in connection with this, efforts were begun to restructure planning and to make it less indicative.

Thus, the 1976 Law on Social Planning put formal planning on a contractual basis, beginning with the 1976–80 period. In principle, plan construction is based on the annual and five-year plans drawn up by enterprises to cover all phases of their operations. Government bodies also construct such plans, as do banks and other work units in the social sector. On the basis of plans prepared at lower levels—adjusted to conform to goals of the political leadership—the federal government adopts the social plan. However, the process of arriving at five-year plan targets is more than ever one of negotiation between firms, banks, and different levels of government. (The 1976–80 plan came out late because of protracted bargaining.)[1]

Once targets are negotiated, the various parties are required to make a commitment to their achievement by signing contracts called "social compacts" and "self-management agreements." The latter (but not the social compacts) are legally binding, and the Social Accounting Service is charged with enforcement. Both types of contracts are designed to make plans and policies less voluntary, once agreement has been reached between the firms and government bodies involved. The original goal was for bottom-up planning, under supervision of the League of Communists and the federal government, to eventually replace the market—not by doing away with interfirm relations, but by monitoring and guiding these more closely. A system governed by command-economy-type allocations and quotas would emerge, but these targets would be arrived at "democratically." This is consciously patterned after the socialist system envisaged by Marx, but we can scarcely ignore the fact that, in plan negotiations, the party is the most powerful bargaining force.[2]

As in any system of planning, Yugoslavia's contractual approach requires firms and government bodies to exchange information about future production and investment. Public authorities must harmonize the plans of different enterprises and aggregate these into a consistent global plan—ultimately for the country as a whole—which details growth priorities for the five years to come. Yugoslav firms are also supposed to exchange information among themselves and to reveal their intentions regarding future expansion. One goal is to dovetail the plans of suppliers and users of producer goods, thereby avoiding excess capacity and bottlenecks in production, which may result from mistaken forecasts as the structure of the economy changes. For all this to work, however, firms and government bodies would have to take the social compacts and self-management agreements more seriously than they have to date. Social compacts between republics have proved especially hard to enforce. Often, they designate goals without detailing any means for achieving these. But even the self-management agreements appear to be widely violated. Planning nevertheless consumes many resources, and most social sector firms participate actively in plan formation—in part, because this raises their chances of getting desired investment projects into the plan, which raises the likelihood that finance will be available.

Despite their loss of direct leverage over economic activity, the federal government and the League of Communists are able to impose their industrial priorities, provided these do not create too much conflict between the regions. Thus, the federation has agreed to build duplicate production facilities in nearly every republic and autonomous region. The cost of this policy is high, not only because of uneconomic duplication, but also because Yugoslavia has promoted industries in which it has an efficiency disadvantage vis-à-vis Western and Asian nations. A recent government inquiry (the Kraigher Commission on Economic Stabilization) recommended reducing the role of social compacts and SMAs to allow Yugoslavia to move toward a unified domestic market. This process has begun. The Commission also recommended reducing Yugoslavia's total tax burden, and shifting away from indirect toward direct taxation—in part, to make the tax burden more neutral between labor and capital.

B. Fiscal and Monetary Policies

Not only has the federal government lost part of its former leverage over investment, but spending and taxing authority have shifted to lower government levels. Federal expenditure has been running less than 20 percent of total public sector outlays or 6 percent of gross domestic product in recent years, much below ratios common in Western countries. The federation has had clear entitlement only to half the basic sales tax (which rose to 75 percent in 1987) and to part of customs revenues. Together, these have covered 55–60 percent of its expenditure. The rest has come mainly from negotiated contributions by republic-level governments to the federal budget. The federation has little leverage over spending of lower government levels, and most of its own outlays go for defense or entitlement programs, including pensions. The upshot is that Yugoslavia has had no real fiscal policy to combat the business cycle. As a basic rule, public sector budgets have been kept in balance. However, the National Bank of Yugoslavia has effectively run large deficits with the rest of the economy—in part, to finance easy credit which has been part of the soft budget constraint.

The soft budget constraint plus the fact that Yugoslavs hold most of their savings in foreign currencies (mainly deutsche marks), whose value in dinars rises with devaluation, has also made it nearly impossible to have an effective monetary policy. As open market operations are still of minor importance, monetary policy is largely a matter of direct interaction between the National Bank and the business or commercial banks. Its basic tools are changes in reserve requirements and (more importantly) variations in the amounts business banks may borrow from the central bank. As in Japan and West Germany, business banks are heavily in debt to the central bank, which has an active rediscount policy. The National Bank will lend to the commercial banks (rediscount their loans) up to ceilings normally 15–20 percent of a bank's short-term deposits. In this way, a bank can transform a percentage of its loans into money, by effectively transferring them, along with part of the associated risk, to the National Bank. Central-bank loans to the business banks—mainly through the rediscount mechanism—are the major source of money supply expansion.

Thus, the National Bank lends large sums to commercial banks at low interest (rediscount) rates and absorbs part of the risk associated with the latters' lending. The central bank also suggests lending priorities to the business banks, who must commit themselves in advance as to how they will lend borrowed funds, and it has made some loans directly to industry, generally on especially favorable terms. On balance, promotion of priority industries through selective taxation and credit allocation in Yugoslavia resembles the same process in Japan, with the notable exception that Japan has a unitary, rather than a federal, structure of government. However, the experiences of the two countries diverge when it comes to overall tightening of money and credit. Historically, each country's government has preferred easy credit to ensure ready financing of output expansion. But sometimes a need arises to tighten credit, in order to reduce inflation, make firms more cost conscious, weed out inefficient enterprises, and improve the balance of payments. (Tight credit restricts domestic demand, which reduces the demand for imports and encourages firms to seek export markets.) The Bank of Japan has never been timid about jolting the system by setting and enforcing credit ceilings for commercial banks that force the latter to curtail their loans.

But in Yugoslavia, such forceful action has been rare. Even when credit is relatively easy to get, many firms do not pay their debts on time because the penalty for this has been low. Yugoslav enterprises also find it profitable to remain illiquid, and accumulating business debts has become a major means of borrowing.[3] While banks and government bodies have guaranteed many of these debts, they are often overextended and therefore forced to selectively default themselves, in effect. Since bankruptcy is usually ruled out—and there is an effective floor on wages— restriction of bank credit mainly causes firms to postpone paying more debt for longer periods of time. Because the debts of one enterprise are the accounts receivable of others, the failure to pay spreads rapidly from firm to firm. One company often cannot pay its debts even when it wants to because it cannot collect enough of what it is owed by its customers. The ratio of accounts receivable to total sales tends to rise rapidly. In this sense, Yugoslavia goes into a liquidity crisis. The flow of money between firms tends to stagnate, the number of court cases involving uncollected debts skyrockets, and eventually, the payment of reasonable wages is endangered.[4]

Subsequently, political pressure on the National Bank, and especially on its republic-level branches, to expand the flow of credit to the business banks beyond previously set ceilings becomes irresistible. Eventually, the central bank gives in. The authorities thus find a tight monetary policy impossible to sustain, and illiquidity and inflation often go hand-in-hand. According to Tyson:

> ironically, . . . liquidity crises cause the reversal of the restrictive monetary policies that led to their appearance in the first place. Unfortunately, . . . this reversal also necessitates sacrifice of the macro-economic goals, notably price stability, that originally fostered . . . the monetary restrictions. Thus, the willingness of enterprises to default on outstanding debt explains not only the recurrence of liquidity crises, but also the inability . . . to maintain macroeconomic stability [with] monetary policy.[5]

A 1976 law partially monetizes accounts receivable—provided they are guaranteed in the manner described earlier—which makes it easier for firms to get around restrictive monetary policy and to undermine it.

Although not all firms have good access to credit, the supply of credit and money in Yugoslavia has been a function of the demand for it, ultimately by firms and government bodies. This tends to make the money supply and the rate of inflation politically determined by the need to maintain the ability of firms in the social sector to pay reasonable wages—meaning that one enterprise cannot be allowed to fall too far behind the others. The Kraigher Commission, whose report was adopted by the Yugoslav Parliament in 1983, recommended reducing the annual rate of inflation to 10 percent by end-1985, as well as establishing positive real interest rates, and moving toward elimination of price controls. However, real interest rates remain negative, and official consumer price inflation has continued to rise, at least through mid-1989.

In Japan, a major purpose of tight monetary policy has been to safeguard the balance of payments—by reducing domestic demand for home-produced goods, which gives an extra incentive to export, and also by reducing the demand for imports. As in the case of Yugoslavia, Japan's growth rate has fluctuated markedly from year to year, this instability being made tolerable by institutional constraints on laying workers off. In protecting its own balance of payments, Yugoslavia's main substitute for a tight monetary policy has been repeated devaluation of the dinar, which lost more than 95 percent of its value in terms of the U.S. dollar between early 1979 and late 1986. Direct controls over imports have also been tightened drastically during the last few years, producing supply bottlenecks and increasing excess capacity.

Like Yugoslavia, Japan often protects domestic firms from import competition. The Japanese import about the same quantity of manufactures as Switzerland, despite a population over eighteen times as large. But Japan protects domestic manufacturing in order to develop its export potential, and managers who receive help, but fail to become export-oriented, will suffer career setbacks. Yugoslav managers are selected and promoted to a greater extent on the basis of noneconomic criteria, and industrial priorities are determined more on ideological grounds, which has led Yugoslavia to subsidize heavy industries year after year, despite their modest export potential and rapacious appetite for imports. Nevertheless, since early 1987, Yugoslav authorities have made stronger efforts to target and control the growth of money and credit, although not yet with apparent success.

11-2. The Organization of Agriculture

Like most socialist nations, with whom it shares a common ideological heritage, Yugoslavia has assigned a low investment priority to agriculture. The Kraigher Commission noted that "every village had the ambition to erect a factory chimney," which was in line with the Communists' attitude toward economic development. Yugoslavia was a food surplus nation before 1970—exporting more food than it imported—but it subsequently became a food deficit nation, largely because of low investment in agriculture. It has regained the status of net food exporter during the 1980s. Yet, on average, each Yugoslav farmer produced just enough food to feed himself and six other people in 1980, one of the lowest support ratios in Europe.[6]

Unlike most socialist countries, the bulk of Yugoslav agriculture has not been collectivized. It consists mainly of 2.1 million small private farms, which cover over 80 percent of the agricultural land. In 1985, private farmers raised more than 80 percent of all livestock and accounted for about 70 percent of total value added in farming. However, because own consumption is high, accounting for over half its output, the private sector supplied only 51 percent of all marketed produce. The rest of production and marketing came from self-managed farm cooperatives, which own over 17 percent of the arable land, and operate along the same organizational lines as worker managed firms in industry. Output in socialist agriculture has grown many times more rapidly than production on private farms, because the former enjoys better access to all nonlabor inputs. In particular, socialist agriculture is much more capital intensive; in a typical year, more is invested there than in private farming. Most tractors are in private hands, although there was just one tractor for every 2.5 private farms in 1985 vs. an average of 9 per social sector farm. Moreover, the average social sector farm covered nearly 1,200 acres of cultivable land in 1985 vs. an average of 8 to 9 acres for private farms. Value added per acre is higher in the socialist sector and value added per worker was about 4 times as high in 1985, although investment yields appear to be higher in the private sector. Around 80 percent of social sector output comes from the northern, more developed parts of the country, where these farms occupy the best land—generally, the sites of large estates before World War II. As in other countries, Yugoslavia's farm labor force is aging. About 25 percent are 60 years or older, and at least 40 percent are over 50. Nearly half of Yugoslavia's private farms (accounting for about 30 percent of the land area of the private sector) are now worked by pensioners for extra income or by individuals who are not professional farmers.

Over 40 percent of Yugoslavia's private farmers cooperate with the social sector in some way—meaning, in particular, that they depend on it for fertilizer, credit, marketing, and technical help. About 250,000 private peasants also cooperate with their neighbors in ''self-managed associations of peasant farmers,'' through which they engage in joint production, marketing, saving, and finance. These associations have their own workers' councils, and farmers pool some of their land, as well as labor, tools, machinery, seed, and other inputs. Private ownership of land is retained, although the associations can accumulate savings and buy land to be jointly owned by their members. In the future, the private sector will probably have greater access to credit and technology than heretofore, although the emphasis will be on acquiring this through the self-managed associations and in the context of peasant cooperation.

Although influential Communists periodically call for collectivization of agriculture, the 1974 Constitution guarantees the right of private ownership. According to a recent Yugoslav publication, ''The League of Communists . . . has clearly declared for the view that the socialist transformation of the countryside is a matter for the farmers themselves. The peasantry may not be the object of Socialist change . . . in which forces outside the villages try to 'introduce Socialism' by political action or administrative measures.''[7] It is widely believed that efforts to forcefully socialize agriculture would cause a peasant uprising. Thus, the land area of the socialist sector is now scheduled to expand slowly, through purchase of land from private farmers who leave the countryside, as over 6.5 million farm family members have done since 1948. Despite the out-migration from agriculture, the average private farm was smaller in 1985 than in 1960, because of the acreage ceiling, the legal right to divide inherited land among offspring, and acquisition of land by individuals to farm part-time.

Thus, there have been suggestions to raise the 25-acre (10-hectare) legal ceiling on private farms to enable them to use modern machinery and land more efficiently, and such a proposal is now expected to become law. In the past, these suggestions have been rejected on ideological grounds—the private property mentality is supposed to wither away under socialism—or on grounds that such a move would lead to greater inequality in the villages. However, beginning in the 1970s, many peasants abandoned their farms and emigrated to Western Europe, in search of better jobs. A number have since returned. Nevertheless, during the 1970s and on into the latter 1980s, 1–2 million acres of potentially productive land have lain untilled. To a degree, this has resulted from the tendency to starve private farmers of credit and supplies, and to a degree, from relatively low farm incomes and the aging of the farm population. However, acreage ceilings have also played a role, and for various reasons, the socialist sector has been unable to establish itself on the unused land. Thus, in 1975, Slovenia raised the legal ceiling on farm size to about 50 acres in hilly areas and to more than 100 acres for sheep or cattle breeders in mountainous regions. Private farmers may also rent additional land beyond their ownership ceilings. Croatia recently raised the ownership limit to about 50 acres in lowlands and to 100 acres in hilly areas. Finally, Montenegro allows private farms of up to 71 acres (29 hectares) in mountainous areas.

Although the share of population gaining its livelihood mainly from agriculture has fallen from 73 percent to under 19 percent since World War II, there are still up to 700,000 underemployed farmers. Most Yugoslav farm labor is now provided by women, and most farm families farm part-time and have additional sources of income. The typical farmer works only about 140 days per year. Partly for this reason, per capita agricultural output is lower in Yugoslavia than in any other East European country, although the percentage of labor force in farming is higher. The share of agriculture in gross domestic product at factor cost has also fallen—from 43 percent to about 14 percent over 1947–85—and its 1985 share of gross fixed investment was 8.9 percent. The Kraigher Report recommended raising the latter to at least 12 percent, while increasing the outputs of farm machinery, fertilizers, and pesticides, expanding irrigation and drainage to 16 percent of the arable land from just over 2 percent in 1985, and building large numbers of new storage facilities.

Most of these recommendations will not be met by the year 2000, their target date, and most are not new. A 1973 social compact, the Green Plan, which ran to 1985, also pledged greater investment in infrastructure, as well as modernization, increased irrigation, and introduction of high-yielding seed varieties. Several of these programs have been successful, but the Green Plan's basic goal of a 39 percent rise in gross farm output over the 12 years was not met. (Instead, the increase was about 25 percent.) Agriculture's investment share was lower in most of these years than the 9.7 percent achieved in 1973. Historically, prices received by farmers have also been lower, relative to prices of other goods and services, than they would have been if all prices had responded freely to supply and demand. This remains true. However, over 1970–85, wholesale farm prices rose 60 percent faster than wholesale prices of industrial inputs for agriculture (machinery, fertilizer, tools, etc.), so that the terms of trade moved favorably, both to private farmers and to farms in the social sector. Because of this and rising labor productivity, real incomes from private agriculture rose over 1980–85, whereas they were falling in most branches of industry. Retail food prices soared to more than 40 times their 1970 level by 1985. In the latter year, 47–48 percent of total expenditure on personal consumption went for food and beverages. Although calorie intake per Yugoslav was high, the cereal content of food consumption was also higher than desirable from a nutritional standpoint.[8]

11-3. The Organization of Foreign Trade

Foreign trade remains the most controlled sector of the Yugoslav economy. Until the latter 1970s, all import and export orders went through the Foreign Trade Ministry, and fewer than 100 enterprises were allowed to trade directly with foreign governments or firms, although one enterprise often traded on behalf of another. A foreign-trade bank, the Yugoslav Bank for International Economic Cooperation, finances most trade. To a degree, government restraints on foreign trade were relaxed by the 1976 Law of Associated Labor. It formalized the present self-management structure and allowed any manufacturing OAL or BOAL to register as a foreign trade enterprise, provided it could demonstrate the necessary funds, personnel, and expertise. At present, more than 1,100 firms have so registered and have established representation abroad, although most of these are interested in imports, rather than exports, so that the number of firms with substantial exports is still fairly low. Moreover, the federal government and the League of Communists have continued to impose their industrial priorities on the structure of imports.

The first steps to free foreign trade and payments were taken in 1952, when the era of command planning was drawing to a close. The dinar was devalued from 50 to 300 = $1 U.S. This proved to be the first of many devaluations, and in 1965, a currency reform exchanged one new dinar for every one hundred old. In mid-1988, about 2,400 new dinars (240,000 old dinars) were exchanging for $1 U.S. Even so, the goal of convertibility for the dinar has not yet been realized, and it is still overvalued vis-à-vis Western currencies. Holders of dinars cannot exchange them freely for dollars, deutsche marks, francs, or yen, etc. Instead, foreign exchange is rationed among would-be importers, tourists, and firms or banks wanting to invest abroad. Formal or informal import quotas exist for most goods. Historically, firms which earned foreign currencies from exports or tourism, etc., have been allowed to keep shares of foreign exchange earnings (the "retention quota," recently around 45 percent), in order to increase the incentive to export. However, a 1985 law abolished this right, as part of an effort to move toward a unified foreign exchange market in which the opportunity to buy convertible currencies is more uniform from one firm to another, and exchange rates move closer to market-clearing levels.

By rationing Western currencies, the government restricts the demand for them by holders of dinars and keeps down their prices in terms of the dinar— which subsidizes firms and individuals with relatively high access to imported goods and penalizes others, who find it more difficult or impossible to buy abroad. Originally, Yugoslavia carried this type of discrimination further by using a system of multiple exchange rates set up in the mid-1950s. For example, in 1955, the basic unofficial exchange rate for trade was about 600 (old) dinars—$1 U.S. But virtually no one used this rate. An importer with a low priority might be assigned a "coefficient of exchange" equal to two, while one with a high priority received a coefficient equal to one-half. The first importer had to pay 1,200 dinars for each U.S. dollar he was allowed, while the second had to pay 300. A similar practice favored some exporters over others. The effect was to subsidize imports of machinery, equipment, raw materials, and fuel, while penalizing imports of light industrial goods. These priorities remain intact today.

Like other East European nations, Yugoslavia has followed a foreign trade strategy of import substitution since World War II. The decision of these countries to emphasize capital intensive heavy industry at home was necessarily a decision in favor of import substitution, since they had previously imported these goods. Unfortunately, the effort to reduce dependence on imports has failed, partly because the countries in question have no comparative advantage in heavy industry. With some exceptions, their products bear a significant cost or quality disadvantage vis-à-vis Western or Asian competition. Moreover, heavy industry is a voracious user of imported raw materials, fuel, and machinery, which in Yugoslavia's case have accounted for over 60 percent of total imports in most recent years. For every one percent increase in growth of real GNP, Yugoslavia has had to raise her imports by more than one percent. It is now more dependent on imports than it was when the postwar import substitution strategy began.

If we look at changes in the composition of exports over 1947–86, we find that, initially, industry and agriculture (plus forestry) each accounted for half the total by value. But by 1986, nearly 85 percent of all exports were industrial products, and the share of capital goods rose from virtually nothing in 1952 to about 18 percent in 1962, since which time it has generally been in the 15–20 percent range. Consumer goods declined from 44 percent to about 32 percent of all exports, while raw materials and intermediate goods showed a small net decrease. Unfortunately, it is exports of food, semiprocessed goods, raw materials, and some manufactured consumer products that sell best in Western markets, where Yugoslavia has its trade deficit.

In this context, the most dramatic changes in the composition of exports occur when we classify them by stage of production. In 1947, over half were raw materials, farm products and other unprocessed goods, while only 7 percent were finished goods. By 1986, over 74 percent were finished goods, and only 5–6 percent were unprocessed. The greatest export growth came in chemicals, machinery, metal goods, electrical goods, and metallurgy, while food, drink, tobacco, and textiles rose more slowly than the average. Yet, Yugoslavia has an import surplus (trade deficit) in the former group of industries and an export surplus in the latter group. The raw materials requirements of three industries—petroleum refining, chemicals, and steel—have accounted for over half the total trade deficit during the 1980s. By contrast, there has been a large trade surplus in consumer goods, partly because imports in this category have been most severely constrained by quotas and exchange controls.

As early as 1961, Yugoslavia's balance of payments was in crisis, despite import controls and export subsidies. In that year, it had to borrow $275 million from the IMF and from Western countries, and it consequently came under Western pressure to liberalize its trade and payments systems, with a view to moving toward dinar convertibility. However, the balance of payments subsequently grew worse—it has generally been a problem area since—and while multiple exchange rates disappeared in 1965, Yugoslavia has never been able to get rid of differential export subsidies (averaging about 20 percent of the value of manufactured exports during the 1980s), coupled with import controls. There is also an intricate tariff structure, whose rates the federal government can raise or lower by half on short notice, whenever "market stability" requires this.[9] Despite such restrictions, Yugoslavia's balance of trade has been continually in deficit since World War II, and foreign debt—mainly to Western nations and institutions—was estimated at about $23 billion in mid-1987. In per capita terms, this is one of the highest debts in Eastern Europe, although Yugoslavia is also one of the poorest of these countries. In 1987, debt servicing costs came to more than a third of Yugoslavia's convertible currency receipts from exports and invisibles (although this was also the lowest debt servicing ratio since 1982).

We should distinguish between Yugoslavia's trade with other socialist or with developing nations, on one hand, and its trade with OECD countries (mainly developed Western nations and Japan) on the other. Yugoslavia's export problems are almost entirely with the latter, since its manufactures often enjoy quality or design advantages over domestic products in socialist and third-world markets. It therefore exports mainly processed goods to these areas, in exchange for raw materials and fuel, whereas trade with the West consists mainly of unprocessed or semiprocessed exports, in return for manufactured goods. Sometimes, it has found it hard to import enough from the centrally planned economies to satisfy trade agreements.[10] By contrast, it has been losing export market shares in the OECD almost continually since 1965.

Nevertheless, while it is an associate member of COMECON, the socialist trading bloc comprising the USSR and its allies (plus Romania), just 33 percent of Yugoslavia's foreign trade was with all other socialist nations combined in 1987, the smallest share of any socialist nation except China. This share has been falling, while the OECD share has been rising (to 54 percent in 1987). Although Yugoslavia has a preferential trade agreement with the EEC, around half its trade deficit has been with this group, partly because of trade barriers against its farm exports. However, Yugoslav producers have also not been sufficiently cost or quality conscious, nor have they tried hard enough to adapt their products to Western export markets. On paper, there has been improvement. Yugoslav exports rose from 60 percent of imports in 1980 to 90 percent of imports in 1987. But this was mainly due to tighter constraints on imports, whose volume in 1987 was less than 70 percent of the 1980 level (vs. a 25 percent volume expansion of exports). Import controls reduce economic growth, but are necessary because the trade deficit must be financed by workers' remittances, tourism, and foreign loans. Of these, only tourism has potential for further expansion.

On balance, Yugoslav firms have a low incentive to export to convertible currency markets and a high propensity to import. The dollar cost to the country of imported fuel was almost twenty times as great in 1982 as in 1972, and the dinar cost was more than fifty times as high. Largely, this was because of a 50 percent volume expansion of fuel imports over 1974–80—just when their prices were soaring—which exceeded the growth of real GNP. Subsequently, import controls were tightened, and the dollar cost of imported fuel has declined (partly because of the fall of world oil prices), although its dinar cost has continued to rise. Underlying this is a weak incentive to economize at the enterprise level, as well as a continuing promotion of heavy industry, including chemicals, which became more irrational following the oil-price explosions of 1974 and 1979. In addition, import substitution, together with regional duplication of production facilities, has resulted in too little specialization—or too wide a range of products being exported—and a failure to realize important scale economies.

Unlike producers in Hungary and elsewhere in Eastern Europe, Yugoslav firms have not been openly shielded from oil price increases or from changes in other import and export prices. Yet, in the competitive scramble to expand exports that followed the first energy crisis in 1973–74, Yugoslavia also lost manufacturing market shares in the OECD and to an even greater extent in the EEC. Yugoslavia shares with other socialist nations a state of excess demand on its domestic market plus a network of taxes and subsidies that tend to divorce wages and salaries from enterprise performance. Given the excess demand, increases in import prices can be entirely passed along to customers, since domestic prices depend on costs of production. The government has been unable (or has lacked the political will) to restrain domestic demand enough to force Yugoslav manufacturers to seek convertible-currency export markets. In 1984, however, producers of raw materials and crude oil were exporting these commodities, even as Yugoslavia was importing massive quantities of the same products for its own industries. (Domestic price controls on these items were severe, and exporters were keeping more than their legal retention quotas of scarce foreign exchange.)

Since 1984, however, Yugoslavia has made a stronger effort to specialize according to comparative advantage and to move toward dinar convertibility, with some success (and in line with a recommendation of the Kraigher Commission).

11-4. Concluding Comments on the Yugoslav Economy and Socialism

Yugoslavia's postwar leaders inherited some of its most intractable social and economic problems—in particular, those of ethnic diversity, underdevelopment, rural underemployment, and regional income inequality. External political pressures on the country have resulted largely from a fierce determination to remain independent. Given the constraints, its leaders have shown ingenuity in turning adversity into advantage, and courage in launching and developing the experiment in workers' self-management. By balancing diverse interests and drawing maximum advantage from nonalignment, while sustaining high rates of saving and investment, they were able to maintain rapid growth up to the second energy crisis in 1979–80. Together with emigration, this provided a safety valve for pressures that might otherwise have become intolerable. Several times since 1946, observers as diverse as American business experts and Mao Zedong have forecast the demise of the ''Yugoslav system.'' Today, China's leaders are borrowing elements of this same system.

However, we may also wonder whether Yugoslavia's unsolved economic problems will not eventually catch up with it. As in the USSR and most of Eastern Europe, the net effect of reforms since the early 1960s on the autonomy of enterprises, on their responsibility for profits and losses, and on the rules under which new firms are founded or old ones expand into new markets, has been limited. The main result of Yugoslavia's search for a system during this period has been to raise the relative power of regional governments. This has not increased efficiency, although it may have helped to contain ethnic tensions. However, the environment in which Yugoslavia finds itself during the 1980s is harsher than it was two decades earlier. The death of Tito has removed one of history's great leaders, who rose above the storm of competing regional interests to give the nation efficient crisis management. The energy crisis has dealt Yugoslavia a double blow, by closing the safety valve of expanding employment opportunities in Western Europe and by raising the cost of its import substitution strategy. Moreover, opportunities for extensive growth of industrial output, obtained mainly from large investments, have greatly declined.

In this context, we recall Marx's forecast of the evolution of modern capitalism. Because of a persistent tendency for the rate of profit to fall, such economies would not be able to maintain high rates of investment, in his view. Thus, they are condemned to a worsening series of cyclical fluctuations of output and employment, which, in combination with declining average growth and rising average unemployment over each cycle, would ultimately lead to their downfall and replacement by state socialism. Although modern socialist economies are alternatives, rather than successors to modern capitalism, they have maintained high rates of investment. Yugoslavia has generally invested 30–35 percent or more of its gross domestic product, a higher percentage than Japan or virtually any Western nation. While a large share of this investment has consisted of inventory build-up, the fixed capital-to-labor ratio has also risen rapidly, especially in industry.

As this has happened, the marginal productivity of capital has fallen—according to one estimate, by about two-thirds over 1955–74—and there is little doubt that the decline has continued since.[11] The same phenomenon has been documented for the Soviet Union and can be considered a socialist version of the falling rate of profit, since capital's marginal productivity is an index of the return on investment. The effect on capital's marginal productivity of diminishing returns—which have resulted from the rise of the capital-to-labor ratio—has swamped the effect of technological progress (which generally causes capital productivity to rise). The resulting fall in growth has been sharpened by the balance-of-payments constraint on imports of raw materials, energy, and sophisticated machinery and machine tools. Growth has become more and more expensive to buy with sacrifices of present consumption, and these savings are mostly involuntary, being generated largely by taxation and inflationary credit creation.

Unlike some East European countries, Yugoslavia does have a labor reserve of at least one million people, who would like to work in the social sector. Potentially, their employment would reduce the average capital intensity of production and could help to generate a renewal of growth. However, it may be hard to expand employment to efficient levels in profitable social sector firms, because they may be unwilling to take on new employees (or to divide the pie into more slices), when this causes net income per worker to fall. This would restrict the number of social sector jobs and keep incomes there higher, while depressing average incomes in the private sector—mainly in agriculture—by expanding the numbers who work there. It would also increase the number of unemployed. In the context of section 3-5, those with rights to good jobs, earnings, and benefits (notably housing) in the social sector are insiders, while those unable to obtain such jobs, but who are qualified to hold or to train for them, are outsiders. Such job rationing could help to explain the coexistence of declining extensive growth and a large labor reserve currently seeking employment. But during the 1980s, there is another explanation as well—namely, the balance-of-payments constraint on imports, which restricts the growth of production and the number of jobs.

Despite its commitment to self-management, Yugoslavia shares basic features with other socialist economies. These include: the leading role of the League of Communists in economic and political life; priority development of heavy industry, with comparative neglect of agriculture and services; politicization of investment decisions and of the appointment and promotion of economic decision makers; an excess demand in many domestic markets, along with administrative, cost-plus pricing; a soft budget constraint for enterprises; and a large bureaucracy for administering and planning the economy. These tend to discourage enterprise initiative and competition, and they reduce the return on efforts to improve quality and cost control. Whereas Yugoslavia was on the cutting edge of reform in the 1950s and 1960s, it has since been leap-frogged by China, Hungary, and, possibly, other socialist nations.

If Yugoslavia's leaders are to surmount the economic problems of the post-Tito era, they will have to expand exports, while reducing the import content of domestic production. They will also have to pay a lower price for growth, in foregone present consumption and balance-of-payments deficits, and generate more employment for given output expansion than in the recent past. This will require them to swallow several bitter pills that most East European nations have been regurgitating for over twenty years. To begin with, they will finally have to end the investment priority for heavy industry, that was originally advocated by Lenin and subsequently adopted by all socialist nations.[12] It will then become important to end regional and local duplication of production facilities, in order to realize scale economies and to achieve more rational location patterns. In addition, Yugoslavia will have to promote industries in which it can reasonably hope to develop a cost or quality advantage vis-à-vis the rest of the world—including agriculture, labor-intensive lines of manufacturing, and industries based on mineral resources. Over time, it may be able to evolve a comparative advantage in capital and then in knowledge-intensive industries, following a pattern set in Japan and other Asian countries. In any event, a shift of priorities will be necessary, if Yugoslavia is to achieve a satisfactory balance of payments, but this alone will not be enough.

It will also have to end the greenhouse environment in which many firms are preserved year after year—even when they develop no export potential—through combinations of protected markets for their products and frequent subsidies. This will require the National Bank to get control over the supplies of money and credit and governments at all levels to end price controls (along with pressure on firms to fix prices via the SMAs) for most products. At the enterprise level, wages will have to depend more closely on enterprise profitability before taxes and subsidies, and the claims on profits and losses associated with entrepreneurship will have to rise. Barriers to entry at all levels (national, regional, local) will have to fall, in line with the Kraigher Commission's recommendation that the internal Yugoslav market be unified. This will require at least a further reduction of the role of SMAs and social compacts. While redistribution through the budget from well-to-do regions to poor must continue, recycling of funds within the same ethnic area, from efficient to inefficient firms, will have to be cut back. To make it easier for new competition to enter a market and to raise the influence of prospective investment yields on access to loanable funds, bank employees or their elected representatives should have more say in hiring and firing bank directors and in approving lending policies, thereby ending this departure from workers' management. Based on their record in providing jobs, as well as goods and services in demand, private firms also deserve greater freedom to get established and better access to finance, especially if they agree to become self-managed when they exceed a specified size.

The above proposals represent a logical step forward in the development of self-management, as well as a return to Yugoslavia's reform intentions of the mid-1960s. According to Marx, the main potential source of human welfare lies in creating goods and services for others. If so, a major part of the prospective gain from socialism would result from the ability of workers, who control production, to turn out goods and services possessing a high use value with which their enterprises become identified in the minds of customers. Ultimately, it may become possible to rely entirely on intrinsic motivation without actually tying pay to performance.

However, the journey to this level of social consciousness will be long and arduous, as Marx realized. He therefore assumed that, in the initial stages of socialism, claims to income based on differential labor contributions would be necessary. During this period of bourgeois right, profit sharing within each enterprise would also be required, in order to build team spirit and collective identification of workers with their firm and its products. Later, this would be a basis for extending collective identification beyond the enterprise, and eventually for building the social consciousness envisaged by Marx and Engels. Then and only then, if they were right, will this consciousness allow decoupling of extrinsic rewards from contributions, without impairing efficiency.

In the meantime, building team spirit based on efficient performance requires a hard budget constraint at the enterprise level, including a real possibility of bankruptcy, as well as decentralized pricing and workable competition (and, thus, low barriers to entry and exit for domestic producers). The latter two are necessary to make prices more rational guides to production and profits a better measure of performance, as well as to countervail any tendencies to restrict employment and output below efficient levels. However, because bourgeois right creates income differentials, as well as social tensions that sit ill at ease with the orthodox view of a classless society, socialist systems have been under pressure to avoid this stage or to move quickly past it by suppressing differences between firms. But this has created worse problems, without necessarily reducing social inequality. Workers and managers have been protected from customer acceptance as a measure of enterprise success, resulting in swollen costs and low use value of production, along with the range of problems which stem from this.

Partly because of pressure from the International Monetary Fund, whose credit Yugoslavia needs, and partly because of the threat of runaway inflation, as well as a more favorable attitude toward reform in Eastern Europe, Yugoslav authorities have made new efforts to push reform forward in 1987–88. A start has been made in reducing the role of price controls and administered pricing, as well as in liberalizing foreign trade and payments. Attempts to more firmly control the expansion of money and credit are continuing, and real interest rates are supposed to become and remain positive. To this end, the principal of each loan of one year or more and of each savings deposit of three months or more has been indexed to (and will therefore increase with) the retail price index.

Finally, Yugoslavia passed a tough bankruptcy law in 1987, as well as a law to link earnings more closely to enterprise performance. The first law requires loss-making firms to go into receivership if they are unable to solve their financial problems within 140 days. In most cases of bankruptcy, priority is given to meeting creditors' claims, rather than to paying wages and salaries. The second law has triggered a wave of strikes and protests, partly because it also mandates real wage cuts of 20 percent (30 percent since May 1988) in unprofitable firms. These protests gained new subsidies for loss-makers, and it is presently unclear how much the budget constraint has really hardened. Establishing a riskier, more competitive environment for Yugoslav firms will pose political risks for government at all levels, as well as for the League of Communists. But the alternative is likely to be further reduction of real incomes, a sharpening of regional tensions, and, ultimately, a threat to Yugoslavia's survival, as well as to its ambition of providing a unique and successful socialist alternative.

Notes

1. Moreover, "As for the 15 social compacts the Plan assumed would specify production and investment targets for regions and firms and the policy measures needed to achieve them, by June 1977, only three such compacts had been concluded." Ellen Commisso, "Yugoslavia in the 1970s: Self-Management and Bargaining," Department of Political Science, University of California at San Diego, 1978, p. 18. From 1989, Yugoslavia no longer constructs annual plans.

2. See sections 4-1 and 4-2 above, along with the references cited there, for a discussion of the socialist system envisaged by Marx.

3. Laura D'Andrea-Tyson, "Liquidity Crises in the Yugoslav Economy: An Alternative to Bankruptcy?" *Soviet Studies*, April 1977. See, as well Svetozar Pejovich, "The Banking System and the Investment Behavior of the Yugoslav Firm," in M. Bornstein, ed., *Plan and Market* (New Haven: Yale University Press, 1973).

4. For instance, in 1968, there were nearly 600,000 court edicts ordering firms to fulfill their contractual obligations. See Pejovich, "The Banking System," p. 308. This situation persisted well into 1972, affecting over 2,000 firms employing some 800,000 workers. The short-term bank accounts of these companies were blocked by the Social Accounting Service, except for use in debt repayment.

5. Tyson, "Liquidity Crises in the Yugoslav Economy," p. 286.

6. This ratio is low, even for Eastern Europe. For example, in the USSR, each farmer supports nine other people and in East Germany, seventeen.

7. See Klime Corba and Savo Cukanovich, "Self-Management Associations of Peasant Farmers," *Yugoslav Survey*, February 1981, p. 92. See, as well, Ivan Loncarevic, "Prices and Private Agriculture in Yugoslavia," *Soviet Studies*, October 1987.

8. See Thad Alton, et al., "Agricultural Output, Expenses and Depreciation, Gross Product, and Net Product in Eastern Europe, 1965, 1970, and 1975–86," Research Project on National Income in East-Central Europe, Occasional Paper OP-96, New York, July 1987, Table 18, pp. 50–51; and Miladin Raichevich, "Living Standards, 1976–84," *Yugoslav Survey*, August 1985.

9. Imports are classified in four basic categories: (LB) "fully liberalized" imports, which in practice are subject to foreign exchange quotas; (LBO) partially restricted imports, whose degree of restriction depends on the current balance of payments and availability of foreign exchange; (K) imports subject to physical volume quotas; and (D) imports subject to license.

10. Historically, trade with other socialist nations has been mainly on a bilateral clearing basis, so that little currency has actually changed hands. Every year, Yugoslavia's trade with each of these countries should approximately balance, but goods produced in COMECON are not very competitive in the Yugoslav market. This has created problems. For example, "In 1969 . . . despite excess production of light bulbs at home . . . a license was granted for the import of 19.5 million bulbs from Poland and Czechoslovakia. . . . In 1970, despite surplus stocks of 100 million home-produced eggs . . . the Yugoslav market was flooded with imports of old Polish eggs." D. A. Dyker, "The Yugoslav Deficit on Balance of Payments," *European Economic Review*, 3, 1974, pp. 337–38. While the practice of bilateral clearing has declined, it persists with the Soviet Union, as well as with East Germany and Czechoslovakia.

the Yugoslav Miracle?'' *Economic Journal,* June 1980, especially Table 5, p. 301. Also see Miroslav Prica, "Economic Investment and Changes in the Structure of the Economy," *Yugoslav Survey,* November 1982, especially Table V, p. 54, and Lazar Drakul, "Economic Development, 1971–1982," *Yugoslav Survey,* May 1984, pp. 63–65. Also see the discussion above in section 5-1.

12. Marxians trace these priorities to *Das Kapital,* but this is doubtful. See Shumpei Kumon, *The "Scheme of Reproduction" as a Model of Planned Growth* (Tokyo: University of Tokyo, 1970). See, as well, V. I. Lenin, "On the So-Called Market Question," in his *Collected Works* (Moscow: Foreign Languages Publishing House, 1960), Vol. 1, pp. 75–125.

Questions for Review, Discussion, Examination

1. In principle, the 1976 Law on Social Planning made plan targets more binding than they had been over 1954–75, while providing for "democratic" plan formation. How is this achieved? Are these targets binding, in practice?

2. The Kraigher Commission recommended reducing the role of self-management agreements and social compacts in the Yugoslav economy to allow Yugoslavia to move toward a more unified domestic market. Why do you think that one effect of these agreements has been to fragment the domestic market?

*3. (a) What are the main tools of monetary policy in Yugoslavia?

(b) Why has there been a basic bias toward easy money and why has it been nearly impossible to sustain a tight monetary policy?

(c) Why has there been some tendency for illiquidity and inflation to go hand-in-hand?

4. In what way is agriculture in Yugoslavia organized differently than Yugoslav industry? In what way is Yugoslav agriculture organized differently than agriculture in most other socialist countries? Indicate the relative importance of the private sector.

In what ways has the growth of agriculture been restricted to provide more resources for industry?

5. Although a substantial rural-to-urban migration has occurred, the average size of private farms has fallen since 1960. Why is this? In what ways has the private sector been restricted?

*6. What has been Yugoslavia's basic foreign trade policy since World War II? How does this fit in with the basic growth strategy and in what other ways has its handling of foreign trade resembled practice in other socialist countries?

7. Why has Yugoslavia found it difficult to export to Western markets? How has this forced it to curtail economic growth during the 1980s? Has its basic growth strategy also played a role in this?

Why do you think Yugoslavia's trade deficit did not force curtailment of growth before 1980?

Finally, are Yugoslavia's trade problems with socialist countries the same as those with OECD nations? Briefly explain any differences.

*8. Does evidence suggest that Yugoslav growth has been mainly extensive or intensive? What has happened to the marginal productivity of capital? Explain how this can be consistent with the existence of a large reserve of unemployed labor.

9. What basic features does Yugoslavia share with other socialist economies that are inhibiting growth during the 1980s (although some of these features may have been beneficial earlier on, especially during periods of hostility with the USSR)?

*10. Development of social consciousness would ultimately allow decoupling of extrinsic rewards from productive contributions, with no impairment of efficiency, in the Marxian vision of socialism and its progress toward full communism. (In the end, "From each according to his abilities, to each according to his needs" would at last prevail.)

Why, then, is it important to maintain a hard budget constraint in the early stages of socialism, regardless of whether we accept the Marxian view, and what is the cost of suppressing "bourgeois right" too quickly?

* = more difficult.

Suggested Further Readings

Note: A wealth of data and analyses of the Yugoslav economy is published in English by the federal government of Yugoslavia in the quarterly journal, *Yugoslav Survey*. See, as well, the various OECD reports on Yugoslavia and *Eastern European Economics*, a journal of translations.

Adizes, Ichak. *Industrial Democracy: Yugoslav Style*. New York: Free Press, 1971.
Antanaskovich, Srboljub. "The Passenger Car Industry." *Yugoslav Survey* 27 (May 1986): 89–104.
Bicanich, Rudolph. *Economic Policy in Socialist Yugoslavia*. Cambridge: Cambridge University Press, 1973.
Blagoev, Borislav. "Labour Relations." *Yugoslav Survey* 25 (February 1984): 49–74.
Bombelles, J. T. *Economic Development in Communist Yugoslavia*. Stanford, Calif.: Stanford University Press, 1968.
———. "Transfer of Resources From More to Less Developed Republics and Autonomous Provinces of Yugoslavia, 1971–1980." Research Project on National Income in East-Central Europe, Occasional Paper OP-69, New York (July 1981).
Breznik, Dusan. "Economic Activity of the Population." *Yugoslav Survey* 27 (February 1986): 33–46.
Burkett, John P. "Stabilization Measures in Yugoslavia: An Assessment of the Proposals of Yugoslavia's Commission for Problems of Economic Stabilization." In Vol. 3 of U.S. Congress, Joint Economic Committee. *East European Economies: Slow Growth in the 1980s*. Washington, D.C.: U.S. Government Printing Office, 1986, pp. 561–574.
Cochrane, Nancy. "Yugoslav Agricultural Performance in the 1980s and Prospects for the 1990s." In Vol. 3 of U.S. Congress, Joint Economic Committee. *East European Economics: Slow Growth in the 1980s*. Washington, D.C.: U.S. Government Printing Office 1986, pp. 575–594.
Commisso, Ellen. *Workers' Control Under Plan and Market*. New Haven: Yale University Press, 1979.
Corbe, Klime, and Savo Cukanovich. "Self-Management Associations of Peasant Farmers." *Yugoslavia Survey* 22 (February 1981): 91–102.
D'Andrea-Tyson, Laura. "Liquidity Crises in the Yugoslav Economy: An Alternative to Bankruptcy?" *Soviet Studies* 29 (April 1977a): 284–295.

------. "The Yugoslav Economy in the 1970's: A Survey of Recent Developments and Future Prospects." In U.S. Congress, Joint Economic Committee. *East European Economies Post-Helsinki*. Washington, D.C.: U.S. Government Printing Office, 1977b, pp. 941–996.

D'Andrea-Tyson, Laura, and Gabriel Eichler. "Continuity and Change in the Yugoslav Economy in the 1970s and 1980s." In U.S. Congress, Joint Economic Committee. *East European Economic Assessment, Part I*. Washington, D.C.: U.S. Government Printing Office 1981, pp. 139–214.

Dirlam, Joel, and James Plummer. *An Introduction to the Yugoslav Economy*. Columbus, Oh.: Merrill, 1973.

Dimitrijevich, Dimitrije. "Interest Rates." *Yugoslav Survey* 24 (November 1983): 91–102.

Dyker, D. A. "The Yugoslav Deficit on Balance of Payments." *European Economic Review* 5, 3 (1974): 329–354.

Farkas, R. P. *Yugoslav Economic Development and Political Change*. New York: Praeger, 1975.

Furubotn, Eirik G., and Svetozar Pejovich. "The Role of the Banking System in Yugoslav Economic Planning, 1946–69." *Revue Internationale d'Histoire de la Banque* 87–89, 4 (1971): 51–91.

------. "Property Rights, Economic Decentralization, and the Evolution of the Yugoslav Firm, 1965–72." *Journal of Law and Economics* 16 (October 1973): 275–302.

Gorupich, D., and I. Paj. *Workers' Self-Management in Yugoslav Undertakings*. Ekonomski Institut: Zagreb, 1970.

Granick, D. *Enterprise Guidance in Eastern Europe*. Princeton: Princeton University Press, 1975), part IV.

Gregory, M. B. "Regional Economic Development in Yugoslavia." *Soviet Studies* 25 (October 1973): 213–228.

Hamilton, F. E. Ian. *Yugoslavia: Patterns of Economic Activity*. New York: Praeger, 1968.

Hocevar, Toussaint. "Inter-regional Economic Integration: The Yugoslav Case." Paper presented at Third World Congress for Soviet and East European Studies, Washington, D.C. (October 30–November 4, 1985.

Horvat, Branko. *An Essay on Yugoslav Society*. New York: International Arts and Sciences Press, 1969.

------. "Yugoslav Economic Policy in the Postwar Period: Problems, Ideas, Institutional Developments." *American Economic Review* 61 (June 1971) supplement.

------. *The Yugoslav Economic System*. White Plains, N.Y.: International Arts and Sciences Press, 1976.

Kolaja, Jiri. *Workers' Councils: The Yugoslav Experience*. London: Tavistock, 1965.

Loncarevic, Ivan. "Prices and Private Agriculture in Yugoslavia." *Soviet Studies* 39 (October 1987): 628–650.

Lydall, H. *Yugoslav Socialism: Theory and Practice*. Oxford: Clarendon Press, 1984.

Marsenich, Dragutin. "Economic Development, 1945–1984." *Yugoslav Survey* 27 (February 1986): 69–98.

Milenkovitch, Deborah. "The Case of Yugoslavia." *American Economic Review* 67 (February 1977): 55–60.

Miljkovich, Dusan. "Yugoslavia's Socio-Economic Development, 1947–1972." *Yugoslav Survey* 15 (February 1974): 1–36.

Milovanovich, Rade. "The Status of Yugoslav Citizens Temporarily Working or Residing Abroad." *Yugoslav Survey* 24 (August 1983): 3–20.

Moore, J. H. *Growth with Self-Management: Yugoslav Industrialization in 1952–75*. Stanford, Calif.: Hoover, 1980.

------. "Self-Management in Yugoslavia." In U.S. Congress, Joint Economic Committee. *East European Economic Assessment, Part I*. Washington, D.C.: U.S. Government Printing Office, 1981, pp. 215–229.

Printing Office, 1981, pp. 215–229.

Neuberger, Egon. "The Yugoslav Investment Auctions." *Quarterly Journal of Economics* 73 (February 1959): 88–115.

Nikolich, Miloje. "The Social Accountancy Service." *Yugoslav Survey* 19 (August 1978): 59–74.

Obradovich, Josip. "Participation and Work Attitudes in Yugoslavia." *Industrial Relations* 9 (February 1970): 161–169.

———. "Workers' Participation: Who Participates?" *Industrial Relations* 14 (February 1975): 32–44.

Pejovich, Svetozar. "The Banking System and Investment Behavior of the Yugoslav Firm." In Bornstein, Morris, ed. *Plan and Market*. New Haven: Yale University Press 1975, pp. 285–311.

Penev, Goran. "The Non-Agricultural Population." *Yugoslav Survey* 28 (August 1987): 3–24.

Petrovich, Ruza. "The National Composition of the Population." *Yugoslav Survey* 24 (August 1983): 21–34.

Posrkacha, Dragomir. "Pensions, 1976–82." *Yugoslav Survey* 24 (February 1983): 105–112.

Prasnikar, Janez. "The Yugoslav Self-Managed Firm and its Behavior." *Eastern European Economics* 22 (Winter 1983–84): 3–43.

Prica, Miroslav. "Investment, 1979–1984." *Yugoslav Survey* 27 (February 1986): 99–106.

Raichevich, Bozidar. "Financing General Social Needs in Republics and Autonomous Provinces." *Yugoslav Survey* 24 (November 1983): 55–70.

Raichevich, Bozidar, and Pavle Gligorich. "Resources for Financing Public and Collective Needs, 1981–1985." *Yugoslav Survey* 28 (August 1987): 77–88.

Ramet, P. *Nationalism and Federalism in Yugoslavia, 1963–83*. Bloomington: Indiana University Press, 1984.

Ribnikar, Ivan. "The Yugoslav Monetary System." *The ACES Bulletin* 23 (Spring 1981): 67–78.

Rus, Velijko. "Influence Structure in the Yugoslav Enterprise." *Industrial Relations* 9 (February 1970): 148–160.

Sacks, Stephen R. *Entry of New Competitors in Yugoslav Market Socialism*. Institute of International Studies, Research Series, no. 19. Berkeley: University of California, 1973.

Sapir, André "Economic Growth and Factor Substitution: What Happened to the Yugoslav Miracle?" *Economic Journal* 90 (June 1980): 294–313.

Schrenk, Martin, Cyrus Ardalan, and Nawal El Tatawy. *Yugoslavia: Self-Management Socialism and the Challenges of Development*. Baltimore: Johns Hopkins University Press, 1979.

Singleton, Fred. "Problems of Regional Development: The Case of Yugoslavia." *Jahrbuch der Wirtschaft Osteuropas (Yearbook of East-European Economics)* 2 (1971), Part 2, pp. 375–395.

Singleton, Fred, and Bernard Carter. *The Economy of Yugoslavia*. London: Croom Helm, 1982.

Sirc, Ljubo. *The Yugoslav Economy Under Self–Management*. London: Macmillan, 1979.

Sojich, Milan. "Capital Accumulation and Expansion of Production in the Socialist Economy, 1965–1984." *Yugoslav Survey* 27 (May 1986): 63–78.

"Some Characteristics of Economic Trends Manifest Over the 1981–1985 Period." *Yugoslav Survey* 27 (August 1986): 57–76.

Stefanovich, Mileva. "The Iron and Steel Industry, 1976–82." *Yugoslav Survey* 25 (February 1984): 97–108.

Stojanovic, R., ed. *The Functioning of the Yugoslav Economy*. Armonk, N.Y.: M. E. Sharpe, 1982.

426 COMPARATIVE ECONOMIC SYSTEMS

gress, House of Representatives, Committee on Banking and Currency. *Activities by Various Central Banks to Promote Economic and Social Welfare Programs.* Washington, D.C.: U.S. Government Printing Office 1971, pp. 43–44, 306–332.

Varga, Werner. "Yugoslavia's Battle for Economic Stability." *Eastern European Economics* 19 (Summer 1981): 58–74.

Vucinich, W. S., ed. *Contemporary Yugoslavia: Twenty Years of Socialist Experiment.* Berkeley: University of California Press, 1969.

Vukajlovich, Dragoljub. "Taxation of Private Individuals." *Yugoslav Survey* 25 (February 1984): 75–86.

Wachtel, H. M. "Workers' Management and Inter-Industry Wage Differentials in Yugoslavia." *Journal of Political Economy* 80 (May–June 1972): 540–560.

——. *Workers' Management and Workers' Wages in Yugoslavia.* Ithaca, N.Y.: Cornell University Press, 1973.

World Bank Staff, *Yugoslavia: Development with Decentralization.* Baltimore: Johns Hopkins University Press, 1975.

——. *Yugoslavia: Adjustment Policies and Development Perspectives.* Washington, D.C.: World Bank, 1983.

Zupanov, Josip. "The Producer and Risk." *Eastern European Economics* 7 (Spring 1969): 12–28.

——. "Yugoslavia: A Socialist Alternative." In de Hoghton, Charles, ed. *The Company: Law, Structure, and Reform in Eleven Countries.* London: Allen & Unwin, 1970, pp. 320–336.

——. "Is Enterprise Management Becoming Professionalized?" *International Studies in Management and Organization* 3 (Fall 1973): 42–83.

INDEX

ABOUT THE
AUTHOR

Richard L. Carson received an M.A. in journalism from the University of Minnesota and a Ph.D. in economics from Indiana University. He is presently associate professor of economics at Carleton University in Ottawa, Canada, where he teaches courses in comparative economic systems and economic theory. He has also published extensively in these areas, including articles in the *Canadian Journal of Economics*, the *American Economic Review*, the *ACES Bulletin*, the *Journal of Economics and Businesss*, and the *Eastern Economic Journal*.